A BOOK OF HEROIC VERSE

POETS ARE THE TRUMPETS WHICH SING TO BATTLE. POETS ARE THE UNACKNOWLEDGED LEGISLATORS OF THE WORLD. SHELLEY

A BOOK OF HEROIC VERSE

CHOSEN BY ARTHUR BURRELL

Granger Index Reprint Series

BOOKS FOR LIBRARIES PRESS
FREEPORT, NEW YORK

First Published 1920
Reprinted 1971

INTERNATIONAL STANDARD BOOK NUMBER
0-8369-6295-8

LIBRARY OF CONGRESS CATALOG CARD NUMBER
78-168775

PRINTED IN THE UNITED STATES OF AMERICA
BY
NEW WORLD BOOK MANUFACTURING CO., INC.
HALLANDALE, FLORIDA 33009

INTRODUCTION

THIS collection differs in one particular from the usual anthologies. It strives to show that heroic verse is the verse dealing with heroes, heroic characters, heroic acts, quite irrespective of the nationality or century of the actors themselves. A patriotic hymn is a patriotic hymn, an heroic action is an heroic action, whether the hymn celebrate Thermopylae or Mukden and whether the action takes place outside Bethulia or Ladysmith. Indeed, until a short time ago, Leonidas was more real to British youth than either Wolfe or Clive, and this catholicity is an element in the mutual admiration which makes for world-peace, even though the songs be of war. It follows too, though this has, I think, been little appreciated in books on history or sociology, that it is impossible in such a collection to hide the transcendent merit of man as an individual. I do not say that collective heroism is unknown (for many of the pieces included in this book seem to show its possibility); but it appears to be clear that nowhere does the importance of the single personality show itself so brilliantly as in the individual act, word, thought. Even when, as in a stubborn defence of a town, or as in a sortie, or as in the unnamed, unknown heroism of families under agonising stress, or as in the prolongation of a righteous strike—even when collective heroism seems demonstrated, it will surely be found that the dynamic thrust comes from a character, an attitude, a sacrifice. The crowning example of this is, of course, seen in the history of Christianity, the most absolute monarchy and the most individualistic creed which the world has ever seen. The hero is always in the minority; an heroic majority is unthinkable. This gives to heroic verse its sting and stimulus.

THE EDITOR.

CONTENTS

Contents

PATRIA

BREATHES THERE THE MAN

BREATHES there the man, with soul so dead,
Who never to himself hath said,
   This is my own, my native land.
Whose heart hath ne'er within him burn'd,
As home his footsteps he hath turn'd,
   From wandering on a foreign strand?
If such there breathe, go, mark him well;
For him no Minstrel raptures swell;
High though his titles, proud his name,
Boundless his wealth as wish can claim;
Despite those titles, power, and pelf,
The wretch, concentred all in self,
Living, shall forfeit fair renown,
And, doubly dying, shall go down
To the vile dust, from whence he sprung,
Unwept, unhonour'd, and unsung.

                SIR WALTER SCOTT.

A STATE

  WHAT constitutes a state?
Not high-raised battlement or laboured mound,
  Thick wall or moated gate:
Not cities proud, with spires and turrets crowned:
  Not bays and broad-armed ports,
Where, laughing at the storm, rich navies ride:
  Not starred and spangled courts,
Where low-bred baseness wafts perfume to pride.
  No: men, high-minded men,
With powers as far above dull brutes endued,
  In forest, brake, or den,

3

As beasts excel cold rocks and brambles rude:
   Men who their duties know,
But know their rights; and knowing dare maintain,
   Prevent the long-aim'd blow,
And crush the tyrant while they rend the chain.
   These constitute a state,
And sovereign Law, at the state's collected will,
   O'er thrones and globes elate
Sits empress, crowning good, repressing ill;
   Smit by her sacred frown,
The fiend Discretion like a vapour sinks,
   And e'en the all-dazzling crown
Hides his faint rays and at her bidding shrinks.
   Such was this heaven-loved isle,
Than Lesbos fairer, and the Cretan shore!
   No more shall Freedom smile?
Shall Britons languish, and be men no more?

SIR W. JONES.

OF OLD SAT FREEDOM

OF old sat Freedom on the heights,
   The thunders breaking at her feet:
Above her shook the starry lights:
   She heard the torrents meet.

There in her place she did rejoice,
   Self-gather'd in her prophet-mind,
But fragments of her mighty voice
   Came rolling on the wind.

Then stept she down thro' town and field
   To mingle with the human race,
And part by part to men reveal'd
   The fulness of her face—

Grave mother of majestic works,
   From her isle-altar gazing down,
Who, God-like, grasps the triple forks,
   And, King-like, wears the crown:

Her open eyes desire the truth.
　　The wisdom of a thousand years
Is in them.　May perpetual youth
　　Keep dry their light from tears;

That her fair form may stand and shine,
　　Make bright our days and light our dreams,
Turning to scorn with lips divine
　　The falsehood of extremes!

LORD TENNYSON.

PART OF GRAY'S ELEGY

BENEATH those rugged elms, that yew-tree's shade,
　　Where heaves the turf in many a mouldering heap,
Each in his narrow cell for ever laid,
　　The rude forefathers of the hamlet sleep.

The breezy call of incense-breathing Morn,
　　The swallow twittering from the straw-built shed,
The cock's shrill clarion, or the echoing horn,
　　No more shall rouse them from their lowly bed.

For them no more the blazing hearth shall burn,
　　Or busy housewife ply her evening care;
No children run to lisp their sire's return,
　　Or climb his knees the envied kiss to share.

Oft did the harvest to their sickle yield,
　　Their furrow oft the stubborn glebe has broke;
How jocund thy did drive their team a-field!
　　How bowed the woods beneath their sturdy stroke!

Let not Ambition mock their useful toil,
　　Their homely joys, and destiny obscure;
Nor Grandeur hear with a disdainful smile
　　The short and simple annals of the poor.

The boast of heraldry, the pomp of power,
　　And all that beauty, all that wealth e'er gave,
Awaits alike the inevitable hour.
　　The paths of glory lead but to the grave.

Nor you, ye proud, impute to these the fault,
    If Memory o'er their tomb no trophies raise,
Where through the long-drawn aisle and fretted vault
    The pealing anthem swells the note of praise.

Can storied urn, or animated bust,
    Back to its mansion call the fleeting breath?
Can Honour's voice provoke the silent dust,
    Or Flattery soothe the dull cold ear of Death?

Perhaps in this neglected spot is laid
    Some heart once pregnant with celestial fire;
Hands, that the rod of empire might have swayed,
    Or waked to ecstasy the living lyre.

But Knowledge to their eyes her ample page
    Rich with the spoils of time did ne'er unroll;
Chill Penury repressed their noble rage,
    And froze the genial current of the soul.

Full many a gem of purest ray serene,
    The dark unfathomed caves of ocean bear:
Full many a flower is born to blush unseen,
    And waste its sweetness on the desert air.

Some village Hampden, that, with dauntless breast,
    The little tyrant of his fields withstood,
Some mute inglorious Milton here may rest,
    Some Cromwell guiltless of his country's blood.

The applause of listening senates to command,
    The threats of pain and ruin to despise,
To scatter plenty o'er a smiling land,
    And read their history in a nation's eyes,

Their lot forbade: nor circumscribed alone
    Their growing virtues, but their crimes confined;
Forbade to wade through slaughter to a throne,
    And shut the gates of mercy on mankind;

The struggling pangs of conscious truth to hide,
    To quench the blushes of ingenuous shame,

Or heap the shrine of Luxury and Pride
   With incense kindled at the Muse's flame.

Far from the madding crowd's ignoble strife,
   Their sober wishes never learned to stray;
Along the cool sequestered vale of life
   They kept the noiseless tenor of their way.

                    THOMAS GRAY.

THIS ROYAL THRONE OF KINGS

THIS royal throne of kings, this sceptred isle,
This earth of majesty, this seat of Mars,
This other Eden, demi-paradise,
This fortress built by Nature for herself
Against infection and the hand of war,
This happy breed of men, this little world,
This precious stone set in the silver sea,
Which serves it in the office of a wall
Or as a moat defensive to a house,
Against the envy of less happier lands,
This blessed plot, this earth, this realm, this England,
This nurse, this teeming womb of royal kings,
Fear'd by their breed and famous by their birth,
Renowned for their deeds as far from home,
For Christian service and true chivalry,
As is the sepulchre in stubborn Jewry
Of the world's ransom, blessed Mary's Son,
This land of such dear souls, this dear dear land,
Dear for her reputation through the world,
Is now leased out, I die pronouncing it,
Like to a tenement or pelting farm:
England, bound in with the triumphant sea,
Whose rocky shore beats back the envious siege
Of watery Neptune, is now bound in with shame,
With inky blots and rotten parchment bonds:
That England, that was wont to conquer others,
Hath made a shameful conquest of itself.
Ah, would the scandal vanish with my life,
How happy then were my ensuing death!

                    WILLIAM SHAKESPEARE.

MEN OF ENGLAND

MEN of England! who inherit
  Rights that cost your sires their blood!
Men whose undegenerate spirit
  Has been proved on land and flood:—

By the foes ye've fought uncounted,
  By the glorious deeds ye've done,
Trophies captured—breaches mounted,
  Navies conquer'd—kingdoms won!

Yet, remember, England gathers
  Hence but fruitless wreaths of fame,
If the patriotism of your fathers
  Glow not in your hearts the same.

What are monuments of bravery,
  Where no public virtues bloom?
What avail in lands of slavery,
  Trophied temples, arch, and tomb?

Pageants!—Let the world revere us
  For our people's rights and laws.
And the breasts of civic heroes
  Bared in Freedom's holy cause.

Yours are Hampden's, Russell's glory,
  Sydney's matchless shade is yours,—
Martyrs in heroic story,
  Worth a hundred Agincourts!

We're the sons of sires that baffled
  Crowned and mitred tyranny:—
They defied the field and scaffold
  For their birthrights—so will we!

THOMAS CAMPBELL.

ENGLAND

ENGLAND, with all thy faults, I love thee still,
My country! and, while yet a nook is left
Where English minds and manners may be found,
Shall be constrained to love thee. Though thy clime
Be fickle, and thy year, most part, deformed
With dripping rains, or withered by a frost,
I would not yet exchange thy sullen skies
And fields without a flower, for warmer France
With all her vines; nor for Ausonia's groves
Of golden fruitage, and her myrtle bowers.
To shake thy senate, and from heights sublime
Of patriot eloquence to flash down fire
Upon thy foes, was never meant my task;
But I can feel thy fortunes, and partake
Thy joys and sorrows with as true a heart
As any thunderer there. And I can feel
Thy follies too, and with a just disdain
Frown at effeminates, whose very looks
Reflect dishonour on the land I love.
How, in the name of soldiership and sense,
Should England prosper, when such things, as smooth
And tender as a girl, all-essenced o'er
With odours, and as profligate as sweet,
Who sell their laurel for a myrtle wreath,
And love when they should fight,—when such as these
Presume to lay their hand upon the ark
Of her magnificent and awful cause?
Time was when it was praise and boast enough
In every clime, and travel where we might,
That we were born her children; praise enough
To fill the ambition of a private man,
That Chatham's language was his mother tongue,
And Wolfe's great name compatriot with his own.
Farewell those honours, and farewell with them
The hope of such hereafter! They have fallen
Each in his field of glory: one in arms,
And one in council—Wolfe upon the lap

Of smiling Victory that moment won,
And Chatham, heart-sick of his country's shame!
They made us many soldiers.   Chatham still
Consulting England's happiness at home,
Secured it by an unforgiving frown
If any wronged her.   Wolfe, where'er he fought,
Put so much of his heart into his act,
That his example had a magnet's force,
And all were swift to follow whom all loved.
Those suns are set.   Oh, rise some other such!
Or all that we have left is empty talk
Of old achievements, and despair of new.

WILLIAM COWPER.

TO THE VIRGINIAN VOYAGE

You brave heroic minds,
Worthy your country's name,
That honour still pursue;
Go and subdue,
Whilst loit'ring hinds
Lurk here at home with shame.

Britons, you stay too long;
Quickly aboard bestow you,
And with a merry gale
Swell your stretch'd sail,
With vows as strong
As the winds that blow you.

Your course securely steer,
West and by south forth keep;
Rocks, lee-shores, nor shoals,
When Eolus scowls,
You need not fear;
So absolute the deep.

And cheerfully at sea
Success you still entice

To get the pearl and gold,
And ours to hold
Virginia,
Earth's only Paradise.

Where nature hath in store
Fowl, venison, and fish,
And the fruitful'st soil,
Without your toil,
Three harvests more,
All greater than your wish.

And the ambitious vine
Crowns with his purple mass
The cedar reaching high
To kiss the sky,
The cypress, pine,
And useful sassafras.

To whom the golden age
Still nature's laws doth give,
No other cares attend
But them to defend
From winter's rage,
That long there doth not live.

When as the luscious smell
Of that delicious land,
Above the seas that flows,
The clear wind throws
Your hearts to swell
Approaching the dear strand;

In kenning of the shore
(Thanks to God first given)
O you, the happiest men,
Be frolic then;
Let cannons roar,
Frighting the wide heaven.

And in regions far,
Such heroes bring ye forth,

As those from whom we came;
   And plant our name
Under that star
Not known unto our North.

And as there plenty grows
Of Laurel everywhere,
   Apollo's sacred tree,
   You it may see,
A poet's brows
To crown, that may sing there.

Thy voyages attend
Industrious Hackluit,
   Whose reading shall inflame
   Men to seek fame,
And much commend
To after-times thy wit.

                 MICHAEL DRAYTON.

THE SONG OF THE BOW

WHAT of the bow?
  The bow was made in England:
Of true wood, of yew-wood,
  The wood of English bows;
    So men who are free
    Love the old yew-tree
And the land where the yew-tree grows.

What of the cord?
  The cord was made in England:
A rough cord, a tough cord,
  A cord that bowmen love;
    And so we will sing
    Of the hempen string
And the land where the cord was wove.

What of the shaft?
  The shaft was cut in England:

A long shaft, a strong shaft,
   Barbed and trim and true;
     So we'll drink all together
     To the grey goose-feather
And the land where the grey goose flew.

What of the mark?
   Ah, seek it not in England,
A bold mark, our old mark
   Is waiting over-sea.
     When the strings harp in chorus,
     And the lion flag is o'er us,
It is there that our mark will be.

What of the men?
   The men were bred in England:
The bowmen—the yeomen,
   The lads of dale and fell.
     Here's to you—and to you!
     To the hearts that are true
And the land where the true hearts dwell.

                  SIR ARTHUR CONAN DOYLE.

THE BARD

" RUIN seize thee, ruthless King!
   Confusion on thy banners wait!
Though fanned by Conquest's crimson wing
   They mock the air with idle state.
Helm, nor hauberk's twisted mail,
Nor e'en thy virtues, tyrant, shall avail
To save thy secret soul from nightly fears,
From Cambria's curse, from Cambria's tears!"
Such were the sounds that o'er the crested pride
   Of the first Edward scattered wild dismay,
As down the steep of Snowdon's shaggy side
   He wound with toilsome march his long array:
Stout Glo'ster stood aghast in speechless trance;
" To arms!" cried Mortimer, and couched his quivering
   lance.

On a rock, whose haughty brow
Frowns o'er old Conway's foaming flood,
  Robed in the sable garb of woe
With haggard eyes the Poet stood
(Loose his beard and hoary hair
Streamed like a meteor to the troubled air),
And with a master's hand and prophet's fire
Struck the deep sorrows of his lyre:
" Hark, how each giant oak and desert-cave
  Sighs to the torrent's awful voice beneath!
O'er thee, O King! their hundred arms they wave,
  Revenge on thee in hoarser murmurs breathe;
Vocal no more, since Cambria's fatal day,
To high-born Hoel's harp or soft Llewellyn's lay.

" Cold is Cadwallo's tongue
  That hushed the stormy main:
Brave Urien sleeps upon his craggy bed:
  Mountains, ye mourn in vain
  Modred, whose magic song
Made huge Plinlimmon bow his cloud-topt head.
  On dreary Arvon's shore they lie
Smeared with gore and ghastly pale:
Far, far aloof the affrighted ravens sail;
  The famished eagle screams, and passes by.
Dear lost companions of my tuneful art,
  Dear as the light that visits these sad eyes,
Dear as the ruddy drops that warm my heart,
  Ye died amidst your dying country's cries!—
No more I weep. They do not sleep.
  On yonder cliffs, a grisly band,
I see them sit; they linger yet,
  Avengers of their native land:
With me in dreadful harmony they join,
And weave with bloody hands the tissue of thy line.

" Weave the warp and weave the woof
  The winding-sheet of Edward's race:
Give ample room and verge enough
  The characters of hell to trace.
Mark the year and mark the night
When Severn shall re-echo with affright

The shrieks of death through Berkeley's roof that ring,
Shrieks of an agonising king!
   She-wolf of France, with unrelenting fangs,
That tear'st the bowels of thy mangled mate,
   From thee be born, who o'er thy country hangs
The scourge of Heaven! What terrors round him wait!
Amazement in his van, with Flight combined,
And Sorrow's faded form, and Solitude behind.

" Mighty victor, mighty lord,
   Low on his funeral couch he lies!
No pitying heart, no eye, afford
   A tear to grace his obsequies.
Is the sable warrior fled?
Thy son is gone. He rests among the dead.
The swarm that in thy noontide beam were born?
Gone to salute the rising morn.

" Fair laughs the Morn, and soft the zephyr blows,
   While proudly riding o'er the azure realm
In gallant trim the gilded vessel goes:
   Youth on the prow and Pleasure at the helm:
Regardless of the sweeping Whirlwind's sway,
That hushed in grim repose expects his evening prey.

   " Fill high the sparkling bowl,
The rich repast prepare;
   Reft of a crown, he yet may share the feast:
Close by the regal chair
   Fell Thirst and Famine scowl
   A baleful smile upon their baffled guest.
Heard ye the din of battle bray,
   Lance to lance and horse to horse?
   Long years of havoc urge their destined course,
And through the kindred squadrons mow their way.
   Ye towers of Julius, London's lasting shame,
With many a foul and midnight murder fed,
   Revere his consort's faith, his father's fame,
And spare the meek usurper's holy head!
Above, below, the rose of snow,
   Twined with her blushing foe, we spread:
The bristled boar in infant-gore

Wallows beneath the thorny shade.
Now, brothers, bending o'er the accursed loom,
Stamp we our vengeance deep, and ratify his doom.

" Edward, lo! to sudden fate
  (Weave we the woof; the thread is spun;)
Half of thy heart we consecrate.
  (The web is wove; the work is done.)
Stay, O stay! nor thus forlorn
Leave me unblessed, unpitied, here to mourn:
In yon bright track that fires the western skies
They melt, they vanish from my eyes.
But O! what solemn scenes on Snowdon's height
  Descending slow their glittering skirts unroll?
Visions of glory, spare my aching sight,
  Ye unborn ages, crowd not on my soul!
No more our long-lost Arthur we bewail:
All hail, ye genuine kings! Britannia's issue, hail!

" Girt with many a baron bold
Sublime their starry fronts they rear;
  And gorgeous dames, and statesmen old
In bearded majesty, appear.
In the midst a form divine!
Her eye proclaims her of the Briton-line:
Her lion-port, her awe-commanding face
Attempered sweet to virgin grace.
What strings symphonious tremble in the air,
  What strains of vocal transport round her play?
Hear from the grave, great Taliessin, hear;
  They breathe a soul to animate thy clay.
Bright Rapture calls and, soaring as she sings,
Waves in the eye of Heaven her many-coloured wings.

" The verse adorn again
  Fierce War and faithful Love
And Truth severe, by fairy fiction drest,
  In buskined measures move
Pale Grief and pleasing Pain,
With Horror, tyrant of the throbbing breast.
A voice as of the cherub-choir
  Gales from blooming Eden bear,
  And distant warblings lessen on my ear

That lost in long futurity expire.
Fond impious man, think'st thou yon sanguine cloud,
　Raised by thy breath, has quenched the orb of day?
To-morrow he repairs the golden flood
　And warms the nations with redoubled ray.
Enough for me: with joy I see
　The different doom our fates assign:
Be thine Despair and sceptred Care,
　To triumph and to die are mine."
He spoke, and headlong from the mountain's height
Deep in the roaring tide he plunged to endless night.

THOMAS GRAY.

THE ISLES OF GREECE

THE isles of Greece, the isles of Greece!
　Where burning Sappho loved and sung,
Where grew the arts of war and peace,
　Where Delos rose, and Phœbus sprung!
Eternal summer gilds them yet,
But all except their sun is set.

The Scian and the Teian muse,
　The hero's harp, the lover's lute,
Have found the fame your shores refuse:
　Their place of birth alone is mute
To sounds which echo further west
Than your sires' " Islands of the Blest."

The mountains look on Marathon—
　And Marathon looks on the sea;
And, musing there an hour alone,
　I dreamed that Greece might still be free;
For, standing on the Persian's grave,
I could not deem myself a slave.

A king sate on the rocky brow
　Which looks o'er sea-born Salamis;
And ships by thousands lay below,
　And men in nations;—all were his!
He counted them at break of day,
And when the sun set, where were they?

B

And where are they? and where art thou,
　My country?　On thy voiceless shore
The heroic lay is tuneless now,
　The heroic bosom beats no more!
And must thy lyre, so long divine,
Degenerate into hands like mine?

'Tis something in the dearth of fame,
　Though linked among a fettered race,
To feel at least a patriot's shame,
　Even as I sing, suffuse my face;
For what is left the poet here?
For Greeks a blush, for Greece a tear!

Must we but weep o'er days more blest?
　Must we but blush?　Our fathers bled.
Earth! render back from out thy breast
　A remnant of our Spartan dead!
Of the three hundred grant but three,
To make a new Thermopylæ!

What, silent still? and silent all?
　Ah! no: the voices of the dead
Sound like a distant torrent's fall,
　And answer, " Let one living head,
But one arise,—we come, we come! "
'Tis but the living who are dumb.

In vain—in vain: strike other chords;
　Fill high the cup with Samian wine!
Leave battles to the Turkish hordes,
　And shed the blood of Scio's vine!
Hark! rising to the ignoble call,
How answers each bold Bacchanal!

You have the Pyrrhic dance as yet;
　Where is the Pyrrhic phalanx gone?
Of two such lessons, why forget
　The nobler and the manlier one?
You have the letters Cadmus gave;
Think ye he meant them for a slave?

Fill high the bowl with Samian wine!
  We will not think of themes like these!
It made Anacreon's song divine:
  He served—but served Polycrates:
A tyrant; but our masters then
Were still, at least, our countrymen.

The tyrant of the Chersonese
  Was freedom's best and bravest friend;
That tyrant was Miltiades!
  Oh! that the present hour would lend
Another despot of the kind!
Such chains as his were sure to bind.

Fill high the bowl with Samian wine!
  On Suli's rock and Parga's shore
Exists the remnant of a line
  Such as the Doric mothers bore;
And there, perhaps, some seed is sown
The Heracleidan blood might own.

Trust not for freedom to the Franks—
  They have a king who buys and sells;
In native swords and native ranks
  The only hope of courage dwells:
But Turkish force and Latin fraud
Would break your shield, however broad.

Fill high the bowl with Samian wine!
  Our virgins dance beneath the shade—
I see their glorious black eyes shine;
  But, gazing on each glowing maid,
My own the burning tear-drop laves,
To think such breasts must suckle slaves.

Place me on Sunium's marbled steep,
  Where nothing save the waves and I
May hear our mutual murmurs sweep;
  There, swan-like, let me sing and die:
A land of slaves shall ne'er be mine—
Dash down yon cup of Samian wine!

                          LORD BYRON.

THE PROPHECY OF CAPYS

In the hall-gate sate Capys,
    Capys, the sightless seer;
From head to foot he trembled
    As Romulus drew near.
And up stood stiff his thin white hair,
    And his blind eyes flashed fire:
" Hail! foster child of the wondrous nurse!
    Hail! son of the wondrous sire!

" But thou—what dost thou hear
    In the old man's peaceful hall?
What doth the eagle in the coop,
    The bison in the stall?
Our corn fills many a garner;
    Our vines clasp many a tree;
Our flocks are white on many a hill;
    But these are not for thee.

" For thee no treasure ripens
    In the Tartessian mine:
For thee no ship brings precious bales
    Across the Libyan brine:
Thou shalt not drink from amber;
    Thou shalt not rest on down;
Arabia shall not steep thy locks,
    Nor Sidon tinge thy gown.

" Leave gold and myrrh and jewels,
    Rich table and soft bed,
To them who of man's seed are born,
    Whom woman's milk have fed.
Thou wast not made for lucre,
    For pleasure, nor for rest;
Thou, that art sprung from the War-god's loins,
    And hast tugged at the she-wolf's breast.

" From sunrise unto sunset
    All earth shall hear thy fame:

A glorious city thou shalt build,
   And name it by thy name:
And there, unquenched through ages,
   Like Vesta's sacred fire,
Shall live the spirit of thy nurse,
   The spirit of thy sire.

" The ox toils through the furrow,
   Obedient to the goad;
The patient ass, up flinty paths,
   Plods with his weary load:
With whine and bound the spaniel
   His master's whistle hears;
And the sheep yields her patiently
   To the loud clashing shears.

" But thy nurse will hear no master;
   Thy nurse will bear no load;
And woe to them that shear her,
   And woe to them that goad!
When all the pack, loud baying,
   Her bloody lair surrounds,
She dies in silence, biting hard,
   Amidst the dying hounds.

" Pomona loves the orchard;
   And Liber loves the vine;
And Pales loves the straw-built shed
   Warm with the breath of kine;
And Venus loves the whispers
   Of plighted youth and maid,
In April's ivory moonlight
   Beneath the chestnut shade.

" But thy father loves the clashing
   Of broadsword and of shield:
He loves to drink the steam that reeks
   From the fresh battle-field:
He smiles a smile more dreadful
   Than his own dreadful frown,
When he sees the thick black cloud of smoke
   Go up from the conquered town.

" And such as is the War-god,
   The author of thy line,
And such as she who suckled thee,
   Even such be thou and thine.
Leave to the soft Campanian
   His baths and his perfumes;
Leave to the sordid race of Tyre
   Their dyeing-vats and looms:
Leave to the sons of Carthage
   The rudder and the oar:
Leave to the Greek his marble Nymphs
   And scrolls of wordy lore.

" Thine, Roman, is the pilum:
   Roman, the sword is thine,
The even trench, the bristling mound,
   The legion's ordered line;
And thine the wheels of triumph,
   Which with their laurelled train
Move slowly up the shouting streets
   To Jove's eternal fane.

" Beneath thy yoke the Volscian
   Shall vail his lofty brow:
Soft Capua's curled revellers
   Before thy chairs shall bow:
The Lucumoes of Arnus
   Shall quake thy rods to see;
And the proud Samnite's heart of steel
   Shall yield to only thee.

" The Gaul shall come against thee
   From the land of snow and night;
Thou shalt give his fair-haired armies
   To the raven and the kite.

" The Greek shall come against thee,
   The conqueror of the East.
Beside him stalks to battle
   The huge earth-shaking beast,
The beast on whom the castle
   With all its guards doth stand,

The beast who hath between his eyes
    The serpent for a hand.
First march the bold Epirotes,
    Wedged close with shield and spear;
And the ranks of false Tarentum
    Are glittering in the rear.

" The ranks of false Tarentum
    Like hunted sheep shall fly:
In vain the bold Epirotes
    Shall round their standards die:
And Apennine's grey vultures
    Shall have a noble feast
On the fat and the eyes
    Of the huge earth-shaking beast.

" Hurrah! for the good weapons
    That keep the War-god's land.
Hurrah! for Rome's stout pilum
    In a stout Roman hand.
Hurrah! for Rome's short broadsword,
    That through the thick array
Of levelled spears and serried shields
    Hews deep its gory way.

" Hurrah! for the great triumph
    That stretches many a mile.
Hurrah! for the wan captives
    That pass in endless file.
Ho! bold Epirotes, whither
    Hath the Red King ta'en flight?
Ho! dogs of false Tarentum,
    Is not the gown washed white?

" Hurrah! for the great triumph
    That stretches many a mile.
Hurrah! for the rich dye of Tyre,
    And the fine web of Nile,
The helmets gay with plumage
    Torn from the pheasant's wings,
The belts set thick with starry gems
    That shone on Indian kings,

The urns of massy silver,
  The goblets rough with gold,
The many-coloured tablets bright
  With loves and wars of old,
The stone that breathes and struggles,
  The brass that seems to speak;—
Such cunning they who dwell on high
  Have given unto the Greek.

" Hurrah! for Manius Curius,
  The bravest son of Rome,
Thrice in utmost need sent forth,
  Thrice drawn in triumph home.
Weave, weave, for Manius Curius
  The third embroidered gown:
Make ready the third lofty car,
  And twine the third green crown;
And yoke the steeds of Rosea
  With necks like a bended bow,
And deck the bull, Mevania's bull,
  The bull as white as snow.

" Blest and thrice blest the Roman
  Who sees Rome's brightest day,
Who sees that long victorious pomp
  Wind down the Sacred Way,
And through the bellowing Forum,
  And round the Suppliant's Grove,
Up to the everlasting gates
  Of Capitolian Jove.

" Then where, o'er two bright havens,
  The towers of Corinth frown;
Where the gigantic King of Day
  On his own Rhodes looks down;
Where soft Orontes murmurs
  Beneath the laurel shades;
Where Nile reflects the endless length
  Of dark-red colonnades;
Where in the still deep water,
  Sheltered from waves and blasts,

Bristles the dusky forest
  Of Byrsa's thousand masts;
Where fur-clad hunters wander
  Amidst the northern ice;
Where through the sand of morning-land
  The camel bears the spice;
Where Atlas flings his shadow
  Far o'er the western foam,
Shall be great fear on all who hear
  The mighty name of Rome."

LORD MACAULAY.

THE WORDS OF FAULCONBRIDGE

THIS England never did, nor never shall,
Lie at the proud foot of a conqueror,
But when it first did help to wound itself.
Now these her princes are come home again,
Come the three corners of the world in arms,
And we shall shock them.   Nought shall make us rue,
If England to itself do rest but true.

WILLIAM SHAKESPEARE.

THE ISLAND

DADDY Neptune one day to Freedom did say,
  " If ever I lived upon dry land,
The spot I should hit on would be little Britain; "
  Says Freedom " Why that's my own Island."
    Oh! what a snug little Island,
      A right little, tight little Island!
    Seek all the globe round, none can be found
      So happy as this little Island.

Julius Cæsar the Roman, who yielded to no man,
  Came by water, he couldn't come by land!
And Dane, Pict, and Saxon, their homes turned their backs on
  And all for the sake of our Island.

Oh! what a snug little Island,
    They'd all have a touch at the Island,
Some were shot dead—some of them fled,
    And some stayed to live on the Island.

Then a very great war-man, called Billy the Norman,
    Cried, " Hang it! I never liked my land;
It would be much more handy to leave this Normandy,
    And live on yon beautiful Island."
    Says he, " 'Tis a snug little Island,
        Shan't us go visit the Island? "
    Hop, skip, and jump,—there he was plump,
        And he kicked up a dust in the Island.

Then the Spanish Armada set out to invade her,
    Quite sure if they ever came nigh land,
They couldn't do less than tuck up Queen Bess,
    And take their full swing in the Island.
    Oh! the poor Queen and the Island,
        The drones came to plunder the Island,
    But snug in her hive the Queen was alive,
        And buzz was the word in the I land.

I don't wonder much that the French and the Dutch
    Have since often been tempted to try land,
And I wonder much less they have met no success,
    For why should we give up our Island?
    We'd fight for our right to the Island,
        We'd give them enough of the Island;
    Invaders should just bite at the dust,
        But not a bit more of the Island.

Then long live the King, may his foes e'er be seen
    To perish before they come nigh land;
And may Providence bless, and grant him success in
    Defending the rights of our Island.
    Oh! it's a free little Island,
        A dear little spot is our Island,
    And Britons all can and will die to a man,
        Ere they give up a grain of our Island.

ANON.

THE ROAST BEEF OF OLD ENGLAND

WHEN mighty roast beef was the Englishman's food,
It ennobled our hearts, and enriched our blood,
Our soldiers were brave and our courtiers were good.
    Oh! the roast beef of old England!
    And oh! for old England's roast beef!

Our fathers of old were robust, stout, and strong,
And kept open house, with good cheer, all day long,
Which made their plump tenants rejoice in the song,
    Oh! the roast beef of old England!
    And oh! for old England's roast beef!

When Good Queen Elizabeth sat on the throne,
Ere coffee and tea and such slip-slops were known,
The world was in terror, if e'er she did frown.
    Oh! the roast beef of old England!
    And oh! for old England's roast beef!

In those days, if fleets did presume on the main,
They seldom or never returned back again,
As witness the vaunting Armada of Spain.
    Oh! the roast beef of old England!
    And oh! for old England's roast beef!

RICHARD LEVERIDGE.

JOHN DORY

As it fell on a holy day,
    And upon a holy tide-a,
John Dory bought him an ambling nag,
    To Paris for to ride-a;
      To Paris for to ride-a,
      And upon a holy tide.

The first man that John Dory did meet,
    Was good King John of France-a,

John Dory could well of his courtesie,
But fell down in a trance-a;
But fell down in a trance-a,
At good King John of France.

" A pardon, a pardon, my liege and my King,
For my merie men and me-a,
And all the churles in merie England,
I'll bring them bound to thee-a,
I'll bring them bound to thee-a,
My merie men and me."

And Nicholl was then a Cornish man,
A little beside Bohyde-a;
And he manned forth a good black bark,
With fifty good oars on a side-a,
With fifty good oars on a side-a,
And he dwelt beside Bohyde.

The roaring cannons then were plied,
And dub-a-dub went the drum-a;
The braying trumpets loud they cried,
To courage both all and some-a,
To courage both all and some-a,
And dub-a-dub went the drum.

The grappling-hooks were brought at length,
The brown bill and the sword-a;
John Dory at length, for all his strength,
Was clapt fast under board-a;
Was clapt fast under board-a,
By the brown bill and the sword.

ANON.

HEART OF OAK

COME, cheer up, my lads, 'tis to glory we steer,
To add something new to this wonderful year;
To honour we call you, not press you like slaves,
For who are so free as the sons of the waves?
Heart of oak are our ships, heart of oak are our men,
We always are ready,
Steady, boys, steady!
We'll fight and we'll conquer again and again!

We ne'er see our foes but we wish them to stay,
They never see us but they wish us away,
If they run, why, we follow, and run them ashore,
For if they won't fight us, we cannot do more.
    Heart of oak are our ships, heart of oak are our men,
      We always are ready,
        Steady, boys, steady!
    We'll fight and we'll conquer again and again!

They swear they'll invade us, these terrible foes,
They frighten our women, our children, our beaux;
But should their flat bottoms in darkness get o'er,
Still Britons they'll find to receive them on shore.
    Heart of oak are our ships, heart of oak are our men,
      We always are ready,
        Steady, boys, steady!
    We'll fight and we'll conquer again and again!
                        DAVID GARRICK

RULE, BRITANNIA!

WHEN Britain first at heaven's command,
    Arose from out the azure main,
This was the charter of the land,
    And guardian angels sang this strain,—
      Rule, Britannia! Britannia rule the waves!
      Britons never shall be slaves.

The nations not so blessed as thee,
    Must in their turns to tyrants fall,
While thou shalt flourish great and free,
    The dread and envy of them all.
      Rule, Britannia! Britannia rule the waves!
      Britons never shall be slaves.

Still more majestic thou shalt rise,
    More dreadful from each foreign stroke,
As the loud blast that tears the skies,
    Serves but to root thy native oak.
      Rule, Britannia! Britannia rule the waves!
      Britons never shall be slaves.

Thee haughty tyrants ne'er shall tame,
　All their attempts to bend thee down
Will but arouse thy gen'rous flame
　　To work their woe and thy renown.
　　　　Rule, Britannia! Britannia rule the waves!
　　　　Britons never shall be slaves.

The Muses still with freedom found,
　Shall to thy happy coast repair;
Blest Isle with matchless beauty crown'd,
　　And manly hearts to guard the fair.
　　　　Rule, Britannia! Britannia rule the waves!
　　　　Britons never shall be slaves.

JAMES THOMSON.

THE FATHERLAND

WHERE is the true man's fatherland?
　Is it where he by chance is born?
　Doth not the yearning spirit scorn
In such scant borders to be spanned?
O, yes! his fatherland must be
As the blue heaven wide and free!

Is it alone where freedom is,
　Where God is God, and man is man?
　Doth he not claim a broader span
For the soul's love of home than this?
O, yes! his fatherland must be
As the blue heaven wide and free!

Where'er a human heart doth wear
　Joy's myrtle-wreath or sorrow's gyves,
　Where'er a human spirit strives
After a life more true and fair,
There is the true man's birthplace grand,
His is a world-wide fatherland!

Where'er a single slave doth pine,
  Where'er one man may help another,—
  Thank God for such a birthright, brother,—
That spot of earth is thine and mine!
There is the true man's birthplace grand,
His is a world-wide fatherland!

J. R. LOWELL.

FREEDOM

WE are not free: Freedom doth not consist
In musing with our faces toward the Past,
While petty cares, and crawling interests, twist
Their spider-threads about us, which at last
Grow strong as iron chains, to cramp and bind
In formal narrowness heart, soul, and mind.
Freedom is recreated year by year,
In hearts wide open on the Godward side,
In souls calm-cadenced as the whirling sphere,
In minds that sway the future like a tide.
No broadest creeds can hold her, and no codes;
She chooses men for her august abodes,
Building them fair and fronting to the dawn;
Yet, when we seek her, we but find a few
Light footprints, leading morn-ward through the dew;
Before the day had risen, she was gone.

And we must follow: swiftly runs she on,
And, if our steps should slacken in despair,
Half turns her face, half smiles, through golden hair,
Forever yielding, never wholly won:
That is not love which pauses in the race
Two close-linked names on fleeting sand to trace;
Freedom gained yesterday is no more ours;
Men gather but dry seeds of last year's flowers;
Still there's a charm ungranted, still a grace,
Still rosy Hope, the free, the unattained,
Makes us Possession's languid hand let fall;
'Tis but a fragment of ourselves is gained,—
The Future brings us more, but never all.

J. R. LOWELL.

O MOTHER STATE

O Mother State, how quenched thy Sinai fires!
    Is there none left of thy staunch Mayflower breed?
No spark among the ashes of thy sires,
    Of Virtue's altar-flame the kindling seed?
Are these thy great men, these that cringe and creep,
    And writhe through slimy ways to place and power?—
How long, O Lord, before thy wrath shall reap
    Our frail-stemmed summer prosperings in their flower?
O for one hour of that undaunted stock
That went with Vane and Sydney to the block!

O for a whiff of Naseby, that would sweep,
    With it stern Puritan besom, all this chaff
From the Lord's threshing-floor!   Yet more than half
The victory is attained when one or two,
    Through the fool's laughter and the traitor's scorn,
    Beside thy sepulchre can abide the morn,
Crucified Truth, when thou shalt rise anew.
J. R. Lowell.

THE DESERTED VILLAGE

Ill fares the land, to hastening ills a prey,
Where wealth accumulates, and men decay:
Princes and lords may flourish, or may fade—
A breath can make them, as a breath has made:
But a bold peasantry, their country's pride,
When once destroyed, can never be supplied.

A time there was, ere England's griefs began,
When every rood of ground maintained its man;
For him light labour spread her wholesome store,
Just gave what life required, but gave no more:
His best companions, innocence and health,
And his best riches ignorance of wealth.

But times are altered; trade's unfeeling train
Usurp the land, and dispossess the swain:
Along the lawn, where scattered hamlets rose,
Unwieldy wealth and cumbrous pomp repose;
And every want to luxury allied,
And every pang that folly pays to pride.
Those gentle hours that plenty bade to bloom,
Those calm desires that asked but little room,
Those healthful sports that graced the peaceful scene,
Lived in each look, and brightened all the green;
These, far departing, seek a kinder shore,
And rural mirth and manners are no more.

OLIVER GOLDSMITH.

HARP OF THE NORTH

HARP of the North! that mouldering long hast hung
   On the witch-elm that shades Saint Fillan's spring,
And down the fitful breeze thy numbers flung,
   Till envious ivy did around thee cling,
Muffling with verdant ringlet every string,—
   O minstrel Harp, still must thine accents sleep?
Mid rustling leaves and fountains murmuring,
   Still must thy sweeter sounds their silence keep,
Nor bid a warrior smile, nor teach a maid to weep?

Not thus, in ancient days of Caledon,
   Was thy voice mute amid the festal crowd,
When lay of hopeless love, or glory won,
   Aroused the fearful, or subdued the proud.
At each according pause, was heard aloud
   Thine ardent symphony sublime and high!
Fair dames and crested chiefs attention bow'd;
   For still the burden of thy minstrelsy
Was Knighthood's dauntless deed, and Beauty's matchless
   eye.

O wake once more! how rude soe'er the hand
   That ventures o'er thy magic maze to stray;

C

O wake once more! though scarce my skill command
  Some feeble echoing of thine earlier lay:
Though harsh and faint, and soon to die away,
  And all unworthy of thy nobler strain,
Yet if one heart throb higher at its sway,
  The wizard note has not been touch'd in vain.
Then silent be no more! Enchantress, wake again!

Harp of the North, farewell! The hills grow dark,
  On purple peaks a deeper shade descending;
In twilight copse the glow-worm lights her spark,
  The deer, half-seen, are to the covert wending.
Resume thy wizard elm! the fountain lending,
  And the wild breeze, thy wilder minstrelsy;
Thy numbers sweet with nature's vespers blending,
  With distant echo from the fold and lea,
And herd-boy's evening pipe, and hum of housing bee.

Yet, once again, farewell, thou Minstrel harp!
  Yet, once again, forgive my feeble sway,
And little reck I of the censure sharp
  May idly cavil at an idle lay.
Much have I owed thy strains on life's long way,
  Through secret woes the world has never known,
When on the weary night dawn'd wearier day,
  And bitterer was the grief devour'd alone.
That I o'erlive such woes, Enchantress! is thine own.

Hark! as my lingering footsteps slow retire,
  Some Spirit of the Air has waked thy string!
'Tis now a seraph bold, with touch of fire,
  'Tis now the brush of Fairy's frolic wing.
Receding now, the dying numbers ring
  Fainter and fainter down the rugged dell,
And now the mountain breezes scarcely bring
  A wandering witch-note of the distant spell—
And now, 'tis silent all!—Enchantress, fare thee well!

                  SIR WALTER SCOTT.

I TELL THEE, PRIEST

I TELL thee, priest, when shoemakers make shoes
That are well sewed, with never a stitch amiss,
And use no craft in uttering of the same;
When tailors steal no stuff from gentlemen,
When tanners are with curriers well agreed,
And both so dress their hides that we go dry;
When cutlers leave to sell old rusty blades,
And hide no cracks with solder nor deceit;
When tinkers make no more holes than they found,
When thatchers think their wages worth their work,
When colliers put no dust into their sacks,
When maltmen make us drink no firmentie,
When Davy Diker digs and dallies not,
When smiths shoe horses as they would be shod,
When millers toll not with a golden thumb,
When bakers make not barm bear price of wheat,
When brewers put no baggage in their beer,
When butchers blow not over all their flesh,
When horse-coursers beguile no friends with jades,
When weavers' weight is found in housewives' web;
(But why dwell I so long among these louts?)

When mercers make no bones to swear and lie,
When vintners mix no water with their wine,
When printers pass none errors in their books,
When hatters use to buy none old cast robes,
When goldsmiths get no gains by solder'd crowns,
When upholsters sell feathers without dust,
When pewterers infect no tin with lead,
When drapers draw on gains by giving day,
When parchmentiers put in no ferret silk,
When surgeons heal all wounds without delay:
(Tush, these are toys, but yet my glass showeth all.)

When purveyors provide not for themselves,
When takers take no bribes nor use no brags,
When customers conceal no covine used,
When searchers see all corners in a ship,

(And spy no pence by any sight they see).
When shrives do serve all process as they ought,
When bailiffs strain none other thing but strays,
When auditors their counters cannot change,
When proud surveyors take no parting pence,
When silver sticks not on the teller's fingers,
And when receivers pay as they receive:
When all these folk have quite forgotten fraud,

(Again my priests, a little by your leave.)
When sycophantes can find no place in court,
But are espied for echoes, as they are;
When roisters ruffle not above their rule,
Nor colour craft by swearing " precious coles; "
When fencers' fees are like to apes' rewards,
A piece of bread and therewithall a bob;
When Lais lives not like a lady's peer,
Nor useth art in dyeing of her hair;
When all these things are ordered as they ought,
And see themselves within my glass of steel:
Even then (my priests) may you make holiday,
And pray no more but ordinary prayers.

GEORGE GASCOIGNE.

THE DESTRUCTION OF SENNACHERIB

THE Assyrian came down like the wolf on the fold,
And his cohorts were gleaming in purple and gold;
And the sheen of their spears was like stars on the sea,
When the blue wave rolls nightly on deep Galilee.

Like the leaves of the forest when summer is green,
That host with their banners at sunset were seen:
Like the leaves of the forest when autumn hath blown,
That host on the morrow lay withered and strown.

For the Angel of Death spread his wings on the blast,
And breathed on the face of the foe as he passed:
And the eyes of the sleepers waxed deadly and chill,
And their hearts but once heaved, and for ever grew still!

And there lay the steed with his nostril all wide,
But through it there rolled not the breath of his pride:
And the foam of his gasping lay white on the turf,
And cold as the spray of the rock-beating surf.

And there lay the rider distorted and pale,
With the dew on his brow and the rust on his mail;
The tents were all silent, the banners alone,
The lances unlifted, the trumpet unblown.

And the widows of Ashur are loud in their wail,
And the idols are broke in the temple of Baal;
And the might of the Gentile, unsmote by the sword,
Hath melted like snow in the glance of the Lord!

LORD BYRON.

CHRISTMAS

RING out, wild bells, to the wild sky,
　　The flying cloud, the frosty light:
　　The year is dying in the night;
Ring out, wild bells, and let him die.

Ring out the old, ring in the new,
　　Ring, happy bells, across the snow:
　　The year is going, let him go;
Ring out the false, ring in the true.

Ring out the grief that saps the mind,
　　For those that here we see no more;
　　Ring out the feud of rich and poor,
Ring in redress to all mankind.

Ring out a slowly dying cause,
　　And ancient forms of party strife;
　　Ring in the nobler modes of life,
With sweeter manners, purer laws.

Ring out the want, the care, the sin,
　　The faithless coldness of the times;
　　Ring out, ring out my mournful rhymes,
But ring the fuller minstrel in.

Ring out false pride in place and blood,
　　The civic slander and the spite;
　　Ring in the love of truth and right,
Ring in the common love of good.

Ring out old shapes of foul disease;
　　Ring out the narrowing lust of gold;
　　Ring out the thousand wars of old,
Ring in the thousand years of peace.

Ring in the valiant man and free,
　　The larger heart, the kindlier hand;
　　Ring out the darkness of the land,
Ring in the Christ that is to be.

　　　　　　　　　　　　LORD TENNYSON.

THE PATRIOT

I

IT was roses, roses, all the way,
　　With myrtle mixed in my path like mad.
The house-roofs seemed to heave and sway,
　　The church-spires flamed, such flags they had,
A year ago on this very day!

II

The air broke into a mist with bells,
　　The old walls rocked with the crowds and cries.
Had I said, " Good folks, mere noise repels—
　　But give me your sun from yonder skies! "
They had answered, " And afterward, what else? "

III

Alack, it was I who leaped at the sun,
　　To give it my loving friends to keep.
Nought man could do, have I left undone
　　And you see my harvest, what I reap
This very day, now a year is run.

IV

There's nobody on the house-tops now—
　　Just a palsied few at the windows set—
For the best of the sight is, all allow,
　　At the Shambles' Gate—or, better yet,
By the very scaffold's foot, I trow.

V

I go in the rain, and, more than needs,
　　A rope cuts both my wrists behind,
And I think, by the feel, my forehead bleeds,
　　For they fling, whoever has a mind,
Stones at me for my year's misdeeds.

VI

Thus I entered Brescia, and thus I go!
　　In such triumphs, people have dropped down dead.
" Thou, paid by the World,—what dost thou owe
　　Me? " God might have questioned: but now instead
'Tis God shall requite　I am safer so.

ROBERT BROWNING.

THE COTTER'S SATURDAY NIGHT

THE cheerfu' supper done, wi' serious face,
　　They, round the ingle, form a circle wide;
The sire turns o'er, wi' patriarchal grace,
　　The big ha' Bible, ance his father's pride;
His bonnet rev'rently is laid aside,
　　His lyart haffets [1] wearing thin and bare;
Those strains that once did sweet in Zion glide,
　　He wales [2] a portion with judicious care;
And " Let us worship GOD! " he says, with solemn air.

They chant their artless notes in simple guise;
　　They tune their hearts, by far the noblest aim:
Perhaps " Dundee's " wild-warbling measures rise,
　　Or plaintive " Martyrs," worthy of the name;

[1] Grey temples.　　　[2] Selects.

Or noble " Elgin " beets the heaven-ward flame,
    The sweetest far of Scotia's holy lays:
Compared with these, Italian trills are tame;
    The tickled ear no heartfelt raptures raise;
Nae unison hae they with our Creator's praise.

The priest-like father reads the sacred page,
    How Abram was the friend of GOD on high;
Or, Moses bade eternal warfare wage
    With Amalek's ungracious progeny:
Or how the royal bard did groaning lie
    Beneath the stroke of Heaven's avenging ire;
Or Job's pathetic plaint, and wailing cry;
    Or rapt Isaiah's wild, seraphic fire;
Or other holy seers that tune the sacred lyre.

Perhaps the Christian volume is the theme,
    How guiltless blood for guilty man was shed;
How HE, who bore in Heaven the second name,
    Had not on earth whereon to lay His head:
How His first followers and servants sped,
    The precepts sage they wrote to many a land:
How he, who lone in Patmos banishèd,
    Saw in the sun a mighty angel stand;
And heard great Bab'lon's doom pronounced by Heaven's
    command.

Then kneeling down, to HEAVEN'S ETERNAL KING,
    The saint, the father, and the husband prays:
Hope " springs exulting on triumphant wing,"
    That thus they all shall meet in future days:
There ever bask in uncreated rays,
    No more to sigh or shed the bitter tear,
Together hymning their Creator's praise,
    In such society, yet still more dear;
While circling time moves round in an eternal sphere.

Compared with this, how poor religion's pride,
    In all the pomp of method, and of art,
When men display to congregations wide
    Devotion's every grace, except the heart!

The Power, incensed, the pageant will desert,
    The pompous strain, the sacerdotal stole:
But, haply, in some cottage far apart,
    May hear, well pleased, the language of the soul;
And in His book of life the inmates poor enrol.

Then homeward all take off their several way;
    The youngling cottagers retire to rest:
The parent-pair their secret homage pay,
    And proffer up to Heaven the warm request
That HE, who stills the raven's clamorous nest,
    And decks the lily fair in flowery pride,
Would, in the way His wisdom sees the best,
    For them and for their little ones provide;
But, chiefly, in their hearts with grace divine preside.

From scenes like these old Scotia's grandeur springs,
    That makes her loved at home, revered abroad:
Princes and lords are but the breath of kings,
    " An honest man's the noblest work of GOD; "
And certes, in fair virtue's heavenly road,
    The cottage leaves the palace far behind.
What is a lordling's pomp?—a cumbrous load,
    Disguising oft the wretch of human kind,
Studied in arts of hell, in wickedness refined!

O Scotia! my dear, my native soil!
    For whom my warmest wish to Heaven is sent!
Long may thy hardy sons of rustic toil
    Be blest with health, and peace, and sweet content!
And, oh! may Heaven their simple lives prevent
    From luxury's contagion, weak and vile!
Then, howe'er crown and coronets be rent,
    A virtuous populace may rise the while,
And stand a wall of fire around their much-loved isle.

                      ROBERT BURNS.

MY HEART'S IN THE HIGHLANDS

My heart's in the Highlands, my heart is not here;
My heart's in the Highlands, a-chasing the deer;
A-chasing the wild deer, and following the roe—
My heart's in the Highlands wherever I go.

Farewell to the Highlands, farewell to the North,
The birthplace of valour, the country of worth;
Wherever I wander, wherever I rove,
The hills of the Highlands for ever I love.

Farewell to the mountains high cover'd with snow;
Farewell to the straths and green valleys below;
Farewell to the forests and wild-hanging woods;
Farewell to the torrents and loud-pouring floods.

My heart's in the Highlands, my heart is not here;
My heart's in the Highlands a-chasing the deer;
A-chasing the wild deer, and following the roe—
My heart's in the Highlands wherever I go.

ROBERT BURNS.

PROLOGUES TO HENRY V

O FOR a Muse of fire, that would ascend
The brightest heaven of invention,
A kingdom for a stage, princes to act,
And monarchs to behold the swelling scene!
Then should the warlike Harry, like himself,
Assume the port of Mars; and at his heels,
Leash'd in like hounds, should famine, sword, and fire
Crouch for employment. But pardon, gentles all,
The fla t unraised spirit that hath dar'd
On this unworthy scaffold to bring forth
So great an object: can this cockpit hold
The vasty fields of France? or may we cram
Within this wooden O the very casques

That did affright the air at Agincourt?
O, pardon! since a crooked figure may
Attest in little place a million;
And let us, ciphers to this great accompt,
On your imaginary forces work.
Suppose within the girdle of these walls
Are now confin'd two mighty monarchies,
Whose high-upreared and abutting fronts
The perilous, narrow ocean parts asunder.
Piece out our imperfections with your thoughts;
Into a thousand parts divide one man,
And make imaginary puissance:
Think, when we talk of horses, that you see them
Printing their proud hoofs i' the receiving earth;
For 't is your thoughts that now must deck our kings,
Carry them here and there, jumping o'er times,
Turning the accomplishment of many years
Into an hour-glass: for the which supply,
Admit me Chorus to this history;
Who prologue-like your humble patience pray,
Gently to hear, kindly to judge, our play.

Now all the youth of England are on fire,
And silken dalliance in the wardrobe lies:
Now thrive the armourers, and honour's thought
Reigns solely in the breast of every man.
They sell the pasture now to buy the horse,
Following the mirror of all Christian kings,
With winged heels, as English Mercuries;
For now sits Expectation in the air,
And hides a sword from hilts unto the point
With crowns imperial, crowns, and coronets,
Promis'd to Harry and his followers.
The French, advis'd by good intelligence
Of this most dreadful preparation,
Shake in their fear, and with pale policy
Seek to divert the English purposes.
O England! model to thy inward greatness,
Like little body with a mighty heart,
What mightst thou do, that honour would thee do,
Were all thy children kind and natural!
But see thy fault! France hath in thee found out

A nest of hollow bosoms, which he fills
With treacherous crowns; and three corrupted men,
One, Richard Earl of Cambridge, and the second,
Henry Lord Scroop of Masham, and the third,
Sir Thomas Grey, knight, of Northumberland,
Have, for the gilt of France,—O guilt indeed!—
Confirm'd conspiracy with fearful France;
And by their hands this grace of kings must die,
If hell and treason hold their promises,
Ere he take ship for France, and in Southampton.
Linger your patience on, and well digest
The abuse of distance; force a play.
The sum is paid; the traitors are agreed;
The king is set from London; and the scene
Is now transported, gentles, to Southampton;
There is the playhouse now, there must you sit:
And thence to France shall we convey you safe,
And bring you back, charming the narrow seas
To give you gentle pass; for, if we may,
We'll not offend one stomach with our play.
But, till the king come forth, and not till then,
Unto Southampton do we shift our scene.

    Thus with imagin'd wing our swift scene flies,
In motion of no less celerity
Than that of thought.   Suppose that you have seen
The well-appointed king at Hampton pier
Embark his royalty; and his brave fleet
With silken streamers the young Phœbus fanning:
Play with your fancies, and in them behold
Upon the hempen tackle ship-boys climbing;
Hear the shrill whistle which doth order give
To sounds confus'd; behold the threaden sails,
Borne with the invisible and creeping wind,
Draw the huge bottoms through the furrow'd sea,
Breasting the lofty surge.   O, do but think
You stand upon the rivage and behold
A city on the inconstant billows dancing;
For so appears this fleet majestical,
Holding due course to Harfleur.   Follow, follow!
Grapple your minds to sternage of this navy,
And leave your England, as dead midnight still,

Guarded with grandsires, babies, and old women,
Either past or not arriv'd to pith and puissance;
For who is he, whose chin is but enrich'd
With one appearing hair, that will not follow
These cull'd and choice-drawn cavaliers to France?
Work, work your thoughts, and therein see a siege;
Behold the ordnance on their carriages,
With fatal mouths gaping on girded Harfleur.
Suppose the ambassador from the French comes back;
Tells Harry that the king doth offer him
Katherine his daughter, and with her, to dowry,
Some petty and unprofitable dukedoms.
The offer likes not: and the nimble gunner
With linstock now the devilish cannon touches,
                [Alarum, and chambers go off.
And down goes all before them. Still be kind,
And eke out our performance with your mind.

   Now entertain conjecture of a time
When creeping murmur and the poring dark
Fills the wide vessel of the universe.
From camp to camp through the foul womb of night
The hum of either army stilly sounds,
That the fix'd sentinels almost receive
The secret whispers of each other's watch.
Fire answers fire, and through their paly flames
Each battle sees the other's umber'd face:
Steed threatens steed, in high and boastful neighs
Piercing the night's dull ear; and from the tents
The armourers, accomplishing the knights,
With busy hammers closing rivets up,
Give dreadful note of preparation:
The country cocks do crow, the clocks do toll,
And the third hour of drowsy morning name.
Proud of their numbers and secure in soul,
The confident and over-lusty French
Do the low-rated English play at dice;
And chide the cripple tardy-gaited night,
Who, like a foul and ugly witch, doth limp
So tediously away. The poor condemned English,
Like sacrifices, by their watchful fires
Sit patiently, and inly ruminate

The morning's danger; and their gesture sad,
Investing lank-lean cheeks and war-worn coats,
Presenteth them unto the gazing moon
So many horrid ghosts.   O now, who will behold
The royal captain of this ruin'd band
Walking from watch to watch, from tent to tent,
Let him cry " Praise and glory on his head! "
For forth he goes and visits all his host,
Bids them good morrow with a modest smile,
And calls them brothers, friends, and countrymen.
Upon his royal face there is no note
How dread an army hath enrounded him;
Nor doth he dedicate one jot of colour
Unto the weary and all-watched night,
But freshly looks, and over-bears attaint
With cheerful semblance and sweet majesty;
That every wretch, pining and pale before,
Beholding him, plucks comfort from his looks:
A largess universal like the sun
His liberal eye doth give to every one,
Thawing cold fear, that, mean and gentle all
Behold, as may unworthiness define,
A little touch of Harry in the night.
And so our scene must to the battle fly;
Where—O for pity!—we shall much disgrace
With four or five most vile and ragged foils,
Right ill-dispos'd in brawl ridiculous,
The name of Agincourt.   Yet sit and see,
Minding true things by what their mockeries be.

Vouchsafe to those that have not read the story,
That I may prompt them: and of such as have,
I humbly pray them to admit the excuse
Of time, of numbers, and due course of things,
Which cannot in their huge and proper life
Be here presented.   Now we bear the king
Toward Calais: grant him there; there seen,
Heave him away upon your winged thoughts
Athwart the sea.   Behold, the English beach
Pales in the flood with men, with wives, and boys,
Whose shouts and claps out-voice the deep-mouth'd sea,
Which like a mighty whiffler fore the king

Seems to prepare his way: so let him land,
And solemnly see him set on to London.
So swift a pace hath thought that even now
You may imagine him upon Blackheath;
Where that his lords desire him to have borne
His bruised helmet and his bended sword
Before him through the city: he forbids it,
Being free from vainness and self-glorious pride;
Giving full trophy, signal, and ostent
Quite from himself to God.   But now behold,
In the quick forge and working-house of thought,
How London doth pour out her citizens!
The mayor and all his brethren in best sort,
Like to the senators of the antique Rome,
With the plebeians swarming at their heels,
Go forth and fetch their conquering Cæsar in;
As, by a lower but loving likelihood,
Were now the general of our gracious empress,
As in good time he may, from Ireland coming,
Bringing rebellion broached on his sword,
How many would the peaceful city quit,
To welcome him! much more, and much more cause,
Did they this Harry.   Now in London place him;—
As yet the lamentation of the French
Invites the King of England's stay at home;
The emperor coming in behalf of France,
To order peace between them;—and omit
All the occurrences, whatever chanc'd,
Till Harry's back-return again to France:
There must we bring him; and myself have play'd
The interim, by remembering you 't is past.
Then brook abridgment, and your eyes advance,
After your thoughts, straight back again to France.

WILLIAM SHAKESPEARE.

WAR AND PEACE

WAR

PREPARE, prepare the iron helm of war,
Bring forth the lots, cast in the spacious orb;
The Angel of Fate turns them with mighty hands,
And casts them out upon the darkened earth.
                    Prepare, prepare.

Prepare your hearts for Death's cold hand! prepare
Your souls for flight, your bodies for the earth!
Prepare your arms for glorious victory.
Prepare your eyes to meet a holy God.
                    Prepare, prepare.

Whose fatal scroll is that?   Methinks 'tis mine.
Why sinks my heart, why faltereth my tongue?
Had I three lives, I'd die in such a cause,
And rise, with ghosts, over the well-fought field.
                    Prepare, prepare.

The arrows of Almighty God are drawn.
Angels of Death stand in the low'ring heavens.
Thousands of souls must seek the realms of light,
And walk together on the clouds of heaven.
                    Prepare, prepare.

Soldiers, prepare! Our cause is Heaven's cause;
Soldiers, prepare! Be worthy of our cause:
Prepare to meet our fathers in the sky:
Prepare, O troops that are to fall to-day.
                    Prepare, prepare.

Alfred shall smile, and make his heart rejoice;
The Norman William and the learned Clerk,
And Lion-Heart, and black-browed Edward with
His loyal queen, shall rise, and welcome us.
                    Prepare, prepare!
                              WILLIAM BLAKE.

WAR

PRIVATE Smith of the Royals; the veldt and a slate-black
    sky,
Hillocks of mud, brick-red with blood, and a prayer—half
    curse—to die.
A lung and a Mauser bullet; pink froth and a half-choked cry.

Private Smith of the Royals; a torrent of freezing rain;
A hail of frost on a life half lost; despair and a grinding pain.
And the drip-drip-drip of the Heavens to wash out the brand
    of Cain.

Private Smith of the Royals, self-sounding his funeral knell;
A burning throat that each gasping note scrapes raw like a
    broken shell.
A thirst like a red-hot iron and a tongue like a patch of Hell.

Private Smith of the Royals; the blush of a dawning day;
The fading mist that the sun has kissed—and over the hills
    away
The blest Red Cross like an angel in the trail of the men who
    slay.

But Private Smith of the Royals gazed up at the soft blue
    sky—
The rose-tinged morn like a babe new born and the sweet-
    songed birds on high—
With a fleck of red on his pallid lip and a film of white on
    his eye.

HERBERT CADETT.

THE MINSTREL BOY

THE Minstrel Boy to the war is gone
    In the ranks of death you'll find him,
His father's sword he has girded on,
    And his wild harp slung behind him.

The Soldier's Tear

" Land of song!" said the warrior bard,
  " Tho' all the world betrays thee,
One sword, at least, thy rights shall guard,
  One faithful harp shall praise thee."

The minstrel fell! but the foeman's chain
  Could not bring that proud soul under;
The harp he loved ne'er spoke again,
  For he tore its chords asunder;
And said, " No chain shall sully thee,
  Thou soul of love and bravery.
Thy songs were made for the pure and free,
  They shall never sound in slavery."

THOMAS MOORE.

THE SOLDIER'S TEAR

UPON the hill he turn'd
  To take a last fond look
Of the valley and the village church,
  And the cottage by the brook.
He listen'd to the sounds
  So familiar to his ear,
And the soldier leant upon his sword,
  And wip'd away a tear.

Beside that cottage porch
  A girl was on her knees,
She held aloft a snowy scarf,
  Which flutter'd in the breeze.
She breath'd a prayer for him,
  A prayer he could not hear,
But he paused to bless her as she knelt,
  And wip'd away a tear.

He turn'd and left the spot,
  Oh do not deem him weak,
For dauntless was the soldier's heart,
  Tho' tears were on his cheek.
Go watch the foremost ranks,
  In danger's dark career,
Be sure the hand most daring there,
  Has wip'd away a tear.   ALEXANDER LEE.

LULLABY OF AN INFANT CHIEF

O, HUSH thee, my babie, thy sire was a knight,
Thy mother a lady, both lovely and bright;
The woods and the glens, from the towers which we see,
They all are belonging, dear babie, to thee.

O, fear not the bugle, though loudly it blows,
It calls but the warders that guard thy repose;
Their bows would be bended, their blades would be red,
Ere the step of a foemen draws near to thy bed.

O, hush thee, my babie, the time soon will come,
When thy sleep shall be broken by trumpet and drum;
Then hush thee, my darling, take rest while you may,
For strife comes with manhood, and waking with day.

SIR WALTER SCOTT.

PIBROCH

PIBROCH of Donuil Dhu,
   Pibroch of Donuil,
Wake thy wild voice anew,
   Summon Clan-Conuil.
Come away, come away,
   Hark to the summons!
Come in your war array,
   Gentles and commons.

Come from deep glen, and
   From mountain so rocky,
The war-pipe and pennon
   Are at Inverlochy.
Come every hill-plaid, and
   True heart that wears one,
Come every steel blade, and
   Strong hand that bears one.

Leave untended the herd,
   The flock without shelter;
Leave the corpse uninterr'd,
   The bride at the altar;
Leave the deer, leave the steer,
   Leave nets and barges:
Come with your fighting gear,
   Broadswords and targes.

Come as the winds come, when
   Forests are rended,
Come as the waves come, when
   Navies are stranded:
Faster come, faster come,
   Faster and faster,
Chief, vassal, page and groom,
   Tenant and master.

Fast they come, fast they come;
   See how they gather!
Wide waves the eagle plume,
   Blended with heather.
Cast your plaids, draw your blades,
   Forward each man set!
Pibroch of Donuil Dhu,
   Knell for the onset!

SIR WALTER SCOTT.

A DIRGE

REST on your battle-fields, ye brave.
Let the pines murmur o'er your grave,
Your dirge be in the moaning wave—
   We call you back no more.

O there was mourning when ye fell,
In your own vales a deep-toned knell,
An agony, a wild farewell—
   But that hath long been o'er.

Rest with your still and solemn fame;
The hills keep record of your name,
And never can a touch of shame
    Darken the buried brow.

But we on changeful days are cast
When bright names from their place fall fast;
And ye that with your glory passed,
    We cannot mourn you now.

Felicia Hemans.

THE WAR-HORSE

Hast thou given the horse strength?
Hast thou clothed his neck with thunder?
Canst thou make him afraid as a grasshopper?
The glory of his nostrils is terrible.
He paweth in the valley, and rejoiceth in his strength:
He goeth on to meet the armed men.
He mocketh at fear, and is not affrighted;
Neither turneth he back from the sword.
The quiver rattleth against him,
The glittering spear and the shield.
He swalloweth the ground with fierceness and rage:
Neither believeth he that it is the sound of the trumpet.
He saith among the trumpets, Ha! ha!
And he smelleth the battle afar off,
The thunder of the captains, and the shouting.

Job xxxix.

WAR SONG OF THE RED SEA

I will sing unto the Lord,
    For he hath triumphed gloriously:
The horse and his rider
    Hath he thrown into the sea.

The Lord is my strength and song,
  And he is become my salvation:
He is my God,
    And I will prepare him an habitation;
  My father's God,
    And I will exalt him.
The Lord is a man of war:
  The Lord is his name.
Pharaoh's chariots and his host
    Hath he cast into the sea:
  His chosen captains also
    Are drowned in the Red Sea.
The depths have covered them:
  They sank into the bottom as a stone.

Thy right hand, O Lord,
  Is become glorious in power:
Thy right hand, O Lord,
  Hath dashed in pieces the enemy.
And in the greatness of thine excellency
  Thou hast overthrown them
    That rose up against thee:
Thou sentest forth thy wrath,
  Which consumed them as stubble.
And with the blast of thy nostrils
  The waters were gathered together,
The floods stood upright as an heap,
  And the depths were congealed
    In the heart of the sea.
The enemy said,
  I will pursue, I will overtake,
  I will divide the spoil;
  My lust shall be satisfied upon them;
  I will draw my sword,
  My hand shall destroy them.
Thou didst blow with thy wind
  The sea covered them:
  They sank as lead in the mighty waters.

EXODUS xv.

WAR SONG OF KISHON

THEN sang Deborah and Barak the son of Abinoam on that
    day, saying,
    Praise ye the Lord for the avenging of Israel,
When the people willingly offered themselves.
Hear, O ye kings;
Give ear, O ye princes;
I, even I, will sing unto the Lord;
I will sing praise to the Lord God of Israel.
Lord, when thou wentest out of Seir,
When thou marchedst out of the field of Edom,
The earth trembled, and the heavens dropped,
The clouds also dropped water.
The mountains melted from before the Lord,
Even that Sinai from before the Lord God of Israel.

    In the days of Shamgar the son of Anath,
In the days of Jael, the highways were unoccupied,
And the travellers walked through byways.
The inhabitants of the villages ceased,
They ceased in Israel,
Until that I Deborah arose,
That I arose a mother in Israel.
They chose new gods;
Then was war in the gates:
Was there a shield or spear seen
Among forty thousand in Israel?

    My heart is toward the governors of Israel,
That offered themselves willingly among the people.
Bless ye the Lord.
Speak,
Ye that ride on white asses,
Ye that sit in judgment,
And walk by the way.
They that are delivered from the noise of archers in the places
    of drawing water,
There shall they rehearse the righteous acts of the Lord,
Even the righteous acts toward the inhabitants of his villages
    in Israel:

Then shall the people of the Lord go down to the gates.
Awake, awake, Deborah:
Awake, awake, utter a song:
Arise, Barak,
And lead thy captivity captive, thou son of Abinoam.

Then he made him that remaineth have dominion over the
  nobles among the people:
The Lord made me have dominion over the mighty.
Out of Ephraim was there a root of them against Amalek;
After thee, Benjamin, among thy people;
Out of Machir came down governors,
And out of Zebulun they that handle the pen of the writer.
And the princes of Issachar were with Deborah;
Even Issachar, and also Barak:
He was sent on foot into the valley.
For the divisions of Reuben
There were great thoughts of heart.
Why abodest thou among the sheepfolds,
To hear the bleatings of the flocks?
For the divisions of Reuben
There were great searchings of heart.
Gilead abode beyond Jordan:
And why did Dan remain in ships?
Asher continued on the sea-shore,
And abode in his breaches.
Zebulun and Naphtali were a people that jeoparded their
  lives
Unto the death in the high places of the field.

The kings came and fought,
Then fought the kings of Canaan
In Taanach by the waters of Megiddo;
They took no gain of money.
They fought from heaven;
The stars in their courses fought against Sisera.
The river of Kishon swept them away,
That ancient river, the river Kishon.
O my soul, thou hast trodden down strength.
Then were the horsehoofs broken
By the means of the prancings, the prancings of their mighty
  ones.

Curse ye Meroz, said the angel of the Lord,
Curse ye bitterly the inhabitants thereof;
Because they came not to the help of the Lord,
To the help of the Lord against the mighty.

JUDGES V.

BOADICEA

WHEN the British warrior Queen,
  Bleeding from the Roman rods,
Sought, with an indignant mien,
  Counsel of her country's gods,

Sage beneath a spreading oak
  Sat the Druid, hoary chief,
Every burning word he spoke
  Full of rage, and full of grief:

" Princess! if our aged eyes
  Weep upon thy matchless wrongs,
'Tis because resentment ties
  All the terrors of our tongues.

" Rome shall perish—write that word
  In the blood that she has spilt;
Perish, hopeless and abhorr'd,
  Deep in ruin as in guilt.

" Rome, for empire far renown'd,
  Tramples on a thousand states;
Soon her pride shall kiss the ground—
  Hark! the Gaul is at her gates!

" Other Romans shall arise,
  Heedless of a soldier's name;
Sounds, not arms, shall win the prize,
  Harmony the path to fame.

" Then the progeny that springs
  From the forests of our land,
Armed with thunder, clad with wings,
  Shall a wider world command.

" Regions Cæsar never knew
   Thy posterity shall sway;
Where his eagles never flew,
   None invincible as they."

Such the bard's prophetic words,
   Pregnant with celestial fire,
Bending as he swept the chords
   Of his sweet but awful lyre.

She, with all a monarch's pride,
   Felt them in her bosom glow;
Rush'd to battle, fought and died;
   Dying, hurl'd them at the foe.

Ruffians, pitiless as proud,
   Heaven awards the vengeance due;
Empire is on us bestowed,
   Shame and ruin wait for you!

WILLIAM COWPER.

CHEVY CHACE

GOD prosper long our noble king,
   Our liffes and safetyes all;
A woefull hunting once there did
   In Chevy-Chace befall.

To drive the deere with hound and horne,
   Erle Percy took his way;
The child may rue that is unborne
   The hunting of that day.

The stout Erle of Northumberland
   A vow to God did make,
His pleasure in the Scottish woods
   Three summer days to take;

The cheefest harts in Chevy-Chace
   To kill and beare away:
These tydings to Erle Douglas came,
   In Scotland where he lay.

Who sent Erle Percy present word,
  He wold prevent his sport;
The English Erle not fearing that,
  Did to the woods resort,

With fifteen hundred bow-men bold,
  All chosen men of might,
Who knew full well in time of neede
  To ayme their shafts arright.

The gallant greyhounds swiftly ran,
  To chase the fallow deere;
On Munday they began to hunt,
  Ere day-light did appeare;

And long before high noone they had
  An hundred fat buckes slaine;
Then having din'd, the drovyers went
  To rouze the deare againe.

The bow-men mustered on the hills,
  Well able to endure;
Theire backsides all, with speciall care,
  That day were guarded sure.

The hounds ran swiftly through the woods,
  The nimble deere to take,
That with their cryes the hills and dales
  An eccho shrill did make.

Lord Percy to the quarry went,
  To view the tender deere;
Quoth he, " Erle Douglas promised
  This day to meet me heere;

" But if I thought he wold not come,
  Noe longer wold I stay."
With that, a brave younge gentleman
  Thus to the Erle did say:

 'Loe, yonder doth Erle Douglas come,
  His men in armour bright;

Full twenty hundred Scottish speres,
   All marching in our sight.

" All men of pleasant Tivydale
   Fast by the river Tweede: "
" O cease your sport," Erle Percy said,
   " And take your bowes with speede.

" And now with me, my countrymen,
   Your courage forth advance;
For never was there champion yett
   In Scotland or in France,

" That ever did on horsebacke come,
   But, if my hap it were,
I durst encounter man for man,
   With him to breake a spere."

Erle Douglas on his milke-white steede,
   Most like a baron bold,
Rode formost of his company,
   Whose armour shone like gold.

" Show me," sayd hee, " whose men you bee,
   That hunt soe boldly heere,
That, without my consent, doe chase
   And kill my fallow-deere."

The man that first did answer make
   Was noble Percy hee;
Who sayd, " Wee list not to declare,
   Nor shew whose men wee bee.

" Yet will wee spend our deerest blood,
   Thy cheefest harts to slay; "
Then Douglas swore a solempne oathe,
   And thus in rage did say;

" Ere thus I will out-braved bee,
   One of us two shall dye:
I know thee well, an erle thou art;
   Lord Percy, soe am I.

" But trust me, Percy, pittye it were,
   And great offence, to kill
Any of these our guiltlesse men,
   For they have done no ill.

" Let thou and I the battell trye,
   And set our men aside."
" Accurst bee he," Erle Percy sayd,
   " By whome this is denyed."

Then stept a gallant squier forth,
   Witherington was his name,
Who said, " I wold not have it told
   To Henry our king for shame,

" That ere my captaine fought on foote,
   And I stood looking on:
You bee two erles," sayd Witherington,
   " And I a squier alone.

" Ile doe the best that doe I may,
   While I have power to stand;
While I have power to weeld my sword,
   Ile fight with hart and hand."

Our English archers bent their bowes,
   Their harts were good and trew;
Att the first flight of arrowes sent,
   Full four-score Scots they slew.

Yet bides Earl Douglas on the bent,
   As Chieftain stout and good,
As valiant Captain, all unmov'd
   The shock he firmly stood.

His host he parted had in three,
   As Leader ware and try'd,
And soon his spearmen on their foes
   Bare down on every side.

Throughout the English archery
   They dealt full many a wound;

But still our valiant Englishmen
   All firmly kept their ground.

And throwing strait their bows away,
   They grasp'd their swords so bright:
And now sharp blows, a heavy shower,
   On shields and helmets light.

They clos'd full fast on everye side,
   Noe slacknes there was found;
And many a gallant gentleman
   Lay gasping on the ground.

O Christ! it was a griefe to see,
   And likewise for to heare,
The cries of men lying in their gore,
   And scattered here and there.

At last these two stout erles did meet,
   Like captaines of great might;
Like lyons wood they layd on lode,
   And made a cruell fight.

They fought, untill they both did sweat,
   With swords of tempered steele;
Until the blood, like drops of rain,
   They trickling downe did feele.

" Yeeld thee, Lord Percy," Douglas sayd,
   " In faith I will thee bringe,
Where thou shalt high advancèd bee
   By James our Scottish king.

" Thy ransome I will freely give,
   And thus report of thee,
Thou art the most couragious knight
   That ever I did see."

" Noe, Douglas," quoth Erle Percy then,
   " Thy proffer I doe scorne;
I will not yeelde to any Scott,
   That ever yett was borne."

E

With that, there came an arrow keene
　　Out of an English bow,
Which strucke Erle Douglas to the heart,
　　A deepe and deadlye blow:

Who never spake more words than these,
　　" Fight on, my merry men all;
For why, my life is at an end:
　　Lord Percy sees my fall."

Then leaving liffe, Erle Percy tooke
　　The dead man by the hand;
And said, " Erle Douglas, for thy life
　　Wold I had lost my land!

" O Christ! my verry hart doth bleed
　　With sorrow for thy sake;
For sure, a more renownèd knight
　　Mischance cold never take."

A knight amongst the Scotts there was,
　　Which saw Erle Douglas dye,
Who streight in wrath did vow revenge
　　Upon the Lord Percye;

Sir Hugh Mountgomerye was he call'd,
　　Who, with a spere most bright,
Well-mounted on a gallant steed,
　　Ran fiercely through the fight;

And past the English archers all,
　　Without all dread or feare,
And through Earl Percyes body then
　　He thrust his hatefull spere.

With such a vehement force and might
　　He did his body gore,
The speare ran through the other side
　　A large cloth-yard, and more.

So thus did both these nobles dye,
　　Whose courage none could staine;

An English archer then perceiv'd
   The noble erle was slaine.

He had a bow bent in his hand,
   Made of a trusty tree;
An arrow of a cloth-yard long
   Up to the head drew hee.

Against Sir Hugh Mountgomerye,
   So right the shaft he sett,
The grey goose-wing that was thereon
   In his harts bloode was wett.

This fight did last from breake of day
   Till setting of the sun;
For when they rung the evening bell,
   The battel scarce was done.

With stout Erle Percy, there was slaine,
   Sir John of Egerton,
Sir Robert Ratcliff, and Sir John,
   Sir James, that bold Baròn.

And with Sir George and stout Sir James,
   Both knights of good account,
Good Sir Ralph Rabby there was slaine,
   Whose prowesse did surmount.

For Witherington needs must I wayle,
   As one in doleful dumpes;
For when his legs were smitten off,
   He fought upon his stumpes.

And with Erle Douglas, there was slaine
   Sir Hugh Mountgomerye,
Sir Charles Murray, that from the feeld
   One foote wold never flee.

Sir Charles Murray of Ratcliff, too,
   His sisters sonne was hee;
Sir David Lamb, so well esteem'd,
   Yet savèd cold not bee.

And the Lord Maxwell in like case
    Did with Erle Douglas dye;
Of twenty hundred Scottish speres,
    Scarce fifty-five did flye.

Of fifteen hundred Englishmen,
    Went home but fifty-three;
The rest were slaine in Chevy-Chace,
    Under the greene wood tree.

Next day did many widowes come,
    Their husbands to bewayle;
They washt their wounds in brinish teares,
    But all wold not prevayle.

Theyr bodyes, bathed in purple blood,
    They bore with them away:
They kist them dead a thousand times,
    Ere they were cladd in clay.

This newes was brought to Eddenborrow,
    Where Scotlands king did raigne,
That brave Erle Douglas suddenlye
    Was with an arrow slaine.

" O heavy newes," King James did say;
    " Scottland can witnesse bee,
I have not any captaine more
    Of such account as hee."

Like tydings to King Henry came,
    Within as short a space,
That Percy of Northumberland
    Was slaine in Chevy-Chace.

" Now God be with him," said our king,
    " Sith it will noe better bee;
I trust I have, within my realme,
    Five hundred as good as hee.

" Yett shall not Scotts nor Scotland say,
    But I will vengeance take,

I'll be revengèd on them all,
   For brave Erle Percyes sake."

This vow full well the king perform'd
   After, at Humbledowne;
In one day, fifty knights were slayne,
   With lordes of great renowne.

And of the rest, of small account,
   Did many thousands dye:
Thus endeth the hunting in Chevy-Chace,
   Made by the Erle Percy.

God save our king, and bless this land
   In plentye, joy, and peace;
And grant henceforth, that foule debate
   'Twixt noblemen may cease!
                  PERCY'S RELIQUES.

SCOTS WHA HAE

SCOTS, wha hae wi' Wallace bled,
Scots, wham Bruce has aften led,
Welcome to your gory bed,
           Or to victorie!

Now's the day, and now's the hour;
See the front o' battle lour;
See approach proud Edward's power—
           Chains and slaverie!

Wha will be a traitor knave?
Wha can fill a coward's grave?
Wha sae base as be a slave?
           Let him turn and flee!

Wha for Scotland's king and law
Freedom's sword will strongly draw,
Freeman stand, or freeman fa',
           Let him on wi' me!

By oppression's woes and pains!
By your sons in servile chains!
We will drain our dearest veins,
       But they shall be free!

Lay the proud usurpers low!
Tyrants fall in every foe!
Liberty's in every blow!—
       Let us do or die!
              ROBERT BURNS.

AGINCOURT

FAIR stood the wind for France,
When we our sails advance,
Nor now to prove our chance
     Longer will tarry;
But putting to the main
At Kaux, the mouth of Seine,
With all his martial train
     Landed King Harry.

And taking many a fort
Furnish'd in warlike sort,
Marcheth towards Agincourt
     In happy hour;
Skirmishing day by day
With those that stopp'd his way
Where the French Gen'ral lay
     With all his power.

Which in his height of pride
King Henry to deride,
His ransom to provide
     To the King sending;
Which he neglects the while
As from a nation vile,
Yet with an angry smile
     Their fall portending.

And turning to his men
Quoth our brave Henry then:
" Though they to one be ten,
    Be not amazed:
Yet have we well begun,
Battles so bravely won
Have ever to the sun
    By fame been raised.

" And for myself (quoth he)
This my full rest shall be,
England ne'er mourn for me
    Nor more esteem me:
Victor I will remain
Or on this earth lie slain,
Never shall she sustain
    Loss to redeem me.

" Poitiers and Cressy tell,
When most their pride did swell,
Under our swords they fell:
    No less our skill is
Than when our grandsire great,
Claiming the regal seat,
By many a warlike feat
    Lopp'd the French Lilies."

The Duke of York so dread
The eager vaward led;
With the main Henry sped
    Amongst his henchmen;
Exeter had the rear,
A braver man not there,—
O Lord, how hot they were
    On the false Frenchmen!

They now to fight are gone:
Armour on armour shone,
Drum now to drum did groan,—
    To hear was wonder.
That with the cries they make
The very earth did shake;

Trumpet to trumpet spake,
    Thunder to thunder.

Well it thine age became,
O noble Erpingham,
Which did'st the signal aim
    To our hid forces;
When from a meadow by,
Like a storm suddenly,
The English archery
    Struck the French horses,

With Spanish yew so strong,
Arrows a cloth-yard long,
That like to serpents stung
    Piercing the weather;
None from his fellow starts,
But playing manly parts,
And like true English hearts,
    Stuck close together.

When down their bows they threw
And forth their bilboes drew
And on the French they flew,
    Not one was tardy;
Arms were from shoulders sent,
Scalps to the teeth were rent,
Down the French peasants went,
    Our men were hardy.

This while our noble King,
His broad-sword brandishing,
Down the French host did ding,
    As to o'erwhelm it;
And many a deep wound lent,
His arms with blood besprent,
And many a cruel dent
    Bruised his helmet.

Gloster, that Duke so good,
Next of the Royal blood,
For famous England stood

With his brave brother;
Clarence, in steel so bright,
Though but a maiden knight,
Yet in that furious fight
 Scarce such another.

Warwick in blood did wade,
Oxford the foe invade,
And cruel slaughter made
 Still as they ran up:
Suffolk his axe did ply,
Beaumont and Willoughby
Bare them right doughtily,
 Ferrers and Fanhope.

Upon Saint Crispin's day
Fought was this noble fray
Which fame did not delay
 To England to carry:
O when shall English men
With such acts fill a pen,
Or England breed again
 Such a King Harry!

     Michael Drayton.

AGINCOURT

West.   O that we now had here
But one ten thousand of those men in England
That do no work to-day!
 K. Hen.   What's he that wishes so?
My cousin Westmoreland? No, my fair cousin:
If we are mark'd to die, we are enow
To do our country loss; and if to live,
The fewer men, the greater share of honour.
God's will! I pray thee, wish not one man more.
By Jove, I am not covetous for gold,
Nor care I who doth feed upon my cost;
It yearns me not if men my garments wear;
Such outward things dwell not in my desires:

But if it be a sin to covet honour,
I am the most offending soul alive.
No, faith, my coz, wish not a man from England:
God's peace! I would not lose so great an honour
As one man more, methinks, would share from me
For the best hope I have. O, do not wish one more!
Rather proclaim it, Westmoreland, through my host,
That he which hath no stomach to this fight,
Let him depart; his passport shall be made
And crowns for convoy put into his purse:
We would not die in that man's company
That fears his fellowship to die with us.
This day is call'd the feast of Crispian:
He that outlives this day, and comes safe home,
Will stand a tip-toe when this day is named,
And rouse him at the name of Crispian.
He that shall live this day, and see old age,
Will yearly on the vigil feast his neighbours,
And say "To-morrow is Saint Crispian:"
Then will he strip his sleeve and show his scars,
And say "These wounds I had on Crispin's day."
Old men forget; yet all shall be forgot,
But he'll remember with advantages
What feats he did that day: then shall our names,
Familiar in his mouth as household words,
Harry the king, Bedford and Exeter,
Warwick and Talbot, Salisbury and Gloucester,
Be in their flowing cups freshly remember'd.
This story shall the good man teach his son;
And Crispin Crispian shall ne'er go by,
From this day to the ending of the world,
But we in it shall be remembered;
We few, we happy few, we band of brothers;
For he to-day that sheds his blood with me
Shall be my brother; be he ne'er so vile,
This day shall gentle his condition:
And gentlemen in England now a-bed
Shall think themselves accursed they were not here,
And hold their manhoods cheap whiles any speaks
That fought with us upon Saint Crispin's day.

WILLIAM SHAKESPEARE.

FLODDEN

At length the freshening western blast
Aside the shroud of battle cast;
And, first, the ridge of mingled spears
Above the brightening cloud appears;
And in the smoke the pennons flew,
As in the storm the white sea-mew.
Then mark'd they, dashing broad and far,
The broken billows of the war,
And plumed crests of chieftains brave,
Floating like foam upon the wave;
  But nought distinct they see:
Wide raged the battle on the plain;
Spears shook, and falchions flash'd amain;
Fell England's arrow-flight like rain;
Crests rose, and stoop'd, and rose again,
  Wild and disorderly.
Amid the scene of tumult, high
They saw Lord Marmion's falcon fly:
And stainless Tunstall's banner white,
And Edmund Howard's lion bright,
Still bear them bravely in the fight:
  Although against them come,
Of gallant Gordons many a one,
And many a stubborn Highlandman,
And many a rugged Border clan,
  With Huntly, and with Home.

Far on the left, unseen the while,
Stanley broke Lennox and Argyle;
Though there the western mountaineer
Rush'd with bare bosom on the spear,
And flung the feeble targe aside,
And with both hands the broadsword plied.
'Twas vain:—But Fortune, on the right,
With fickle smile, cheer'd Scotland's fight.
Then fell that spotless banner white,
  The Howard's lion fell;
Yet still Lord Marmion's falcon flew
With wavering flight, while fiercer grew

Around the battle-yell.
The Border slogan rent the sky!
A Home! a Gordon! was the cry:
    Loud were the clanging blows;
Advanced,—forced back,—now low, now high
    The pennon sunk and rose;
As bends the bark's mast in the gale,
When rent are rigging, shrouds, and sail,
    It waver'd 'mid the foes.
No longer Blount the view could bear:
" By Heaven, and all its saints! I swear
    I will not see it lost!
Fitz-Eustace, you with Lady Clare
May bid your beads, and patter prayer,—
    I gallop to the host."
And to the fray he rode amain,
Follow'd by all the archer train.
The fiery youth, with desperate charge,
Made, for a space, an opening large,—
    The rescued banner rose,—
But darkly closed the war around,
Like pine-tree, rooted from the ground,
    It sunk among the foes.
Then Eustace mounted too:—yet staid
As loath to leave the helpless maid,
    When, fast as shaft can fly,
Blood-shot his eyes, his nostrils spread,
The loose rein dangling from his head,
Housing and saddle bloody red,
    Lord Marmion's steed rush'd by;
And Eustace, maddening at the sight,
    A look and sign to Clara cast
    To mark he would return in haste,
Then plunged into the fight.

Ask me not what the maiden feels,
    Left in that dreadful hour alone:
Perchance her reason stoops, or reels;
    Perchance a courage, not her own,
    Braces her mind to desperate tone.—
The scatter'd van of England wheels:—
    She only said, as loud in air

The tumult roar'd, " Is Wilton there? "—
They fly, or, madden'd by despair,
Fight but to die,—" Is Wilton there? "
With that, straight up the hill there rode
Two horsemen, drench'd with gore,
And in their arms, a helpless load,
    A wounded knight they bore.
His hand still strain'd the broken brand;
His arms were smear'd with blood and sand.
Dragg'd from among the horses' feet,
With dinted shield, and helmet beat,
The falcon-crest and plumage gone,
Can that be haughty Marmion! . . .
Young Blount his armour did unlace,
And, gazing on his ghastly face,
    Said—" By Saint George, he's gone!
That spear-wound has our master sped,
And see the deep cut on his head!
    Good-night to Marmion."—
" Unnurtured Blount! thy brawling cease:
He opes his eyes," said Eustace; " peace! "

When, doff'd his casque, he felt free air,
Around 'gan Marmion wildly stare:—
" Where's Harry Blount? Fitz-Eustace where?
Linger ye here, ye hearts of hare!
Redeem my pennon,—charge again!
Cry—' Marmion to the rescue! '—Vain!
Last of my race, on battle-plain
That shout shall ne'er be heard again!—
Yet my last thought is England's—fly,
    To Dacre bear my signet ring:
    Tell him his squadrons up to bring.—
Fitz-Eustace, to Lord Surrey hie;
    Tunstall lies dead upon the field,
    His life-blood stains the spotless shield:
    Edmund is down:—my life is reft;
    The Admiral alone is left.
    Let Stanley charge with spur of fire,—
    With Chester charge, and Lancashire,
    Full upon Scotland's central host,
    Or victory and England's lost.—

Must I bid twice?—hence, varlets! fly
Leave Marmion here alone—to die."
They parted, and alone he lay;
Clare drew her from the sight away,
Till pain wrung forth a lowly moan,
And half he murmur'd,—" Is there none,
    Of all my halls have nurst,
Page, squire, or groom, one cup to bring
Of blessed water from the spring,
    To slake my dying thirst!"

O, Woman! in our hours of ease
Uncertain, coy, and hard to please,
    And variable as the shade
By the light quivering aspen made;
When pain and anguish wring the brow,
A ministering angel thou!—
Scarce were the piteous accents said,
When, with the Baron's casque, the maid
    To the nigh streamlet ran:
Forgot were hatred, wrongs, and fears;
The plaintive voice alone she hears,
    Sees but the dying man.
She stoop'd her by the runnel's side,
    But in abhorrence backward drew;
For, oozing from the mountain's side,
Where raged the war, a dark-red tide
    Was curdling in the streamlet blue.
Where shall she turn?—behold her mark
    A little fountain cell,
Where water, clear as diamond-spark,
    In a stone basin fell.
Above, some half-worn letters say,
𝕯rink. weary. pilgrim. drink. and. pray.
𝕱or. the. kind. soul. of. 𝕾ybil. 𝕲rey.
    𝖂ho. built. this. cross. and. well.
She fill'd the helm, and back she hied,
And with surprise and joy espied
    A monk supporting Marmion's head:
A pious man, whom duty brought
To dubious verge of battle fought,
    To shrieve the dying, bless the dead.

Deep drank Lord Marmion of the wave,
And, as she stoop'd his brow to lave—
" Is it the hand of Clare," he said,
" Or injured Constance, bathes my head? "
   Then, as remembrance rose,—
" Speak not to me of shrift or prayer!
   I must redress her woes.
Short space, few words, are mine to spare;
Forgive and listen, gentle Clare! "—
   " Alas! " she said, " the while,—
O, think of your immortal weal!
In vain for Constance is your zeal;
   She—died at Holy Isle."—
Lord Marmion started from the ground,
As light as if he felt no wound;
Though in the action burst the tide,
In torrents, from his wounded side.
" Then it was truth,"—he said—" I knew
That the dark presage must be true.—
I would the Fiend, to whom belongs
The vengeance due to all her wrongs,
   Would spare me but a day!
For wasting fire, and dying groan,
And priests slain on the altar-stone,
   Might bribe him for delay.
It may not be!—this dizzy trance—
Curse on yon base marauder's lance,
And doubly cursed my failing brand!
A sinful heart makes feeble hand."
Then, fainting, down on earth he sunk,
Supported by the trembling Monk.

With fruitless labour, Clara bound,
And strove to stanch the gushing wound:
The Monk, with unavailing cares,
Exhausted all the Church's prayers.
Ever, he said, that, close and near,
A lady's voice was in his ear,
And that the priest he could not hear,
   For that she ever sung,
" *In the lost battle, borne down by the flying,*
Where mingles war's rattle with groans of the dying ! "

So the notes rung;—
" Avoid thee, Fiend!—with cruel hand,
Shake not the dying sinner's sand!—
O, look, my son, upon yon sign
Of the Redeemer's grace divine;
   O, think on faith and bliss!—
By many a death-bed I have been,
And many a sinner's parting seen,
   But never aught like this."—
The war, that for a space did fail,
Now trebly thundering swell'd the gale,
   And—STANLEY! was the cry;
A light on Marmion's visage spread,
   And fired his glazing eye;
With dying hand, above his head,
He shook the fragment of his blade,
   And shouted " Victory!—
Charge, Chester, charge!   On, Stanley, on!"
Were the last words of Marmion.

By this, though deep the evening fell,
Still rose the battle's deadly swell,
For still the Scots, around their King,
Unbroken, fought in desperate ring.
Where's now their victor vaward wing,
   Where Huntly, and where Home?—
O, for a blast of that dread horn,
On Fontarabian echoes borne,
   That to King Charles did come,
When Rowland brave, and Olivier,
And every paladin and peer,
   On Roncesvalles died!
Such blast might warn them, not in vain,
To quit the plunder of the slain,
And turn the doubtful day again,
   While yet on Flodden side,
Afar, the Royal Standard flies,
And round it toils, and bleeds, and dies,
   Our Caledonian pride!
In vain the wish—for far away,
While spoil and havoc mark their way,
Near Sybil's Cross the plunderers stray.—

" O, Lady," cried the Monk, " away! "
   And placed her on her steed,
And led her to the chapel fair,
   Of Tillmouth upon Tweed.
There all the night they spent in prayer,
And at the dawn of morning, there
She met her kinsman, Lord Fitz-Clare.

But as they left the dark'ning heath,
More desperate grew the strife of death.
The English shafts in volleys hail'd,
In headlong charge their horse assail'd;
Front, flank, and rear, the squadrons sweep
To break the Scottish circle deep,
   That fought around their King.
But yet, though thick the shafts as snow,
Though charging knights like whirlwinds go,
Though bill-men ply the ghastly blow,
   Unbroken was the ring;
The stubborn spear-men still made good
Their dark impenetrable wood,
Each stepping where his comrade stood,
   The instant that he fell.
No thought was there of dastard flight;
Link'd in the serried phalanx tight,
Groom fought like noble, squire like knight,
   As fearlessly and well;
Till utter darkness closed her wing
O'er their thin host and wounded King.
Then skilful Surrey's sage commands
Led back from strife his shatter'd bands;
   And from the charge they drew,
As mountain-waves, from wasted lands,
   Sweep back to ocean blue.
Then did their loss his foemen know;
Their King, their Lords, their mightiest low,
They melted from the field as snow,
When streams are swoln and south winds blow,
   Dissolves in silent dew.
Tweed's echoes heard the ceaseless plash,
   While many a broken band,
Disorder'd, through her currents dash,

F

To gain the Scottish land;
To town and tower, to down and dale,
To tell red Flodden's dismal tale,
And raise the universal wail.
Tradition, legend, tune, and song,
Shall many an age that wail prolong:
Still from the sire the son shall hear
Of the stern strife, and carnage drear,
    Of Flodden's fatal field,
Where shiver'd was fair Scotland's spear,
    And broken was her shield!

SIR WALTER SCOTT.

IVRY

Now glory to the Lord of Hosts, from whom all glories are!
And glory to our Sovereign Liege, King Henry of Navarre!
Now let there be the merry sound of music and of dance,
Through thy corn-fields green, and sunny vines, oh pleasant
    land of France!
And thou, Rochelle, our own Rochelle, proud city of the
    waters,
Again let rapture light the eyes of all thy mourning daughters.
As thou wert constant in our ills, be joyous in our joy,
For cold, and stiff, and still are they who wrought thy walls
    annoy.
Hurrah! Hurrah! a single field hath turned the chance of
    war,
Hurrah! Hurrah! for Ivry, and Henry of Navarre.

Oh! how our hearts were beating, when, at the dawn of day,
We saw the army of the League drawn out in long array;
With all its priest-led citizens, and all its rebel peers,
And Appenzel's stout infantry, and Egmont's Flemish spears.
There rode the brood of false Lorraine, the curses of our land;
And dark Mayenne was in the midst, a truncheon in his hand:
And, as we looked on them, we thought of Seine's empurpled
    flood,
And good Coligni's hoary hair all dabbled with his blood;
And we cried unto the living God, who rules the fate of war,
To fight for His own holy name, and Henry of Navarre.

The King is come to marshal us, in all his armour drest,
And he has bound a snow-white plume upon his gallant crest.
He looked upon his people, and a tear was in his eye;
He looked upon the traitors, and his glance was stern and
high.
Right graciously he smiled on us, as rolled from wing to wing,
Down all our line, a deafening shout, " God save our Lord
the King!"
" And if my standard-bearer fall, as fall full well he may,
" For never saw I promise yet of such a bloody fray,
" Press where ye see my white plume shine, amidst the ranks
of war,
" And be your oriflamme to-day the helmet of Navarre."

Hurrah! the foes are moving.   Hark to the mingled din
Of fife, and steed, and trump, and drum, and roaring culverin.
The fiery Duke is pricking fast across Saint André's plain,
With all the hireling chivalry of Guelders and Almayne.
Now by the lips of those ye love, fair gentlemen of France,
Charge for the golden lilies,—upon them with the lance.
A thousand spurs are striking deep, a thousand spears in rest,
A thousand knights are pressing close behind the snow-white
crest;
And in they burst, and on they rushed, while, like a guiding
star,
Amidst the thickest carnage blazed the helmet of Navarre.

Now, God be praised, the day is ours.   Mayenne hath turned
his rein.
D'Aumale hath cried for quarter.   The Flemish count is
slain.
Their ranks are breaking like thin clouds before a Biscay gale;
The field is heaped with bleeding steeds, and flags, and cloven
mail.
And then we thought on vengeance, and, all along our van,
" Remember St. Bartholomew," was passed from man to
man.
But out spake gentle Henry, " No Frenchman is my foe:
" Down, down with every foreigner, but let your brethren
go."
Oh! was there ever such a knight, in friendship or in war,
As our Sovereign Lord, King Henry, the soldier of Navarre?

Right well fought all the Frenchmen who fought for France
   to-day:
And many a lordly banner God gave them for a prey.
But we of the religion have borne us best in fight;
And the good Lord of Rosny has ta'en the cornet white.
Our own true Maximilian the cornet white hath ta'en,
The cornet white with crosses black, the flag of false Lorraine.
Up with it high; unfurl it wide; that all the hosts may know
How God hath humbled the proud house which wrought His
   church such woe.
Then on the ground, while trumpets sound their loudest
   point of war.
Fling the red shreds, a footcloth meet for Henry of Navarre.

Ho! maidens of Vienna; Ho! matrons of Lucerne;
Weep, weep, and rend your hair for those who never shall
   return.
Ho! Philip, send, for charity, thy Mexican pistoles,
That Antwerp monks may sing a mass for thy poor spear-
   men's souls.
Ho! gallant nobles of the League, look that your arms be
   bright;
Ho! burghers of Saint Genevieve, keep watch and ward
   to-night.
For our God hath crushed the tyrant, our God hath raised
   the slave,
And mocked the counsel of the wise, and the valour of the
   brave.
Then glory to His holy name, from whom all glories are;
And glory to our Sovereign Lord, King Henry of Navarre.

                    LORD MACAULAY.

NASEBY

OH! wherefore come ye forth, in triumph from the North,
   With your hands, and your feet, and your raiment all red?
And wherefore doth your rout send forth a joyous shout?
   And whence be the grapes of the wine-press which ye tread?

Oh evil was the root, and bitter was the fruit,
   And crimson was the juice of the vintage that we trod;

For we trampled on the throng of the haughty and the strong,
    Who sate in the high places, and slew the saints of God.

It was about the noon of a glorious day of June,
    That we saw their banners dance, and their cuirasses shine,
And the Man of Blood was there, with his long essenced hair,
    And Astley, and Sir Marmaduke, and Rupert of the Rhine.

Like a servant of the Lord, with his Bible and his sword,
    The General rode along us to form us to the fight,
When a murmuring sound broke out, and swell'd into a shout,
    Among the godless horsemen upon the tyrant's right.

And hark! like the roar of the billows on the shore,
    The cry of battle rises along their charging line!
For God! for the Cause! for the Church! for the Laws!
    For Charles King of England, and Rupert of the Rhine!

The furious German comes, with his clarions and his drums,
    His bravoes of Alsatia, and pages of Whitehall;
They are bursting on our flanks. Grasp your pikes, close
    your ranks;
    For Rupert never comes but to conquer or to fall.

They are here! They rush on! We are broken! We are
    gone!
Our left is borne before them like stubble on the blast.
O Lord, put forth thy might. O Lord, defend the right!
    Stand back to back, in God's name, and fight it to the last.

Stout Skippon hath a wound; the centre hath given ground:
    Hark! hark!—What means the trampling of horsemen on
    our rear?
Whose banner do I see, boys? 'Tis he, thank God, 'tis he,
    boys.
    Bear up another minute: brave Oliver is here.

Their heads all stooping low, their points all in a row,
    Like a whirlwind on the trees, like a deluge on the dykes,
Our cuirassiers have burst on the ranks of the Accurst,
    And at a shock have scattered the forest of his pikes.

Fast, fast, the gallants ride, in some safe nook to hide
  Their coward heads, predestined to rot on Temple Bar;
And he—he turns, he flies:—shame on those cruel eyes
  That bore to look on torture, and dare not look on war.

Ho! comrades, scour the plain; and, ere ye strip the slain,
  First give another stab to make your search secure,
Then shake from sleeves and pockets their broad-pieces and
    lockets,
  The tokens of the wanton, the plunder of the poor.

Fools! your doublets shone with gold, and your hearts were
    gay and bold,
  When you kissed your lily hands to your lemans to-day;
And to-morrow shall the fox, from her chambers in the rocks,
  Lead forth her tawny cubs to howl above the prey.

Where be your tongues that late mocked at heaven and hell
    and fate,
  And the fingers that once were so busy with your blades,
Your perfum'd satin clothes, your catches and your oaths,
  Your stage-plays and your sonnets, your diamonds and
    your spades?

Down, down, for ever down with the mitre and the crown,
  With the Belial of the Court, and the Mammon of the Pope;
There is woe in Oxford Halls: there is wail in Durham's
    Stalls:
  The Jesuit smites his bosom: the Bishop rends his cope.

And She of the seven hills shall mourn her children's ills,
  And tremble when she thinks on the edge of England's
    sword;
And the Kings of earth in fear shall shudder when they hear
  What the hand of God hath wrought for the Houses and
    the Word.

LORD MACAULAY.

THE BURIAL OF SIR JOHN MOORE

NOT a drum was heard, not a funeral note,
  As his corpse to the rampart we hurried;
Not a soldier discharged his farewell shot,
  O'er the grave where our hero we buried.

We buried him darkly, at dead of night,
  The sods with our bayonets turning;
By the struggling moonbeam's misty light,
  And the lantern dimly burning.

No useless coffin enclosed his breast,
  Not in sheet nor in shroud we wound him;
But he lay like a warrior taking his rest,
  With his martial cloak around him.

Few and short were the prayers we said,
  And we spoke not a word of sorrow;
But we steadfastly gazed on the face that was dead,
  And we bitterly thought of the morrow.

We thought, as we hollowed his narrow bed,
  And smoothed down his lonely pillow,
That the foe and the stranger would tread o'er his head,
  And we far away on the billow!

Lightly they'll talk of the spirit that's gone,
  And o'er his cold ashes upbraid him;—
But little he'll reck, if they let him sleep on,
  In a grave where a Briton has laid him.

But half of our heavy task was done
  When the clock struck the hour for retiring;
And we heard the distant and random gun
  That the foe was sullenly firing.

Slowly and sadly we laid him down,
  From the field of his fame fresh and gory;
We carved not a line, and we raised not a stone—
  But we left him alone with his glory!

                                        CHARLES WOLFE.

HOHENLINDEN

On Linden, when the sun was low,
All bloodless lay th' untrodden snow,
And dark as winter was the flow
Of Iser, rolling rapidly:

But Linden saw another sight,
When the drum beat at dead of night,
Commanding fires of death to light
The darkness of her scenery.

By torch and trumpet fast array'd,
Each horsemen drew his battle-blade,
And furious every charger neigh'd,
To join the dreadful revelry.

Then shook the hills with thunder riven,
Then rush'd the steed to battle driven,
And louder than the bolts of heaven,
Far flash'd the red artillery.

But redder yet that light shall glow
On Linden's hills of stainèd snow,
And bloodier yet the torrent flow
Of Iser, rolling rapidly.

'Tis morn, but scarce yon level sun
Can pierce the war-clouds, rolling dun,
Where furious Frank, and fiery Hun,
Shout in their sulph'rous canopy.

The combat deepens. On, ye brave,
Who rush to glory, or the grave!
Wave, Munich! all thy banners wave,
And charge with all thy chivalry!

Few, few, shall part where many meet!
The snow shall be their winding-sheet,
And every turf beneath their feet
Shall be a soldier's sepulchre.

THOMAS CAMPBELL.

WATERLOO

Stop!—for thy tread is on an empire's dust!
An earthquake's spoil is sepulchred below!
Is the spot mark'd with no colossal bust?
Nor column trophied for triumphal show?
None: but the moral's truth tells simpler so.
As the ground was before, thus let it be;
How that red rain hath made the harvest grow!
And is this all the world hath gain'd by thee,
Thou first and last of fields! king-making victory? . ₔ ₔ

There was a sound of revelry by night,
And Belgium's capital had gather'd then
Her Beauty and her Chivalry, and bright
The lamps shone o'er fair women and brave men;
A thousand hearts beat happily; and when
Music arose, with its voluptuous swell,
Soft eyes look'd love to eyes which spake again,
And all went merry as a marriage bell;—
But hush! hark! a deep sound strikes like a rising knell!

Did ye not hear it? No; 'twas but the wind,
Or the car rattling o'er the stony street:
On with the dance! let joy be unconfined;
No sleep till morn, when Youth and Pleasure meet
To chase the glowing hours with flying feet—
But hark!—that heavy sound breaks in once more,
As if the clouds its echo would repeat;
And nearer, clearer, deadlier than before!
Arm! arm! it is!—it is!—the cannon's opening roar!

Within a window'd niche of that high hall
Sat Brunswick's fated chieftain; he did hear
That sound the first amidst the festival,
And caught its tone with Death's prophetic ear;
And when they smiled because he deem'd it near,
His heart more truly knew that peal too well
Which stretch'd his father on a bloody bier,
And roused the vengeance blood alone could quell;
He rush'd into the field, and, foremost fighting, fell!

Ah! then and there was hurrying to and fro,
And gathering tears and tremblings of distress,
And cheeks all pale, which but an hour ago
Blush'd at the praise of their own loveliness;
And there were sudden partings, such as press
The life from out young hearts, and choking sighs
Which ne'er might be repeated! Who could guess
If evermore should meet those mutual eyes,
Since upon night so sweet such awful morn could rise!

And there was mounting in hot haste; the steed,
The mustering squadron, and the clattering car,
Went pouring forward with impetuous speed,
And swiftly forming in the ranks of war;
And the deep thunder, peal on peal, afar;
And near, the beat of the alarming drum
Roused up the soldier, ere the morning star;
While throng'd the citizens with terror dumb,
Or whispering with white lips—" The foe! they come, they
     come!"

And wild and high the " Cameron's gathering " rose—
The war note of Lochiel, which Albyn's hills
Have heard—and heard too have her Saxon foes—
How in the noon of night that pibroch thrills,
Savage and shrill! But with the breath which fills
Their mountain pipe, so fill the mountaineers
With the fierce native daring, which instils
The stirring memory of a thousand years;
And Evan's, Donald's fame rings in each clansman's ears!

And Ardennes waves above them her green leaves,
Dewy with nature's tear-drops, as they pass
Grieving—if aught inanimate e'er grieves—
Over the unreturning brave—alas!
Ere evening to be trodden like the grass,
Which now beneath them, but above shall grow
In its next verdure; when this fiery mass
Of living valour, rolling on the foe,
And burning with high hope, shall moulder cold and low!

Last noon beheld them full of lusty life,
Last eve in Beauty's circle proudly gay;

The midnight brought the signal-sound of strife;
The morn the marshalling in arms; the day
Battle's magnificently stern array!
The thunder-clouds close o'er it, which, when rent,
The earth is cover'd thick with other clay,
Which her own clay shall cover, heap'd and pent,
Rider and horse,—friend, foe—in one red burial blent!

LORD BYRON.

THE CHARGE OF THE LIGHT BRIGADE

I

HALF a league, half a league,
  Half a league or.ward,
All in the valley of Death,
  Rode the six hundred.
"Forward, the Light Brigade!
Charge for the guns!" he said:
Into the valley of Death
  Rode the six hundred.

II

"Forward, the Light Brigade!"
Was there a man dismay'd?
Not tho' the soldier knew
  Some one had blunder'd:
Their's not to make reply,
Their's not to reason why,
Their's but to do and die:
Into the valley of Death
  Rode the six hundred.

III

Cannon to right of them,
Cannon to left of them,
Cannon in front of them
  Volley'd and thunder'd;
Storm'd at with shot and shell,
Boldly they rode and well,
Into the jaws of Death,
Into the mouth of Hell
  Rode the six hundred.

IV

Flash'd all their sabres bare,
Flash'd as they turn'd in air
Sabring the gunners there,
Charging an army, while
   All the world wonder'd:
Plunged in the battery-smoke
Right thro' the line they broke;
Cossack and Russian
Reel'd from the sabre-stroke
   Shatter'd and sunder'd.
Then they rode back, but not—
   Not the six hundred.

V

Cannon to right of them,
Cannon to left of them,
Cannon behind them
   Volley'd and thunder'd;
Storm'd at with shot and shell,
While horse and hero fell,
They that had fought so well
Came thro' the jaws of Death,
Back from the mouth of Hell,
All that was left of them,
   Left of six hundred.

VI

When can their glory fade?
O the wild charge they made!
   All the world wonder'd.
Honour the charge they made!
Honour the Light Brigade,
   Noble six hundred!

LORD TENNYSON.

SONG

Soldier, rest! thy warfare o'er,
   Sleep the sleep that knows not breaking;
Dream of battled fields no more,
   Days of danger, nights of waking.
In our isle's enchanted hall,
   Hands unseen thy couch are strewing,
Fairy strains of music fall,
   Every sense in slumber dewing.
Soldier, rest! thy warfare o'er,
Dream of fighting fields no more:
Sleep the sleep that knows not breaking,
Morn of toil, nor night of waking.

No rude sound shall reach thine ear,
   Armour's clang, nor war-steed champing,
Trump nor pibroch summon here
   Mustering clan, or squadron tramping,
Yet the lark's shrill fife may come
   At the day-break from the fallow,
And the bittern sound his drum,
   Booming from the sedgy shallow.
Ruder sounds shall none be near
Guards nor warders challenge here,
Here's no war-steed's neigh and champing,
Shouting clans, or squadrons stamping.

Huntsman, rest! thy chase is done,
   While our slumbrous spells assail ye,
Dream not, with the rising sun,
   Bugles here shall sound reveillé.
Sleep! the deer is in his den;
   Sleep! thy hounds are by thee lying;
Sleep! nor dream in yonder glen,
   How thy gallant steed lay dying.
Huntsman, rest! thy chase is done,
Think not of the rising sun,
For at dawning to assail ye,
Here no bugles sound reveillé.

Sir Walter Scott.

BOAT SONG

HAIL to the Chief who in triumph advances!
    Honour'd and bless'd be the ever-green Pine!
Long may the tree, in his banner that glances,
    Flourish, the shelter and grace of our line!
        Heaven send it happy dew,
        Earth lend it sap anew,
    Gayly to bourgeon, and broadly to grow,
        While every Highland glen
        Sends our shout back agen,
    " Roderigh Vich Alpine dhu, ho! ieroe!"

Ours is no sapling, chance-sown by the fountain,
    Blooming at Beltane, in winter to fade;
When the whirlwind has stripp'd every leaf on the mountain,
    The more shall Clan-Alpine exult in her shade.
        Moor'd in the rifted rock,
        Proof to the tempest's shock,
    Firmer he roots him the ruder it blow;
        Menteith and Breadalbane, then,
        Echo his praise agen,
    " Roderigh Vich Alpine dhu, ho! ieroe!"

Proudly our pibroch has thrill'd in Glen Fruin,
    And Bannochar's groans to our slogan replied;
Glen Luss and Ross-dhu, they are smoking in ruin,
    And the best of Loch Lomond lie dead on her side.
        Widow and Saxon maid
        Long shall lament our raid,
    Think of Clan Alpine with fear and with woe;
        Lennox and Leven-glen
        Shake when they hear agen,
    " Roderigh Vich Alpine dhu, ho! ieroe!"

Row, vassals, row, for the pride of the Highlands!
    Stretch to your oars, for the ever-green Pine!
O! that the rose-bud that graces yon islands,
    Were wreathed in a garland around him to twine!

O that some seedling gem,
Worthy such noble stem,
Honour'd and bless'd in their shadow might grow
Loud should Clan-Alpine then
Ring from the deepmost glen,
" Roderigh Vich Alpine dhu, ho! ieroe!"

SIR WALTER SCOTT.

THE BOLD DRAGOON

'Twas a Maréchal of France, and he fain would honour gain,
And he long'd to take a passing glance at Portugal from Spain;
   With his flying guns this gallant gay,
   And boasted corps d'armée—
O he fear'd not our dragoons, with their long swords, boldly
   riding,
   Whack, fal de ral, etc.

To Campo Mayor come, he had quietly sat down,
Just a fricassee to pick, while his soldiers sack'd the town,
   When, 'twas peste! morbleu! mon Général,
   Hear the English bugle-call!
And behold the light dragoons, with their long swords, boldly
   riding,
   Whack, fal de ral, etc.

Right about went horse and foot, artillery and all,
And, as the devil leaves a house, they tumbled through the
   wall;
   They took no time to seek the door,
   But, best foot set before—
O they ran from our dragoons, with their long swords, boldly
   riding,
   Whack, fal de ral, etc.

Those valiant men of France they had scarcely fled a mile,
When on their flank there sous'd at once the British rank and
   file;
   For Long, De Grey, and Otway, then
   Ne'er minded one to ten,
But came on like light dragoons, with their long swords,
   boldly riding,
   Whack, fal de ral, etc.

Three hundred British lads they made three thousand reel,
Their hearts were made of English oak, their swords of
  Sheffield steel,
   Their horses were in Yorkshire bred,
   And Beresford them led;
So huzza for brave dragoons, with their long swords, boldly
  riding,
   Whack, fal de ral, etc.

Then here's a health to Wellington, to Beresford, to Long,
And a single word of Bonaparte before I close my song:
   The eagles that to fight he brings
   Should serve his men with wings,
When they meet the bold dragoons, with their long swords,
  boldly riding,
   Whack, fal de ral, etc.

SIR WALTER SCOTT.

THE DANCE OF DEATH

NIGHT and morning were at meeting
  Over Waterloo;
Cocks had sung their earliest greeting;
  Faint and low they crew,
For no paly beam yet shone
On the heights of Mount Saint John;
Tempest-clouds prolonged the sway
Of timeless darkness over day;
Whirlwind, thunder-clap, and shower,
Mark'd it a predestined hour.
Broad and frequent through the night
Flash'd the sheets of levin-light;
Muskets, glancing lightnings back,
Show'd the dreary bivouac
  Where the soldier lay,
Chill and stiff, and drench'd with rain,
Wishing dawn of morn again,
  Though death should come with day.

'Tis at such a tide and hour,
Wizard, witch, and fiend have power,

And ghastly forms through mist and shower
  Gleam on the gifted ken;
And then the affrighted prophet's ear
Drinks whispers strange of fate and fear
Presaging death and ruin near
  Among the sons of men;—
Apart from Albyn's war-array,
'Twas then grey Allan sleepless lay;
Grey Allan, who, for many a day,
Had follow'd stout and stern,
Where, through battle's rout and reel,
Storm of shot and hedge of steel,
Led the grandson of Lochiel,
  Valiant Fassiefern.
Through steel and shot he leads no more,
Low laid 'mid friends' and foemen's gore—
But long his native lake's wild shore,
And Sunart rough and high Ardgower,
  And Morven long shall tell,
And proud Bennevis hear with awe,
How, upon bloody Quatre-Bras,
Brave Cameron heard the wild hurra
  Of conquest as he fell.

'Lone on the outskirts of the host,
The weary sentinel held post,
And heard, through darkness far aloof,
The frequent clang of courser's hoof,
Where held the cloak'd patrol their course,
And spurr'd 'gainst storm the swerving horse;
But there are sounds in Allan's ear,
Patrol nor sentinel may hear,
And sights before his eye aghast
Invisible to them have pass'd,
  When down the destined plain,
'Twixt Britain and the bands of France,
Wild as marsh-borne meteor's glance,
Strange phantoms wheel'd a revel dance,
  And doom'd the future slain.—
Such forms were seen, such sounds were heard
When Scotland's James his march prepared
  For Flodden's fatal plain;

Such, when he drew his ruthless sword,
As Choosers of the Slain, adored
   The yet unchristen'd Dane.
An indistinct and phantom band,
They wheel'd their ring-dance hand in hand,
With gestures wild and dread;
The Seer, who watch'd them ride the storm,
Saw through their faint and shadowy form
   The lightnings flash more red;
And still their ghastly roundelay
Was of the coming battle-fray,
   And of the destined dead.

Song

Wheel the wild dance
While lightnings glance,
   And thunders rattle loud,
And call the brave
To bloody grave,
To sleep without a shroud.

Our airy feet,
So light and fleet,
   They do not bend the rye
That sinks its head when whirlwinds rave,
And swells again in eddying wave,
   As each wild gust blows by;
But still the corn,
At dawn of morn,
   Our fatal steps that bore,
At eve lies waste,
A trampled paste
   Of blackening mud and gore.

Wheel the wild dance
While lightnings glance,
   And thunders rattle loud,
And call the brave
To bloody grave,
   To sleep without a shroud.

Wheel the wild dance!
Brave sons of France,
For you our ring makes room;
Make space full wide
For martial pride,
　For banner, spear, and plume.
Approach, draw near,
Proud Cuirassier!
　Room for the men of steel!
Through crest and plate
The broadsword's weight
Both head and heart shall feel.

Wheel the wild dance!
While lightnings glance,
　And thunders rattle loud,
And call the brave
To bloody grave,
　To sleep without a shroud.

Sons of the Spear!
You feel us near
　In many a ghastly dream;
With fancy's eye
Our forms you spy,
　And hear our fatal scream.
With clearer sight
Ere falls the night,
Just when to weal or woe
Your disembodied souls take flight
On trembling wing—each startled sprite
　Our choir of death shall know.

Wheel the wild dance
While lightnings glance,
　And thunders rattle loud,
And call the brave
To bloody grave,
　To sleep without a shroud.

Burst, ye clouds, in tempest showers,
Redder rain shall soon be ours—

See the east grows wan—
Yield we place to sterner game,
Ere deadlier bolts and direr flame
Shall the welkin's thunders shame;
Elemental rage is tame
　　To the wrath of man.
　　　　　　　　　Sir Walter Scott.

BORDER BALLAD

March, march, Ettrick and Teviotdale,
　Why the deil dinna ye march forward in order?
March, march, Eskdale and Liddesdale,
　All the Blue Bonnets are bound for the Border.
　　Many a banner spread,
　　Flutters above your head,
　Many a crest that is famous in story.
　　Mount and make ready then,
　　Sons of the mountain glen,
Fight for the Queen and our old Scottish glory.

Come from the hills where your hirsels are grazing,
　Come from the glen of the buck and the roe;
Come to the crag where the beacon is blazing,
　Come with the buckler, the lance, and the bow.
　　Trumpets are sounding,
　　War-steeds are bounding,
　Stand to your arms, and march in good order,
　　England shall many a day
　　Tell of the bloody fray,
When the Blue Bonnets came over the Border.
　　　　　　　　　Sir Walter Scott.

BONNY DUNDEE

To the Lords of Convention 'twas Claver'se who spoke,
" Ere the King's crown shall fall there are crowns to be broke;
So let each Cavalier who loves honour and me,
Come follow the bonnet of Bonny Dundee.

" Come fill up my cup, come fill up my can,
Come saddle your horses, and call up your men;
Come open the West Port, and let me gang free,
And it's room for the bonnets of Bonny Dundee! "

Dundee he is mounted, he rides up the street,
The bells are rung backward, the drums they are beat;
But the Provost, douce man, said, " Just e'en let him be,
The Gude Town is weel quit of that Deil of Dundee."
    Come fill up my cup, etc.

As he rode down the sanctified bends of the Bow,
Ilk carline was flyting and shaking her pow;
But the young plants of grace they look'd couthie and slee,
Thinking, luck to thy bonnet, thou Bonny Dundee!
    Come fill up my cup, etc.

With sour-featured Whigs the Grassmarket was cramm'd
As if half the West had set tryst to be hang'd:
There was spite in each look, there was fear in each ee,
As they watch'd for the Bonnets of Bonny Dundee.
    Come fill up my cup, etc.

These cowls of Kilmarnock had spits and had spears,
And lang-hafted gullies to kill Cavaliers;
But they shrunk to close-heads, and the causeway was free,
At the toss of the bonnet of Bonny Dundee.
    Come fill up my cup, etc.

He spurr'd to the foot of the proud Castle rock,
And with the gay Gordon he gallantly spoke;
" Let Mons Meg and her marrows speak twa words or three,
For the love of the bonnet of Bonny Dundee."
    Come fill up my cup, etc.

The Gordon demands of him which way he goes—
" Where'er shall direct me the shade of Montrose!
Your Grace in short space shall hear tidings of me,
Or that low lies the bonnet of Bonny Dundee.
    Come fill up my cup, etc.

" There are hills beyond Pentland, and lands beyond Forth,
If there's lords in the Lowlands, there's chiefs in the North;
There are wild Duniewassals three thousand times three,
Will cry *hoigh !* for the bonnet of Bonny Dundee.
    Come fill up my cup, etc.

" There's brass on the target of barken'd bull-hide;
There's steel in the scabbard that dangles beside;
The brass shall be burnish'd, the steel shall flash free,
At a toss of the bonnet of Bonny Dundee.
    Come fill up my cup, etc.

" Away to the hills, to the caves, to the rocks—
Ere I own an usurper, I'll couch with the fox;
And tremble, false Whigs, in the midst of your glee,
You have not seen the last of my bonnet and me ! "
    Come fill up my cup, etc.

He waved his proud hand, and the trumpets were blown,
The kettle-drums clash'd, and the horsemen rode on,
Till on Ravelston's cliffs and on Clermiston's lee,
Died away the wild war-notes of Bonny Dundee.

    Come fill up my cup, come fill up my can,
    Come saddle the horses and call up the men,
    Come open your gates, and let me gae free,
    For it's up with the bonnets of Bonny Dundee!
                Sir Walter Scott,

THE PIPES AT LUCKNOW

Pipes of the misty moorlands,
    Voice of the glens and hills;
The droning of the torrents,
    The treble of the rills !
Not the braes of broom and heather,
    Nor the mountains dark with rain,
Nor maiden bower, nor border tower,
    Have heard your sweetest strain !

Dear to the Lowland reaper,
    And plaided mountaineer,—
To the cottage and the castle
    The Scottish pipes are dear;—
Sweet sounds the ancient pibroch
    O'er mountain, loch, and glade;
But the sweetest of all music
    The Pipes at Lucknow played.

Day by day the Indian tiger
    Louder yelled, and nearer crept;
Round and round the jungle-serpent
    Near and nearer circles swept.
" Pray for rescue, wives and mothers,—
    Pray to-day! " the soldier said;
" To-morrow, death's between us
    And the wrong and shame we dread."

O, they listened, looked, and waited,
    Till their hope became despair;
And the sobs of low bewailing
    Filled the pauses of their prayer.
Then up spake a Scottish maiden,
    With her ear unto the ground:
" Dinna ye hear it?—dinna ye hear it?
    The pipes o' Havelock sound! "

Hushed the wounded man his groaning;
    Hushed the wife her little ones;
Alone they heard the drum-roll
    And the roar of Sepoy guns.
But to sounds of home and childhood
    The Highland ear was true;
As her mother's cradle-crooning
    The mountain pipes she knew.

Like the march of soundless music
    Through the vision of the seer,
More of feeling than of hearing,
    Of the heart than of the ear,
She knew the droning pibroch,
    She knew the Campbell's call:
" Hark! hear ye no' MacGregor's,—
    The grandest o' them all! "

O, they listened, dumb and breathless,
  And they caught the sound at last;
Faint and far beyond the Goomtee
  Rose and fell the piper's blast!
Then a burst of wild thanksgiving
  Mingled woman's voice and man's;
" God be praised!—the march of Havelock!
  The piping of the clans!"

Louder, nearer, fierce as vengeance,
  Sharp and shrill as swords at strife,
Came the wild MacGregor's clan-call
  Stinging all the air to life.
But when the far-off dust-cloud
  To plaided legions grew,
Full tenderly and blithesomely
  The pipes of rescue blew!

Round the silver domes of Lucknow,
  Moslem mosque and Pagan shrine,
Breathed the air to Britons dearest,
  The air of Auld Lang Syne.
O'er the cruel roll of war-drums
  Rose that sweet and homelike strain;
And the tartan clove the turban,
  As the Goomtee cleaves the plain.

Dear to the corn-land reaper
  And plaided mountaineer,—
To the cottage and the castle
  The piper's song is dear.
Sweet sounds the Gaelic pibroch
  O'er mountain, glen, and glade;
But the sweetest of all music
  The Pipes at Lucknow played!

                              J. G. WHITTIER.

MARSTON MOOR

"To horse! to horse, Sir Nicholas! The clarion's note is
    high.
To horse, to horse, Sir Nicholas! The big drum makes reply.
Ere this hath Lucas marched, with his gallant cavaliers,
And the bray of Rupert's trumpets grows fainter on our ears.
To horse! to horse, Sir Nicholas! White Guy is at the door,
And the vulture whets his beak o'er the field of Marston
    Moor."

Up rose the Lady Alice from her brief and broken prayer,
And she brought a silken standard down the narrow turret-
    stair.
Oh! many were the tears that those radiant eyes had shed
As she worked the bright word *Glory* in the gay and glancing
    thread;
And mournful was the smile which o'er those beauteous
    features ran
As she said: "It is your lady's gift; unfurl it in the van!"

"It shall flutter, noble wench, where the best and boldest
    ride,
Through the steel-clad files of Skippon, the black dragoons
    of Pride;
The recreant soul of Fairfax will feel a sicklier qualm,
And the rebel lips of Oliver give out a louder psalm,
When they see my lady's gewgaw flaunt bravely on their
    wing,
And hear her loyal soldiers' shout, 'For God and for the
    King!'"

'Tis noon. The ranks are broken, along the loyal line
They fly, the braggarts of the court, the bullies of the Rhine.
Stout Langley's cheer is heard no more, and Astley's helm
    is down,
And Rupert sheathes his rapier with a curse and with a
    frown,
And cold Newcastle mutters, as he follows in the flight,
"The German boar had better far have supped in York
    to-night."

The knight is all alone, his steel cap cleft in twain,
His good buff jerkin crimsoned o'er with many a gory stain;
Yet still he waves the standard, and cries amid the rout,
" For Church and King, fair gentlemen!   Spur on, and fight
   it out!"
And now he wards a Roundhead's pike, and now he hums a
   stave,
And here he quotes a stage-play, and there he fells a knave.

God speed to thee, Sir Nicholas! Thou hast no thought of fear;
God speed to thee, Sir Nicholas! But fearful odds are here.
The traitors ring thee round, and with every blow and thrust,
" Down, down," they cry, " with Belial!   Down with him to
   the dust!"
" I would," quoth grim old Oliver, " that Belial's trusty sword
This day were doing battle for the Saints and for the Lord!"

The Lady Alice sits with her maidens in her bower,
The grey-haired warden watches from the castle's highest
   tower.
" What news?   What news, old Anthony? "—" The field is
   lost and won;
The ranks of war are melting as the mists beneath the sun;
And a wounded man speeds hither—I'm old and cannot see,
Or sure I am that sturdy step my master's step should be!"

" I bring thee back the standard from as rude and rough a fray
As e'er was proof of soldier's thews, or theme for minstrel's lay.
Bid Hubert fetch the silver bowl, and liquor *quantum suff.*;
I'll make a shift to drain it, ere I part with boot and buff,
Though Guy through many a gaping wound is breathing out
   his life,
And I come to thee a landless man, my fond and faithful wife.

" Sweet! we will fill our money-bags, and freight a ship for
   France,
And mourn in merry Paris for this poor realm's mischance;
Or if the worst betide me, why better axe or rope,
Then life with Lenthall for a king, and Peters for a pope!
Alas! alas, my gallant Guy!   Out on the crop-eared boor
That sent me, with my standard, on foot from Marston
   Moor!"

W. M. PRAED.

THE SOLDIER'S RETURN

O! DAY thrice lovely! when at length the soldier
Returns home into life; when he becomes
A fellow-man among his fellow-men.
The colours are unfurled, the cavalcade
Marshals, and now the buzz is hushed, and hark!
Now the soft peace-march beats, home, brothers, home!
The caps and helmets are all garlanded
With green boughs, the last plundering of the fields.
The city gates fly open of themselves,
The ramparts are all filled with men and women,
With peaceful men and women, that send onwards
Kisses and welcomings upon the air:
From all the towers rings out the merry peal,
The joyous vespers of a bloody day.
O happy man, O fortunate! for whom
The well-known door, the faithful arms are open,
The faithful tender arms with mute embracing.

S. T. COLERIDGE.

THE PRAYER OF HABAKKUK

O LORD, I have heard thy speech, and was afraid:
O Lord, revive thy work in the midst of the years;
In wrath remember mercy.
God came from Teman,
And the Holy one from Mount Paran:
His glory covered the heavens,
And the earth was full of His praise.
Before Him went the pestilence,
And burning coals went forth at His feet:
And His brightness was as the light:
He had bright beams coming out of His side,
And there was the hiding of His power:
Thy bow was made quite naked.
I saw the tents of Cushan in affliction,

And the curtains of the land of Midian did tremble.
He stood and measured the earth:
He beheld, and drove asunder the nations;
And the everlasting mountains were scattered,
The perpetual hills did bow.
Thou didst cleave the earth with rivers:
Thou didst walk through the sea with Thine horses,
Through the heap of great waters.
The mountains saw Thee and they trembled,
The stream of water overflowed:
The deep uttered his voice,
And lifted up his hands on high:
The sun and moon stood still in their habitation:
At the light of Thine arrows they went,
And at the shining of Thy glittering spear.
Was the Lord displeased against the rivers?
Was Thy wrath against the sea,
That Thou didst ride upon Thine horses
And Thy chariots of salvation?
They came out as a whirlwind to scatter me:
Their rejoicing was as to devour the poor secretly;
Thou didst march through the land in indignation,
Thou didst thresh the heathen in anger.
When I heard, my belly trembled:
My lips quivered at the voice:
Rottenness entered into my bones,
And I trembled in myself,
That I might rest in the day of trouble:
When he cometh up unto the people,
He will invade them with his troops.
Although the fig-tree shall not blossom,
Neither shall fruit be in the vines,
The labour of the olive shall fail,
And the fields shall yield no meat;
The flock shall be cut off from the fold,
And there shall be no herd in the stalls:
Yet I will rejoice in the Lord,
I will joy in the God of my salvation.
The Lord God is my strength,
And He will make my feet like hinds' feet,
And He will make me to walk upon mine high places.

HABAKKUK III.

DISARMAMENT

" Put up the sword! " The voice of Christ once more
Speaks, in the pauses of the cannon's roar,
O'er fields of corn by fiery sickles reaped
And left dry ashes; over trenches reaped
With nameless dead; o'er cities starving slow
Under a rain of fire; through wards of woe
Down which a groaning diapason runs
From tortured brothers, husbands, lovers, sons
Of desolate women in their far-off homes,
Waiting to hear the step that never comes!
O men and brothers! let that voice be heard.
War fails, try peace; put up the useless sword!

Fear not the end. There is a story told
In Eastern tents, when autumn nights grow cold,
And round the fire the Mongol shepherds sit
With grave responses listening unto it:
Once, on the errands of his mercy bent,
Buddha, the holy and benevolent,
Met a fell monster, huge and fierce of look,
Whose awful voice the hills and forests shook.
" O son of peace! " the giant cried, " thy fate
Is sealed at last, and love shall yield to hate."
The unarmed Buddha looking, with no trace
Of fear or anger, in the monster's face,
In pity said: " Poor fiend, even thee I love."
Lo! as he spake the sky-tall terror sank
To hand-breadth size; the huge abhorrence shrank
Into the form and fashion of a dove;
And where the thunder of its rage was heard,
Circling above him sweetly sang the bird:
" Hate hath no harm for love," so ran the song;
" And peace unweaponed conquers every wrong! "

J. G. Whittier.

THE SOLDIER

Now in myself I notice take,
  What life we soldiers lead,
My hair stands up, my heart doth ache,
  My soul is full of dread;
      And to declare
      This horrid fear,
    Throughout my bones I feel
      A shiv'ring cold
      On me lay hold
    And run from head to heel.

It is not loss of limbs or breath
  Which hath me so dismay'd,
Nor mortal wounds, nor groans of death
  Have made me thus array'd:
      When cannons roar,
      I start no more
    Than mountains from their place,
      Nor feel I fears,
      Though swords and spears
  Are darted at my face.

A soldier it would ill become
  Such common things to fear,
The shouts of war, the thund'ring drum,
  His courage up doth cheer:
      Though dust and smoke
      His passage choke,
    He boldly marcheth on,
      And thinketh scorn
      His back to turn,
  Till all be lost or won.

The flashing fires, the whizzing shot,
  Distemper not his wits;
The barbed steed he dreadeth not,
  Nor him who thereon sits;

But through the field,
With sword and shield,
He cutteth forth his way,
And through a flood
Of reeking blood,
Wades on without dismay.

That whereupon the dread begins
Which thus apalleth me,
Is that huge troop of crying sins
Which rife in soldiers be;
The wicked mind,
Wherewith I find
Into the field they go,
More terror hath,
Than all the wrath
And engines of the foe.

Defend me, Lord! from those misdeeds
Which my profession shame
And from the vengeance that succeeds
When we are so to blame:
Preserve me far
From acts of war,
Where Thou dost peace command;
And in my breast
Let mercy rest,
Though justice use my hand.

Be Thou my leader to the field,
My head in battle arm;
Be Thou a breastplate and a shield,
To keep my soul from harm;
For live or die,
I will rely
On Thee, O Lord! alone;
And in this trust,
Though fall I must,
I cannot be undone.

GEORGE WITHER.

ENGLAND

Let it flame or fade, and the war roll down like a wind,
We have proved we have hearts in a cause, we are noble still,
And myself have awaked, as it seems, to the better mind;
It is better to fight for the good, than to rail at the ill;
I have felt with my native land, I am one with my kind,
I embrace the purpose of God, and the doom assign'd.

LORD TENNYSON.

SIR GALAHAD

My good blade carves the casques of men,
    My tough lance thrusteth sure,
My strength is as the strength of ten,
    Because my heart is pure.
The shattering trumpet shrilleth high,
    The hard brands shiver on the steel,
The splinter'd spear-shafts crack and fly,
    The horse and rider reel:
They reel, they roll in clanging lists,
    And when the tide of combat stands,
Perfume and flowers fall in showers,
    That lightly rain from ladies' hands.

How sweet are looks that ladies bend
    On whom their favours fall!
For them I battle till the end,
    To save from shame and thrall:
But all my heart is drawn above,
    My knees are bow'd in crypt and shrine:
I never felt the kiss of love,
    Nor maiden's hand in mine.
More bounteous aspects on me beam,
    Me mightier transports move and thrill;
So keep I fair thro' faith and prayer
    A virgin heart in work and will.

When down the stormy crescent goes,
  A light before me swims,
Between dark stems the forest glows,
  I hear a noise of hymns:
Then by some secret shrine I ride;
  I hear a voice, but none are there;
The stalls are void, the doors are wide
  The tapers burning fair.
Fair gleams the snowy altar-cloth,
  The silver vessels sparkle clean,
The shrill bell rings, the censer swings,
  And solemn chaunts resound between

Sometimes on lonely mountain-meres
  I find a magic bark;
I leap on board: no helmsman steers:
  I float till all is dark.
A gentle sound, an awful light!
  Three angels bear the holy Grail:
With folded feet, in stoles of white,
  On sleeping wings they sail.
Ah, blessed vision! blood of God!
  My spirit beats her mortal bars,
As down dark tides the glory slides,
  And star-like mingles with the stars.

When on my goodly charger borne
  Thro' dreaming towns I go,
The cock crows ere the Christmas morn,
  The streets are dumb with snow.
The tempest crackles on the leads,
  And, ringing, springs from brand and mail;
But o'er the dark a glory spreads,
  And gilds the driving hail.
I leave the plain, I climb the height;
  No branchy thicket shelter yields;
But blessed forms in whistling storms
  Fly o'er waste fens and windy fields.

A maiden knight—to me is given
  Such hope, I know not fear;
I yearn to breathe the airs of heaven
  That often meet me here.

I muse on joy that will not cease,
    Pure spaces clothed in living beams,
Pure lilies of eternal peace,
    Whose odours haunt my dreams;
And, stricken by an angel's hand,
    This mortal armour that I wear,
This weight, and size, this heart and eyes,
    Are touch'd, are turn'd to finest air.

The clouds are broken in the sky,
    And thro' the mountain-walls
A rolling organ-harmony
    Swells up, and shakes and falls.
Then move the trees, the copses nod,
    Wings flutter, voices hover clear:
" O just and faithful knight of God!
    Ride on! the prize is near."
So pass I hostel, hall, and grange;
    By bridge and ford, by park and pale,
All-arm'd I ride, whate'er betide,
    Until I find the holy Grail.

LORD TENNYSON.

THE SOLDIER'S DREAM

OUR bugles sang truce—for the night-cloud had lower'd,
    And the sentinel stars set their watch in the sky;
And thousands had sunk on the ground overpower'd,
    The weary to sleep, and the wounded to die.

When reposing that night on my pallet of straw,
    By the wolf-scaring fagot that guarded the slain;
At the dead of the night a sweet vision I saw,
    And thrice ere the morning I dreamt it again.

Methought from the battle-field's dreadful array,
    Far, far I had roam'd on a desolate track:
'Twas Autumn—and sunshine arose on the way
    To the home of my fathers, that welcomed me back.

I flew to the pleasant fields traversed so oft
  In life's morning march, when my bosom was young;
I heard my own mountain-goats bleating aloft,
  And knew the sweet strain that the corn-reapers sung.

Then pledged we the wine-cup, and fondly I swore,
  From my home and my weeping friends never to part;
My little ones kiss'd me a thousand times o'er,
  And my wife sobb'd aloud in her fulness of heart.

Stay, stay with us—rest, thou art weary and worn;
  And fain was their war-broken soldier to stay;—
But sorrow return'd with the dawning of morn,
  And the voice in my dreaming ear melted away,
                       THOMAS CAMPBELL.

HORATIUS

LARS PORSENA of Clusium
  By the Nine Gods he swore
That the great house of Tarquin
  Should suffer wrong no more.
By the Nine Gods he swore it,
  And named a trysting day,
And bade his messengers ride forth,
East and west and south and north,
  To summon his array.

East and west and south and north
  The messengers ride fast,
And tower and town and cottage
  Have heard the trumpet's blast.
Shame on the false Etruscan
  Who lingers in his home,
When Porsena of Clusium
  Is on the march for Rome.

And now hath every city
  Sent up her tale of men;
The foot are fourscore thousand,
  The horse are thousands ten.

Before the gates of Sutrium
    Is met the great array.
A proud man was Lars Porsena
    Upon the trysting day.

For all the Etruscan armies
    Were ranged beneath his eye,
And many a banished Roman,
    And many a stout ally;
And with a mighty following
    To join the muster came
The Tusculan Mamilius,
    Prince of the Latian name.

But by the yellow Tiber
    Was tumult and affright:
From all the spacious champaign
    To Rome men took their flight.
A mile around the city,
    The throng stopped up the ways;
A fearful sight it was to see
    Through two long nights and days.

But the Consul's brow was sad,
    And the Consul's speech was low,
And darkly looked he at the wall,
    And darkly at the foe.
" Their van will be upon us
    Before the bridge goes down;
And if they once may win the bridge,
    What hope to save the town? "

Then out spake brave Horatius,
    The Captain of the Gate:
" To every man upon this earth
    Death cometh soon or late.
And how can man die better
    Than facing fearful odds,
For the ashes of his fathers,
    And the temples of his Gods,

" And for the tender mother
    Who dandled him to rest,

And for the wife who nurses
   His baby at her breast,
And for the holy maidens
   Who feed the eternal flame,
To save them from false Sextus
   That wrought the deed of shame?

" Hew down the bridge, Sir Consul,
   With all the speed ye may;
I, with two more to help me,
   Will hold the foe in play.
In yon strait path a thousand
   May well be stopped by three.
Now who will stand on either hand,
   And keep the bridge with me? "

Then our spake Spurius Lartius;
   A Ramnian proud was he:
" Lo, I will stand at thy right hand,
   And keep the bridge with thee."
And out spake strong Herminius;
   Of Titian blood was he:
" I will abide on thy left side,
   And keep the bridge with thee."

" Horatius," quoth the Consul,
   " As thou sayest, so let it be."
And straight against that great array
   Forth went the dauntless Three.
For Romans in Rome's quarrel
   Spared neither land nor gold,
Nor son nor wife, nor limb nor life,
   In the brave days of old.

Then none was for a party;
   Then all were for the state;
Then the great man helped the poor,
   And the poor man loved the great:
Then lands were fairly portioned;
   Then spoils were fairly sold:
The Romans were like brothers
   In the brave days of old.

Now Roman is to Roman
   More hateful than a foe,
And the Tribunes beard the high,
   And the Fathers grind the low.
As we wax hot in faction,
   In battle we wax cold:
Wherefore men fight not as they fought
   In the brave days of old.

Now while the Three were tightening
   Their harness on their backs,
The Consul was the foremost man
   To take in hand an axe:
And Fathers mixed with Commons
   Seized hatchet, bar, and crow,
And smote upon the planks above,
   And loosed the props below.

Meanwhile the Tuscan army,
   Right glorious to behold,
Came flashing back the noonday light,
Rank behind rank, like surges bright
   Of a broad sea of gold.
Four hundred trumpets sounded
   A peal of warlike glee,
As that great host, with measured tread,
And spears advanced, and ensigns spread,
Rolled slowly towards the bridge's head,
   Where stood the dauntless Three.

The Three stood calm and silent,
   And looked upon the foes,
And a great shout of laughter
   From all the vanguard rose:
And forth three chiefs came spurring
   Before that deep array;
To earth they sprang, their swords they drew,
And lifted high their shields, and flew
   To win the narrow way.

Stout Lartius hurled down Aunus
   Into the stream beneath:

Herminius struck at Seius,
  And clove him to the teeth:
At Picus brave Horatius
  Darted one fiery thrust;
And the proud Umbrian's gilded arms
  Clashed in the bloody dust.

But now no sound of laughter
  Was heard among the foes.
A wild and wrathful clamour
  From all the vanguard rose.
Six spears' lengths from the entrance
  Halted that deep array,
And for a space no man came forth
  To win the narrow way.

But meanwhile axe and lever
  Have manfully been plied;
And now the bridge hangs tottering
  Above the boiling tide.
" Come back, come back, Horatius! "
  Loud cried the Fathers all.
" Back, Lartius! back, Herminius!
  Back, ere the ruin fall! "

Back darted Spurius Lartius;
  Herminius darted back:
And, as they passed, beneath their feet
  They felt the timbers crack.
But when they turned their faces,
  And on the farther shore
Saw brave Horatius stand alone,
  They would have crossed once more.

But with a crash like thunder
  Fell every loosened beam,
And, like a dam, the mighty wreck
  Lay right athwart the stream:
And a long shout of triumph
  Rose from the walls of Rome,
As to the highest turret-tops
  Was splashed the yellow foam.

Alone stood brave Horatius,
  But constant still in mind;
Thrice thirty thousand foes before,
  And the broad flood behind.
" Down with him! " cried false Sextus,
  With a smile on his pale face.
" Now yield thee," cried Lars Porsena,
  " Now yield thee to our grace."

Round turned he, as not deigning
  Those craven ranks to see;
Nought spake he to Lars Porsena,
  To Sextus nought spake he;
But he saw on Palatinus
  The white porch of his home;
And he spake to the noble river
  That rolls by the towers of Rome.

" Oh, Tiber! father Tiber!
  To whom the Romans pray,
A Roman's life, a Roman's arms,
  Take thou in charge this day! "
So he spake, and speaking sheathed
  The good sword by his side,
And with his harness on his back,
  Plunged headlong in the tide.

No sound of joy or sorrow
  Was heard from either bank;
But friends and foes in dumb surprise,
With parted lips and straining eyes,
  Stood gazing where he sank;
And when above the surges
  They saw his crest appear,
All Rome sent forth a rapturous cry,
And even the ranks of Tuscany
  Could scarce forbear to cheer.

But fiercely ran the current,
  Swollen high by months of rain:
And fast his blood was flowing;
  And he was sore in pain,

And heavy with his armour,
  And spent with changing blows:
And oft they thought him sinking,
  But still again he rose.

And now he feels the bottom;
  Now on dry earth he stands;
Now round him throng the Fathers
  To press his gory hands;
And now, with shouts and clapping,
  And noise of weeping loud,
He enters through the River-Gate,
  Borne by the joyous crowd.

They gave him of the corn-land,
  That was of public right,
As much as two strong oxen
  Could plough from morn till night;
And they made a molten image,
  And set it up on high,
And there it stands unto this day
  To witness if I lie.

It stands in the Comitium
  Plain for all folk to see;
Horatius in his harness,
  Halting upon one knee:
And underneath is written,
  In letters all of gold,
How valiantly he kept the bridge
  In the brave days of old.

And in the nights of winter,
  When the cold north winds blow,
And the long howling of the wolves
  Is heard amidst the snow;
When round the lonely cottage
  Roars loud the tempest's din,
And the good logs of Algidus
  Roar louder yet within;

When the oldest cask is opened,
  And the largest lamp is lit;

When the chestnuts glow in the embers,
And the kid turns on the spit;
When young and old in circle
Around the firebrands close;
When the girls are weaving baskets,
And the lads are shaping bows;

When the goodman mends his armour,
And trims his helmet's plume;
When the goodwife's shuttle merrily
Goes flashing through the loom;
With weeping and with laughter
Still is the story told,
How well Horatius kept the bridge
In the brave days of old.

LORD MACAULAY.

WAR-HORSE

FAST, fast, with heels wild spurning,
The dark-grey charger fled:
He burst through ranks of fighting men;
He sprang o'er heaps of dead.
His bridle far out-streaming,
His flanks all blood and foam,
He sought the southern mountains,
The mountains of his home.
The pass was steep and rugged,
The wolves they howled and whined;
But he ran like a whirlwind up the pass,
And he left the wolves behind.
Through many a startled hamlet
Thundered his flying feet;
He rushed through the gate of Tusculum,
He rushed up the long white street;
He rushed by tower and temple,
And paused not from his race
Till he stood before his master's door
In the stately market-place.
And straightway round him gathered
A pale and trembling crowd,

And when they knew him, cries of rage
  Brake forth, and wailing loud:
And women rent their tresses
  For their great prince's fall;
And old men girt on their old swords,
  And went to man the wall.

LORD MACAULAY.

THE BATTLE

THEN the fierce trumpet-flourish
  From earth to heaven arose,
The kites know well the long stern swell
  That bids the Romans close.
Then the good sword of Aulus
  Was lifted up to slay:
Then, like a crag down Apennine,
  Rushed Auster through the fray.
But under those strange horsemen
  Still thicker lay the slain;
And after those strange horses
  Black Auster toiled in vain.
Behind them Rome's long battle
  Came rolling on the foe,
Ensigns dancing wild above,
  Blades all in line below.
So comes the Po in flood-time
  Upon the Celtic plain:
So comes the squall, blacker than night,
  Upon the Adrian main.
Now, by our Sire Quirinus,
  It was a goodly sight
To see the thirty standards
  Swept down the tide of flight.
So flies the spray of Adria
  When the black squall doth blow,
So corn-sheaves in the flood-time
  Spin down the whirling Po.
False Sextus to the mountains
  Turned first his horse's head;

And fast fled Ferentinum,
   And fast Lanuvium fled.
The horsemen of Nomentum
   Spurred hard out of the fray;
The footmen of Velitræ
   Threw shield and spear away.
And underfoot was trampled,
   Amidst the mud and gore,
The banner of proud Tusculum,
   That never stooped before:
And down went Flavius Faustus,
   Who led his stately ranks
From where the apple blossoms wave
   On Anio's echoing banks,
And Tullus of Arpinum,
   Chief of the Volscian aids,
And Metius with the long fair curls,
   The love of Anxur's maids,
And the white head of Vulso,
   The great Arician seer,
And Nepos of Laurentum,
   The hunter of the deer;
And in the back false Sextus
   Felt the good Roman steel,
And wriggling in the dust he died,
   Like a worm beneath the wheel:
And fliers and pursuers
   Were mingled in a mass;
And far away the battle
   Went roaring through the pass.

Lord Macaulay.

THE WAR SONG

Blow trumpet, for the world is white with May;
Blow trumpet, the long night hath roll'd away!
Blow thro' the living world—" Let the King reign."

Shall Rome or Heathen rule in Arthur's realm?
Flash brand and lance, fall battleaxe upon helm,
Fall battleaxe, and flash brand! Let the King reign.

Strike for the King and live! his knights have heard
That God hath told the King a secret word.
Fall battleaxe, and flash brand!   Let the King reign.

Blow trumpet! he will lift us from the dust.
Blow trumpet! live the strength and die the lust!
Clang battleaxe, and clash brand!   Let the King reign.

Strike for the King and die! and if thou diest,
The King is King, and ever wills the highest.
Clang battleaxe, and clash brand!   Let the King reign.

Blow, for our Sun is mighty in his May!
Blow, for our Sun is mightier day by day!
Clang battleaxe, and clash brand!   Let the King reign.

The King will follow Christ, and we the King
In whom high God hath breathed a secret thing.
Fall battleaxe, and flash brand!   Let the King reign.

Lord TENNYSON.

THY VOICE IS HEARD

THY voice is heard thro' rolling drums,
   That beat to battle where he stands;
Thy face across his fancy comes,
   And gives the battle to his hands:
A moment, while the trumpets blow,
   He sees his brood about thy knee;
The next, like fire he meets the foe,
   And strikes him dead for thine and thee.

LORD TENNYSON.

HOME THEY BROUGHT

HOME they brought her warrior dead:
   She nor swoon'd, nor utter'd cry:
All her maidens, watching, said,
   " She must weep or she will die."

Then they praised him, soft and low,
   Call'd him worthy to be loved,
Truest friend and noblest foe;
   Yet she neither spoke nor moved.

Stole a maiden from her place,
   Lightly to the warrior stept,
Took the face-cloth from the face;
   Yet she neither moved nor wept.

Rose a nurse of ninety years,
   Set his child upon her knee—
Like summer tempest came her tears—
   " Sweet my child, I live for thee."

LORD TENNYSON.

OUR ENEMIES HAVE FALLEN

OUR enemies have fall'n, have fall'n: the seed,
The little seed they laugh'd at in the dark,
Has risen and cleft the soil, and grown a bulk
Of spanless girth, that lays on every side
A thousand arms and rushes to the Sun.

Our enemies have fall'n, have fall'n: they came;
The leaves were wet with women's tears: they heard
A noise of songs they would not understand:
They mark'd it with the red cross to the fall,
And would have strown it, and are fall'n themselves.

Our enemies have fall'n, have fall'n: they came,
The woodmen with their axes: lo the tree!
But we will make it faggots for the hearth,
And shape it plank and beam for roof and floor,
And boats and bridges for the use of men.

Our enemies have fall'n, have fall'n: they struck;
With their own blows they hurt themselves, nor knew
There dwelt an iron nature in the grain:
The glittering axe was broken in their arms,
Their arms were shatter'd to the shoulder-blade.

Our enemies have fall'n, but this shall grow
A night of Summer from the heat, a breadth
Of Autumn, dropping fruits of power; and roll'd
With music in the growing breeze of Time,
The tops shall strike from star to star, the fangs
Shall move the stony bases of the world.

LORD TENNYSON

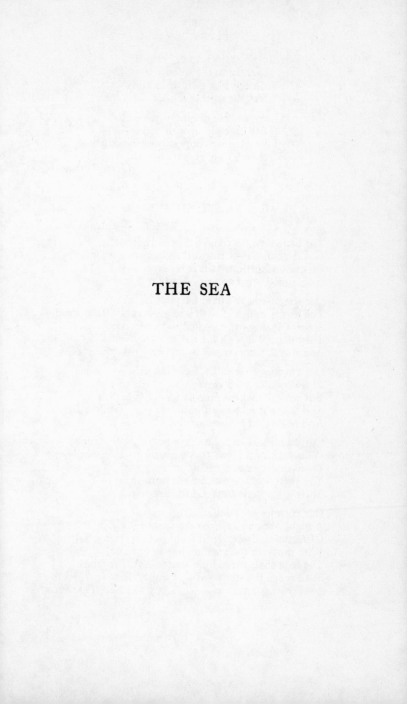

THE SEA

THE SEA

THE Sea! the Sea! the open Sea!
The blue, the fresh, the ever free!
Without a mark, without a bound,
It runneth the earth's wide regions round;
It plays with the clouds; it mocks the skies;
Or like a cradled creature lies.

I'm on the Sea! I'm on the Sea!
I am where I would ever be;
With the blue above, and the blue below,
And silence wheresoe'er I go;
If a storm should come and awake the deep,
What matter? I shall ride and sleep.

I love (oh! how I love) to ride
On the fierce foaming bursting tide,
When every mad wave drowns the moon,
Or whistles aloft his tempest tune,
And tells how goeth the world below,
And why the south-west blasts do blow.

I never was on the dull tame shore,
But I lov'd the great Sea more and more,
And backward flew to her billowy breast,
Like a bird that seeketh its mother's nest;
And a mother she was, and is to me;
For I was born on the open Sea.

The waves were white, and red the morn,
In the noisy hour when I was born;
And the whale it whistled, the porpoise rolled,
And the dolphins bared their backs of gold;
And never was heard such an outcry wild
As welcomed to life the Ocean-child!

I've lived since then, in calm and strife,
Full fifty summers a sailor's life,
With wealth to spend and a power to range,
But never have sought, nor sighed for change;
And Death, whenever he come to me,
Shall come on the wide unbounded Sea!

B. W. PROCTER.

YE MARINERS OF ENGLAND

I

YE Mariners of England!
That guard our native seas;
Whose flag has braved, a thousand years,
The battle and the breeze!
Your glorious standard launch again
To match another foe!
And sweep through the deep,
While the stormy tempests blow;
While the battle rages loud and long,
And the stormy tempests blow.

II

The spirits of your fathers
Shall start from every wave!—
For the deck it was their field of fame,
And Ocean was their grave:
Where Blake and mighty Nelson fell,
Your manly hearts shall glow,
As ye sweep through the deep,
While the stormy tempests blow;
While the battle rages loud and long,
And the stormy tempests blow.

III

Britannia needs no bulwark,
No towers along the steep;
Her march is o'er the mountain-waves,
Her home is on the deep.
With thunders from her native oak,

She quells the floods below,—
As they roar on the shore,
When the stormy tempests blow;
When the battle rages loud and long,
And the stormy tempests blow.

IV

The meteor flag of England
Shall yet terrific burn;
Till danger's troubled night depart,
And the star of peace return.
Then, then, ye ocean-warriors!
Our song and feast shall flow
To the fame of your name,
When the storm has ceased to blow;
When the fiery fight is heard no more,
And the storm has ceased to blow.

THOMAS CAMPBELL.

SIR HUMPHREY GILBERT

SOUTHWARD with fleet of ice
    Sailed the corsair of Death:
Wild and fast blew the blast,
    And the east wind was his breath.

His lordly ships of ice
    Glistened in the sun;
On each side, like pennons wide,
    Flashing crystal streamlets run.

His sails of white sea-mist
    Dripped with silver rain;
But where he passed there were cast
Leaden showers o'er the main.

Eastward from Campobello
    Sir Humphrey Gilbert sailed;
Three days or more seaward he bore,
    Then, alas! the land-wind failed.

Alas! the land-wind failed,
     And ice-cold grew the night:
And never more, on sea or shore,
     Should Sir Humphrey see the light.

He sat upon the deck,
     The Book was in his hand;
" Do not fear! Heaven is as near,"
     He said, " by water as by land! "

In the first watch of the night,
     Without a signal's sound,
Out of the sea mysteriously
     The fleet of Death rose all round.

The moon and the evening star
     Were hanging in the shrouds;
Every mast, as it passed,
     Seemed to rake the passing clouds.

They grappled with their prize,
     At midnight black and cold!
As of a rock was the shock;
     Heavily the ground-swell rolled.

Southward through day and dark,
     They drift in close embrace,
With mist and rain, to the open main;
     Yet there seems no change of place.

Southward, for ever southward,
     They drift through dark and day;
And like a dream, in the Gulf-stream
     Sinking, vanish all away.
                 H. W. LONGFELLOW.

DRAKE'S DRUM

DRAKE he's in his hammock an a thousand miles away,
     Capten art tha sleepin there below?
Slung atween the round shot in Nombre Dios Bay
     An dreamin arl the time o' Plymouth Hoe.

Yarnder lumes the Island, yarnder lie the ships
    Wi' sailor lads a dancin heel and toe,
An the shore lights flashin an the night tide dashin,
    He sees it arl so plainly as he saw it long ago.

Drake he was a Devon man an rewled the Devon seas.
    Capten art tha sleepin there below?
Rovin tho his death fell he went wi' heart at ease
    An dreamin arl the time of Plymouth Hoe.
Take my drum to England; hang et by the shore,
    Strike et when your powder's runnin low.
If the Dons sight Devon I'll quit the port of Heaven
    An drum em up the Channel as we drummed em long ago.

Drake he's in his hammock till the great Armadas come.
    Capten art tha sleepin there below?
Slung atween the round shot listenin for the drum
    An dreamin arl the time o' Plymouth Hoe.
Call him on the deep sea, call him up the Sound,
    Call him when ye sail to meet the foe.
Where the old trade's plying an the old flag flyin
    They shall find him ware and wakin as they found him long
      ago.

Henry Newbolt.

THE ARMADA

Attend, all ye who list to hear our noble England's praise;
I tell of the thrice famous deeds she wrought in ancient days,
When that great fleet invincible against her bore in vain
The richest spoils of Mexico, the stoutest hearts of Spain.

    It was about the lovely close of a warm summer day,
There came a gallant merchant-ship full sail to Plymouth
    Bay;
Her crew hath seen Castile's black fleet, beyond Aurigny's
    isle,
At earliest twilight, on the waves lie heaving many a mile.
At sunrise she escaped their van, by God's especial grace;
And the tall Pinta, till the noon, had held her close in chase.
Forthwith a guard at every gun was placed along the wall;

The beacon blazed upon the roof of Edgecumbe's lofty hall;
Many a light fishing-bark put out to pry along the coast,
And with loose rein and bloody spur rode inland many a post.
With his white hair unbonneted, the stout old sheriff comes;
Behind him march the halberdiers; before him sound the
    drums;
His yeomen round the market cross make clear an ample
    space;
For there behoves him to set up the standard of Her Grace.
And haughtily the trumpets peal, and gaily dance the bells,
As slow upon the labouring wind the royal blazon swells.
Look how the Lion of the sea lifts up his ancient crown,
And underneath his deadly paw treads the gay lilies down.
So stalked he when he turned to flight, on that famed Picard
    field,
Bohemia's plume, and Genoa's bow, and Cæsar's eagle shield.
So glared he when at Agincourt in wrath he turned to bay,
And crushed and torn beneath his claws the princely hunters
    lay.
Ho! strike the flagstaff deep, Sir Knight: ho! scatter flowers,
    fair maids:
Ho! gunners, fire a loud salute: ho! gallants, draw your
    blades:
Thou sun, shine on her joyously; ye breezes, waft her wide;
Our glorious SEMPER EADEM, the banner of our pride.
    The freshening breeze of eve unfurled that banner's massy
    fold;
The parting gleam of sunshine kissed the haughty scroll of
    gold;
Night sank upon the dusky beach, and on the purple sea,
Such night in England ne'er had been, nor e'er again shall be.
From Eddystone to Berwick bounds, from Lynn to Milford
    Bay,
That time of slumber was as bright and busy as the day;
For swift to east and swift to west the ghastly war-flame
    spread,
High on St. Michael's Mount it shone: it shone on Beachy
    Head.
Far on the deep the Spaniard saw, along each southern shire,
Cape beyond cape, in endless range, those twinkling points
    of fire.
The fisher left his skiff to rock on Tamar's glittering waves:

The rugged miners poured to war from Mendip's sunless caves:

O'er Longleat's towers, o'er Cranbourne's oaks, the fiery herald flew:

He roused the shepherds of Stonehenge, the rangers of Beaulieu.

Right sharp and quick the bells all night rang out from Bristol town,

And ere the day three hundred horse had met on Clifton down;

The sentinel on Whitehall gate looked forth into the night,

And saw o'erhanging Richmond Hill the streak of blood-red light.

Then bugle's note and cannon's roar the deathlike silence broke,

And with one start, and with one cry, the royal city woke.

At once on all her stately gates arose the answering fires;

At once the wild alarum clashed from all her reeling spires;

From all the batteries of the Tower pealed loud the voice of fear;

And all the thousand masts of Thames sent back a louder cheer:

And from the furthest wards was heard the rush of hurrying feet,

And the broad streams of pikes and flags rushed down each roaring street;

And broader still became the blaze, and louder still the din,

As fast from every village round the horse came spurring in:

And eastward straight from wild Blackheath the warlike errand went,

And roused in many an ancient hall the gallant squires of Kent.

Southward from Surrey's pleasant hills flew those bright couriers forth;

High on bleak Hampstead's swarthy moor they started for the north;

And on, and on, without a pause, untired they bounded still:

All night from tower to tower they sprang; they sprang from hill to hill:

Till the proud peak unfurled the flag o'er Darwin's rocky dales,

Till like volcanoes flared to heaven the stormy hills of Wales,

Till twelve fair counties saw the blaze on Malvern's lonely
    height,
Till streamed in crimson on the wind the Wrekin's crest of
    light,
Till broad and fierce the star came forth on Ely's stately
    fane,
And tower and hamlet rose in arms o'er all the boundless
    plain;
Till Belvoir's lordly terraces the sign to Lincoln sent,
And Lincoln sped the message on o'er the wide vale of Trent;
Till Skiddaw saw the fire that burned on Gaunt's embattled
    pile,
And the red glare on Skiddaw roused the burghers of Carlisle.

. . . .

LORD MACAULAY.

TOLL FOR THE BRAVE

TOLL for the brave
    The brave that are no more.
All sunk beneath the wave
    Fast by their native shore.

Eight hundred of the brave,
    Whose courage well was tried,
Had made the vessel heel,
    And laid her on her side.

A land-breeze shook the shrouds,
    And she was overset;
Down went the Royal George,
    With all her crew complete.

Toll for the brave.
    Brave Kempenfelt is gone;
His last sea-fight is fought;
    His work of glory done.

It was not in the battle;
    No tempest gave the shock;
She sprang no fatal leak;
    She ran upon no rock.

His sword was in its sheath;
  His fingers held the pen,
When Kempenfelt went down
  With twice four hundred men.

Weigh the vessel up,
  Once dreaded by our foes,
And mingle with our cup
  The tears that England owes.

Her timbers yet are sound,
  And she may float again
Full charged with England's thunder,
  And plough the distant main.

But Kempenfelt is gone,
  His victories are o'er;
And he and his eight hundred
  Shall plough the wave no more.

              WILLIAM COWPER.

THE BATTLE OF THE BALTIC

OF Nelson and the North,
Sing the glorious day's renown,
When to battle fierce came forth
All the might of Denmark's crown,
And her arms along the deep proudly shone;
By each gun the lighted brand,
In a bold determined hand,
And the Prince of all the land
Led them on.

Like leviathans afloat,
Lay their bulwarks on the brine;
While the sign of battle flew
On the lofty British line:
It was ten of April morn by the chime:
As they drifted on their path,
There was silence deep as death;
And the boldest held his breath,
For a time.

But the might of England flush'd
To anticipate the scene;
And her van the fleeter rush'd
O'er the deadly space between.
"Hearts of oak!" our captains cried; when each gun
From its adamantine lips
Spread a death-shade round the ships,
Like the hurricane eclipse
Of the sun.

Again! again! again!
And the havoc did not slack,
Till a feeble cheer the Dane
To our cheering sent us back;—
Their shots along the deep slowly boom:—
Then ceased—and all is wail,
As they strike the shatter'd sail
Or, in conflagration pale,
Light the gloom.

Out spoke the victor then,
As he hail'd them o'er the wave;
"Ye are brothers! ye are men!
And we conquer but to save:—
So peace instead of death let us bring;
But yield, proud foe, thy fleet,
With the crews, at England's feet,
And make submission meet
To our King."

Then Denmark blest our chief,
That he gave her wounds repose;
And the sounds of joy and grief
From her people wildly rose,
As death withdrew his shades from the day.
While the sun look'd smiling bright
O'er a wide and woeful sight,
Where the fires of funeral light
Died away.

Now joy, old England, raise!
For the tidings of thy might,

By the festal cities' blaze,
While the wine cup shines in light;
And yet amidst that joy and uproar,
Let us think of them that sleep,
Full many a fathom deep,
By thy wild and stormy steep,
Elsinore!

Brave hearts! to Britain's pride
Once so faithful and so true,
On the deck of fame that died;
With the gallant good Riou:
Soft sigh the winds of Heaven o'er their grave!
While the billow mournful rolls
And the mermaid's song condoles,
Singing glory to the souls
Of the brave!

THOMAS CAMPBELL.

CHEER, BOYS, CHEER

CHEER, boys, cheer! no more of idle sorrow,
  Courage, true hearts, shall bear us on our way;
Hope points before, and shows the bright to-morrow,
  Let us forget the darkness of to-day.
So farewell, England! Much as we may love thee,
  We'll dry the tears that we have shed before;
Why should we weep to sail in search of fortune?
  So farewell, England! farewell evermore!
Cheer, boys, cheer! for England, mother England,
  Cheer, boys, cheer! the willing strong right hand:
Cheer, boys, cheer! there's work for honest labour—
  Cheer, boys, cheer—in the new and happy land!

Cheer, boys, cheer! the steady breeze is blowing,
  To float us freely o'er the ocean's breast;
The world shall follow in the track we're going,
  The star of empire glitters in the west.
Here we had toil and little to reward it,
  But there shall plenty smile upon our pain;

And ours shall be the mountain and the forest,
　　And boundless prairies ripe with golden grain.
Cheer, boys, cheer! for England, mother England,
　　Cheer, boys, cheer! united heart and hand;
Cheer, boys, cheer! there's wealth for honest labour—
　　Cheer, boys, cheer!—in the new and happy land!
　　　　　　　　　　　　　　　CHARLES MACKAY.

A WET SHEET

A WET sheet and a flowing sea,
　　A wind that follows fast,
And fills the white and rustling sail,
　　And bends the gallant mast;
And bends the gallant mast, my boys,
　　While like the eagle free
Away the good ship flies, and leaves
　　Old England on the lee.

O for a soft and gentle wind!
　　I heard a fair one cry;
But give to me the snoring breeze
　　And white waves heaving high;
And white waves heaving high, my lads,
　　The good ship tight and free—
The world of waters is our home,
　　And merry men are we.

There's tempest in yon horned moon,
　　And lightning in yon cloud;
But hark the music, mariners!
　　The wind is piping loud;
The wind is piping loud, my boys,
　　The lightning flashes free—
While the hollow oak our palace is,
　　Our heritage the sea.
　　　　　　　　　　　　　ALLAN CUNNINGHAM.

ADMIRAL DEATH

Boys are ye callin a toast to night?
  Hear what the sea wind saith,
Fill for a bumper strong and bright
  And here's to Admiral Death.
He's sailed in a hundred builds of boat,
He's fought in a thousand kinds of coat,
He's the senior flag of all afloat,
    And his name is Admiral Death.

Which of you looks for a service free?
  Hear what the sea wind saith,
The rules of the service are but three
  When ye sail with Admiral Death.
Steady your hand in the time of squalls,
Stand to the last by him that falls,
And answer clear to the voice that calls,
    Ay, ay, Admiral Death.

How will ye know him among the rest?
  Hear what the sea wind saith.
By the glint of the stars that cover his breast
  Ye may find Admiral Death.
By the forehead grim with many a scar,
By the voice that rolls like thunder far,
By the tenderest eyes of all that are,
    Ye may know Admiral Death.

Where are the lads that sailed before?
  Hear what the sea wind saith,
Their bones are white by many a shore
  They sleep with Admiral Death.
Oh but they loved him young and old,
For he left the laggard and took the bold,
And the fight was fought and the story's told,
    And they sleep with Admiral Death.

                              HENRY NEWBOLT.

THE TRAVELLER

To men of other minds my fancy flies,
Embosomed in the deep where Holland lies.
Methinks her patient sons before me stand,
Where the broad ocean leans against the land;
And, sedulous to stop the coming tide,
Lift the tall rampire's artificial pride.
Onward, methinks, and diligently slow,
The firm connected bulwark seems to grow,
Spread its long arms amidst the watery roar,
Scoops out an empire, and usurps the shore—
While the pent ocean, rising o'er the pile,
Sees an amphibious world beneath him smile;
The slow canal, the yellow-blossomed vale,
The willow-tufted bank, the gliding sail,
The crowded mart, the cultivated plain—
A new creation rescued from his reign.

OLIVER GOLDSMITH.

A DROWNED SOLDIER

WALKING next day upon the fatal shore,
Among the slaughter'd bodies of their men,
Which the full-stomach'd sea had cast upon
The sands, it was my unhappy chance to light
Upon a face, whose favour when it lived
My astonish'd mind inform'd me I had seen.
He lay in his armour, as if that had been
His coffin; and the weeping sea (like one
Whose milder temper doth lament the death
Of him whom in his rage he slew) runs up
The shore, embraces him, kisses his cheek;
Goes back again and forces up the sands
To bury him; and every time it parts,
Sheds tears upon him; till at last (as if
It could no longer endure to see the man

Whom it had slain, yet loath to leave him), with
A kind of unresolv'd unwilling pace,
Winding her waves one in another (like
A man that folds his arms, or wrings his hands,
For grief), ebb'd from the body and descends,
As if it would sink down into the earth,
And hide itself for shame of such a deed.

CYRIL TOURNEUR.

THE SAILOR BOY

He rose at dawn, and fired with hope,
  Shot o'er the seething harbour-bar,
And reached the ship and caught the rope,
  And whistled to the morning star.

And while he whistled loud and long
  He heard a fierce mermaiden cry
" O boy, tho' thou art young and proud
  I see the place where thou wilt lie.

" The sands and yeasty surges mix
  In caves about the dreary bay,
And on thy ribs the limpet sticks,
  And in thy heart the scrawl shall play."

" Fool," he answered, " death is sure
  To those that stay and those that roam,
But I will nevermore endure
  To sit with empty hands at home.

" My mother clings about my neck,
  My sisters crying ' stay for shame,'
My father raves of death and wreck—
  They are all to blame, they are all to blame.

" God help me! save I take my part
  Of danger on the roaring sea,
A devil rises in my heart
  Far worse than any death to me."

LORD TENNYSON.

THE TEN THOUSAND

HENCE through the continent Ten Thousand Greeks
Urged a retreat whose glory not the prime
Of victories can reach. Deserts in vain
Opposed their course and hostile lands unknown,
And deep rapacious floods dire-bank'd with death;
And mountains in whose jaws Destruction grinned;
Hunger and toil, Armenian snows and storms,
And circling myriads still of barbarous foes.
Greece in their view, and glory yet untouched,
Their steady column pierced the scattering herds
Which a whole empire poured, and held its way
Triumphant, by the sage-exalted chief
Fired and sustained. O light and force of mind,
Almost almighty in severe extremes!
The sea at last from Colchian mountains seen,
Kind-hearted transport round their captains threw
The soldiers' fond embrace; o'erflowed their eyes
With tender floods, and loosed the general voice
To cries resounding loud " The sea! The sea! "

JAMES THOMSON.

HEROES

HOPE

SAY not the struggle nought availeth,
  The labour and the wounds are vain,
The enemy faints not, nor faileth,
  And as things have been they remain.

If hopes were dupes, fears may be liars;
  It may be, in yon smoke concealed,
Your comrades chase e'en now the fliers,
  And, but for you, possess the field.

For while the tired waves, vainly breaking,
  Seem here no painful inch to gain,
Far back, through creeks and inlets making,
  Comes silent, flooding in, the main.

And not by eastern windows only,
  When daylight comes, comes in the light,
In front, the sun climbs slow, how slowly,
  But westward, look, the land is bright.
                              ARTHUR HUGH CLOUGH.

VALOUR

                            IT is held,
That valour is the chiefest virtue, and
Most dignifies the haver: if it be,
The man I speak of cannot in the world
Be singly counterpoised.   At sixteen years,
When Tarquin made a head for Rome, he fought
Beyond the mark of others: our then dictator,
Whom with all praise I point at, saw him fight,
When with his Amazonian chin he drove
The bristled lips before him: he bestrid
An o'erpressed Roman, and i' the consul's view

Slew three opposers: Tarquin's self he met,
And struck him on his knee: in that day's feats,
When he might act the woman in the scene,
He proved best man i' the field, and for his meed
Was brow-bound with the oak. His pupil age
Man-enter'd thus, he waxed like a sea;
And, in the brunt of seventeen battles since,
He lurch'd all swords o' the garland. For this last,
Before and in Corioli, let me say,
I cannot speak him home: he stopp'd the fliers;
And by his rare example, made the coward
Turn terror into sport: as weeds before
A vessel under sail, so men obey'd,
And fell below his stem: his sword (death's stamp)
Where it did mark, it took; from face to foot
He was a thing of blood, whose every motion
Was timed with dying cries: alone he enter'd
The mortal gate o' the city, which he painted
With shunless destiny, aidless came off,
And with a sudden reinforcement struck
Corioli, like a planet: Now all's his:
When by and by the din of war 'gan pierce
His ready sense; then straight his doubled spirit
Re-quicken'd what in flesh was fatigate,
And to the battle came he; where he did
Run reeking o'er the lives of men, as if
'Twere a perpetual spoil: and, till we call'd
Both field and city ours, he never stood
To ease his breast with panting.

WILLIAM SHAKESPEARE.

THE YOUNG HERO

How glorious fall the valiant, sword in hand,
In front of battle for their native land!
But oh! what ills await the wretch that yields,
A recreant outcast from his country's fields!
The mother whom he loves shall quit her home,
An aged father at his side shall roam;
His little ones shall weeping with him go,

And a young wife participate his woe;
While scorn'd and scowl'd upon by every face,
They pine for food, and beg from place to place.

Stain of his breed! dishonouring manhood's form,
All ills shall cleave to him;—Affliction's storm
Shall blind him wandering in the vale of years,
Till, lost to all but ignominious fears,
He shall not blush to leave a recreant's name,
And children, like himself, inured to shame.

But we will combat for our fathers' land,
And we will drain the life-blood where we stand
To save our children:—fight ye side by side,
And serried close, ye men of youthful pride,
Disdaining fear, and deeming light the cost
Of life itself in glorious battle lost.

Leave not our sires to stem the unequal fight,
Whose limbs are nerved no more with buoyant might;
Nor lagging backward, let the younger breast
Permit the man of age (a sight unbless'd)
To welter in the combat's foremost thrust,
His hoary head dishevell'd in the dust,
And venerable bosom bleeding bare.

But youth's fair form, though fallen, is ever fair,
And beautiful in death the boy appears,
The hero boy, that dies in blooming years:
In man's regret he lives, and woman's tears,
More sacred than in life, and lovelier far,
For having perish'd in the front of war.

THOMAS CAMPBELL.

ARMED

ALL furnish'd, all in arms,
All plumed like estridges that wing the wind;
Bated like eagles having lately bathed;
Glittering in golden coats, like images;
As full of spirit as the month of May,

And gorgeous as the sun at midsummer;
Wanton as youthful goats, wild as young bulls.
I saw young Harry,—with his beaver on,
His cuisses on his thighs, gallantly arm'd.—
Rise from the ground like feather'd Mercury,
And vaulted with such ease into his seat,
As if an angel dropp'd down from the clouds,
To turn and wind a fiery Pegasus,
And witch the world with noble horsemanship.

WILLIAM SHAKESPEARE.

THE CITIZENS DEFEND ANGIERS

Alarums and excursions ; then enter a French Herald, *with trumpets, to the gates.*

French Herald. You men of Angiers, open wide your gates,
And let young Arthur, Duke of Bretagne, in,
Who by the hand of France this day hath made
Much work for tears in many an English mother,
Whose sons lie scatter'd on the bleeding ground.
Many a widow's husband grovelling lies,
Coldly embracing the discolour'd earth;
And victory, with little loss, doth play
Upon the dancing banners of the French,
Who are at hand, triumphantly display'd,
To enter conquerors and to proclaim
Arthur of Bretagne England's king and yours.

Enter English Herald, *with trumpets.*

English Herald. Rejoice, you men of Angiers, ring your bells;
King John, your king and England's, doth approach,
Commander of this hot malicious day.
Their armours, that march'd hence so silver-bright,
Hither return all gilt with Frenchmen's blood.
There stuck no plume in any English crest
That is removed by a staff of France;
Our colours do return in those same hands
That did display them when we first march'd forth;

And, like a jolly troop of huntsmen, come
Our lusty English, all with purpled hands,
Dyed in the dying slaughter of their foes.
Open your gates and give the victors way.
  Citizen. Heralds, from off our towers we might behold,
From first to last, the onset and retire
Of both your armies; whose equality
By our best eyes cannot be censured.
Blood hath bought blood, and blows have answer'd blows;
Strength match'd with strength, and power confronted power:
Both are alike; and both alike we like.
One must prove greatest; while they weigh so even,
We hold our town for neither, yet for both.

    Re-enter the two KINGS, *with their powers, severally.*

  King John. France, hast thou yet more blood to cast
      away?
Say, shall the current of our right run on?
Whose passage, vex'd with thy impediment,
Shall leave his native channel and o'erswell
With course disturb'd even thy confining shores,
Unless thou let his silver water keep
A peaceful progress to the ocean.
  King Philip. England, thou hast not sav'd one drop of
      blood,
In this hot trial, more than we of France;
Rather, lost more.   And by this hand I swear,
That sways the earth this climate overlooks,
Before we will lay down our just-borne arms,
We'll put thee down, 'gainst whom these arms we bear,
Or add a royal number to the dead,
Gracing the scroll that tells of this war's loss
With slaughter coupled to the name of kings.
  Bastard. Ha, majesty! how high thy glory towers,
When the rich blood of kings is set on fire!
O, now doth Death line his dead chaps with steel;
The swords of soldiers are his teeth, his fangs;
And now he feasts, mousing the flesh of men,
In undetermin'd differences of kings.—
Why stand these royal fronts amazed thus?
Cry havoc, kings! back to the stained field,
You equal potents, fiery kindled spirits!

Then let confusion of one part confirm
The other's peace; till then, blows, blood, and death!
 King John. Whose party do the townsmen yet admit?
 King Philip. Speak, citizens, for England; who's your
  king?
 Citizen. The king of England, when we know the king.
 King Philip. Know him in us, that here hold up his right.
 King John. In us, that are our own great deputy,
And bear possession of our person here,
Lord of our presence, Angiers, and of you.
 Citizen. A greater power than we denies all this;
And till it be undoubted, we do lock
Our former scruple in our strong-barr'd gates;
King'd of our fears, until our fears, resolv'd,
Be by some certain king purg'd and depos'd.
 Bastard. By heaven, these scroyles of Angiers flout you,
  kings,
And stand securely on their battlements,
As in a theatre, whence they gape and point
At your industrious scenes and acts of death.
Your royal presences be rul'd by me:
Do like the mutines of Jerusalem;
Be friends, awhile, and both conjointly bend
Your sharpest deeds of malice on this town.
By east and west let France and England mount
Their battering cannon charged to the mouths,
Till their soul-fearing clamours have brawl'd down
The flinty ribs of this contemptuous city.
I'd play incessantly upon these jades,
Even till unfenced desolation
Leave them as naked as the vulgar air.
That done, dissever your united strengths,
And part your mingled colours once again,
Turn face to face and bloody point to point;
Then, in a moment, Fortune shall cull forth
Out of one side her happy minion,
To whom in favour she shall give the day,
And kiss him with a glorious victory.
How like you this wild counsel, mighty states?
Smacks it not something of the policy?
 King John. Now, by the sky that hangs above our heads,
I like it well.—France, shall we knit our powers

And lay this Angiers even with the ground,
Then after fight who shall be king of it?
  Bastard. An if thou hast the mettle of a king,
Being wrong'd as we are by this peevish town,
Turn thou the mouth of thy artillery,
As we will ours, against these saucy walls;
And when that we have dash'd them to the ground,
Why then defy each other, and pell-mell
Make work upon ourselves, for heaven or hell.
  King Philip. Let it be so.—Say, where will you assault?
  King John. We from the west will send destruction
Into this city's bosom.
  Austria. I from the north.
  King Philip.   Our thunder from the south
Shall rain their drift of bullets on this town.
  Bastard (aside). O prudent discipline! From north to
    south
Austria and France shoot in each other's mouth:
I'll stir them to it.—Come, away, away!
  Citizen. Hear us, great kings; vouchsafe awhile to stay,
And I shall show you peace and fair-fac'd league,
Win you this city without stroke or wound,
Rescue those breathing lives to die in beds,
That here come sacrifices for the field.
Persever not, but hear me, mighty kings.
  King John. Speak on with favour; we are bent to hear.
  Citizen. That daughter there of Spain, the Lady Blanch,
Is niece to England; look upon the years
Of Lewis the Dauphin and that lovely maid.
If lusty love should go in quest of beauty,
Where should he find it fairer than in Blanch?
If zealous love should go in search of virtue,
Where should he find it purer than in Blanch?
If love ambitious sought a match of birth,
Whose veins bound richer blood than Lady Blanch?
Such as she is, in beauty, virtue, birth,
Is the young Dauphin every way complete:
If not complete of, say he is not she;
And she again wants nothing, to name want,
If want it be not that she is not he.
He is the half part of a blessed man,
Left to be finished by such a she;

And she a fair divided excellence,
Whose fulness of perfection lies in him.
O, two such silver currents, when they join,
Do glorify the banks that bound them in;
And two such shores to two such streams made one,
Two such controlling bounds shall you be, kings,
To these two princes, if you marry them.
This union shall do more than battery can
To our fast-closed gates; for at this match,
With swifter spleen than powder can enforce,
The mouth of passage shall we fling wide ope,
And give you entrance: but without this match,
The sea enraged is not half so deaf,
Lions more confident, mountains and rocks
More free from motion, no, not Death himself
In mortal fury half so peremptory,
As we to keep this city.

 Bastard.   Here's a stay
That shakes the rotten carcass of old Death
Out of his rags! Here's a large mouth, indeed,
That spits forth death and mountains, rocks and seas,
Talks as familiarly of roaring lions
As maids of thirteen do of puppy-dogs!
What cannoneer begot this lusty blood?
He speaks plain cannon fire, and smoke and bounce;
He gives the bastinado with his tongue:
Our ears are cudgell'd; not a word of his
But buffets better than a fist of France.
Zounds! I was never so bethump'd with words
Since I first call'd my brother's father dad.

         WILLIAM SHAKESPEARE.

FATHER AND SON

 Tal. O young John Talbot! I did send for thee,
To tutor thee in stratagems of war;
That Talbot's name might be in thee revived,
When sapless age, and weak unable limbs,
Should bring thy father to his drooping chair
But,—O malignant and ill-boding stars!—
Now thou art come unto a feast of death,

A terrible and unavoided danger:
Therefore, dear boy, mount on my swiftest horse,
And I'll direct thee how thou shalt escape
By sudden flight: come, dally not, begone.

 John. Is my name Talbot? and am I your son?
And shall I fly? O, if you love my mother,
Dishonour not her honourable name,
To make a bastard, and a slave of me:
The world will say—He is not Talbot's blood,
That basely fled, when noble Talbot stood.

 Tal. Fly, to revenge my death, if I be slain.

 John. He that flies so, will ne'er return again.

 Tal. If we both stay, we both are sure to die.

 John. Then let me stay; and, father, do you fly:
Your loss is great, so your regard should be;
My worth unknown, no loss is known in me.
Upon my death the French can little boast;
In yours they will, in you all hopes are lost.
Flight cannot stain the honour you have won;
But mine it will, that no exploit have done:
You fled for vantage every one will swear;
But if I bow, they'll say—it was for fear.
There is no hope, that ever I will stay,
If, the first hour, I shrink, and run away.
Here, on my knee, I beg mortality,
Rather than life preserved with infamy.

 Tal. Shall all thy mother's hopes lie in one tomb?

 John. Ay, rather that I'll shame my mother's womb.

 Tal. Upon my blessing I command thee go.

 John. To fight I will, but not to fly the foe.

 Tal. Part of thy father may be saved in thee.

 John. No part of him, but will be shame in me.

 Tal. Thou never hadst renown, nor canst not lose it.

 John. Yes, your renowned name: Shall flight abuse it?

 Tal. Thy father's charge shall clear thee from that stain.

 John. You cannot witness for me, being slain.
If death be so apparent, then both fly.

 Tal. And leave my followers here, to fight and die:
My age was never tainted with such shame.

 John. And shall my youth be guilty of such blame?
No more can I be sever'd from your side,
Than can yourself yourself in twain divide:

Stay, go, do what you will, the like do I;
For live I will not, if my father die.　　　　　　　*[Exit.*

   Tal. Then here I take my leave of thee, fair son,
Born to eclipse thy life this afternoon.
Come, side by side together live and die:
And soul with soul from France to heaven fly.
　　　　　　　　　　　　　　(*After a while.*)
   Tal. Where is my other life?—mine own is gone;—
O, where's young Talbot, where is valiant John?—
Triumphant death, smear'd with captivity?
Young Talbot's valour makes me smile at thee:
When he perceived me shrink, and on my knee,
His bloody sword he brandish'd over me,
And, like a hungry lion, did commence
Rough needs of rage, and stern impatience:
But when my angry guardant stood alone,
Tend'ring my ruin, and assail'd of none,
Dizzy-eyed fury, and great rage of heart,
Suddenly made him from my side to start
Into the clustering battle of the French:
And in that sea of blood my boy did drench
His overmounting spirit: and there died
My Icarus, my blossom, in his pride.

   Enter Soldiers, bearing the body of JOHN TALBOT.

   Serv. O my dear lord! lo, where your son is borne!
   Tal. Thou antic death, which laugh'st us here to scorn.
Anon, from thy insulting tyranny,
Coupled in bonds of perpetuity,
Two Talbots, winged through the lither sky,
In thy despite, shall 'scape mortality.—
O thou, whose wounds become hard-favour'd death,
Speak to thy father, ere thou yield thy breath:
Brave death by speaking, whether he will, or no;
Imagine him a Frenchman, and thy foe.—
Poor boy! he smiles, methinks: as who should say
Had death been French, then death hath died to-day.
Come, come, and lay him in his father's arms;
My spirit can no longer bear these harms.
Soldiers, adieu! I have what I would have.
Now my old arms are young John Talbot's grave.
　　　　　　　　　　　　　　　WILLIAM SHAKESPEARE.

A COMBAT

Enter HOTSPUR.

Hot. If I mistake not, thou art Harry Monmouth.

P. Hen. Thou speak'st as if I would deny my name.

Hot. My name is Harry Percy.

P. Hen. Why, then I see
A very valiant rebel of the name.
I am the Prince of Wales; and think not, Percy.
To share with me in glory any more:
Two stars keep not their motion in one sphere;
Nor can one England brook a double reign,
Of Harry Percy, and the Prince of Wales.

Hot. Nor shall it, Harry, for the hour is come
To end the one of us. And would to God,
Thy name in arms were now as great as mine!

P. Hen. I'll make it greater, ere I part from thee;
And all the budding honours on thy crest
I'll crop to make a garland for my head.

Hot. I can no longer brook thy vanities.   (*They fight.*)

Enter FALSTAFF.

Fal. Well said Hal! to it, Hal!—Nay, you shall find no
  boy's play here, I can tell you.

Enter DOUGLAS; *he fights with Falstaff, who falls down as if
  he were dead, and exit Douglas. Hotspur is wounded,
  and falls.*

Hot. O, Harry, thou hast robb'd me of my youth;
I better brook the loss of brittle life,
Than those proud titles thou hast won of me!
They wound my thoughts, worse than thy sword my flesh:—
But thought's the slave of life, and life time's fool;
And time, that takes survey of all the world,
Must have a stop. O, I could prophesy,
But that the earthy and cold hand of death
Lies on my tongue:—No, Percy, thou art dust.
And food for—   (*Dies.*)

P. Hen. For worms, brave Percy; Fare thee well, great
  heart!—

Ill-weaved ambition, how much art thou shrunk!
When that this body did contain a spirit,
A kingdom for it was too small a bound;
But now, two paces of the vilest earth
Is room enough.　This earth, that bears thee dead,
Bears not alive so stout a gentleman.
If thou wert sensible of courtesy,
I should not make so dear a show of zeal:—
But let my favours hide thy mangled face!
And, even in thy behalf, I'll thank myself
For doing these fair rites of tenderness.
Adieu, and take thy praise with thee to heaven!
Thy ignominy sleep with thee in the grave,
Be not remember'd in thy epitaph!

　　　　　　　　　　(*He sees Falstaff on the ground.*)

What! old acquaintance! could not all this flesh
Keep in a little life?　Poor Jack, farewell!
I could have better spared a better man.
O, I should have a heavy miss of thee,
If I were much in love with vanity.
Death hath not struck so fat a deer to-day,
Though many dearer, in this bloody fray.
Embowell'd will I see thee by and by:
Till then, in blood by noble Percy lie.　　　　　[*Exit.*

Fal. (*Rising slowly.*) Embowell'd! if thou embowel me
to day, I'll give you leave to powder me, and eat me too,
to-morrow. 'Sblood, 'twas time to counterfeit, or that hot
termagant Scot had paid me scot and lot too.　Counterfeit!
I lie, I am no counterfeit: To die, is to be a counterfeit;
for he is but the counterfeit of a man, who hath not the life
of a man: but to counterfeit dying, when a man thereby
liveth, is to be no counterfeit, but the true and perfect image
of life indeed.　The better part of valour is—discretion; in
the which better part, I have saved my life. 'Zounds, I am
afraid of this gunpowder Percy, though he be dead: How, if
he should counterfeit too, and rise?　I am afraid, he would
prove the better counterfeit.　Therefore I'll make him sure,
yea, and I'll swear I killed him.　Why may not he rise as
well as I?　Nothing confutes me but eyes, and nobody sees
me.　Therefore, sirrah (*stabbing him*), with a new wound in
your thigh, come you along with me.

　　　　　　　　　　(*Takes Hotspur on his back.*)

Re-enter PRINCE HENRY *and* PRINCE JOHN.

P. Hen. Come, brother John, full bravely hast thou flesh'd
Thy maiden sword.

P. John. But, soft! whom have we here?
Did you not tell me, this fat man was dead?

P. Hen. I did; I saw him dead, breathless, and bleeding,
Upon the ground.—
Art thou alive? or is it phantasy
That plays upon our eye-sight? I pr'ythee speak;
We will not trust our eyes, without our ears:—
Thou art not what thou seem'st.

Fal. No, that's certain; I am not a double man: but if I
be not Jack Falstaff, then am I a Jack. There is Percy:
(*throwing the body down*) if your father will do me any honour,
so; if not, let him kill the next Percy himself. I look to be
either earl or duke, I can assure you.

P. Hen. Why, Percy I killed myself, and saw thee dead.

Fal. Didst thou?—Lord! Lord! how this world is given
to lying! I grant you, I was down and out of breath; and so
was he: but we rose both at an instant, and fought a long
hour by Shrewsbury clock. If I may be believed, so; if not,
et them, that should reward valour, bear the sin upon their
own heads. I'll take it upon my death, I gave him this
wound in the thigh; if the man were alive, and would deny it,
I would make him eat a piece of my sword.

P. John. This is the strangest tale that e'er I heard.

P. Hen. This is the strangest fellow, brother John.—
Come, bring your luggage nobly on your back.
For my part, if a lie may do thee grace,
I'll gild it with the happiest terms I have.

(*A retreat is sounded.*)
The trumpet sounds retreat, the day is ours.
Come, brother, let's to the highest of the field,
To see what friends are living, who are dead.

[*Exeunt Prince Henry and Prince John.*

Fal. I'll follow, as they say, for reward. He that rewards
me, Heaven reward him! If I do grow great, I'll grow less,
for I'll purge, and leave sack and live cleanly, as a nobleman
should do.

WILLIAM SHAKESPEARE.

A SWIMMER

Cas. I know that virtue to be in you, Brutus,
As well as I do know your outward favour.
Well, honour is the subject of my story—
I cannot tell, what you and other men
Think of this life; but, for my single self,
I had as lief not be, as live to be
In awe of such a thing as I myself.
I was born free as Cæsar; so were you:
We both have fed as well; and we can both
Endure the winter's cold, as well as he.
For once, upon a raw and gusty day,
The troubled Tiber chafing with her shores,
Cæsar said to me, *Dar'st thou, Cassius, now*
Leap in with me into this angry flood,
And swim to yonder point ?—Upon the word,
Accouter'd as I was, I plunged in,
And bade him follow; so, indeed, he did.
The torrent roar'd; and we did buffet it
With lusty sinews; throwing it aside
And stemming it with hearts of controversy.
But ere we could arrive the point proposed,
Cæsar cried, *Help me, Cassius, or I sink.*
I, as Æneas, our great ancestor,
Did from the flames of Troy upon his shoulder
The old Anchises bear, so, from the waves of Tiber
Did I the tired Cæsar: And this man
Is now become a god; and Cassius is
A wretched creature, and must bend his body,
If Cæsar carelessly but nod on him.
He had a fever when he was in Spain,
And, when the fit was on him, I did mark
How he did shake: 'tis true, this god did shake;
His coward lips did from their colour fly;
And that same eye, whose bend doth awe the world,
Did lose his lustre: I did hear him groan:
Ay, and that tongue of his, that bade the Romans
Mark him, and write his speeches in their books,
Alas! it cried, *Give me some drink, Titinius,*

As a sick girl.   Ye gods, it doth amaze me,
A man of such a feeble temper should
So get the start of the majestic world,
And bear the palm alone.   WILLIAM SHAKESPEARE.

THE TYRANT'S DEATH

THEN she came to the pillar of the bed, which was at
Holofernes' head, and took down his fauchion from thence,

And approached to his bed, and took hold of the hair of
his head, and said, Strengthen me, O Lord God of Israel,
this day.

And she smote twice upon his neck with all her might,
and she took away his head from him,

And tumbled his body down from the bed, and pulled
down the canopy from the pillars; and anon after she went
forth, and gave Holofernes his head to her maid;

And she put it in her bag of meat: so they twain went
together according to their custom unto prayer: and when
they passed the camp, they compassed the valley, and went
up the mountain of Bethulia, and came to the gates thereof.

Then said Judith afar off to the watchman at the gate,
Open, open now the gate: God, even our God, is with us,
to shew his power yet in Jerusalem, and his forces against the
enemy, as he hath even done this day.

Now when the men of her city heard her voice, they made
haste to go down to the gate of their city, and they called
the elders of the city.

And then they ran all together, both small and great, for
it was strange unto them that she was come: so they opened
the gate, and received them, and made a fire for a light, and
stood round about them.

Then she said to them with a loud voice, Praise, praise
God, praise God, I say, for he hath not taken away his mercy
from the house of Israel, but hath destroyed our enemies by
mine hands this night.

So she took the head out of the bag, and shewed it, and
said unto them, Behold the head of Holofernes, the chief
captain of the army of Assur, and behold the canopy, wherein
he did lie in his drunkenness; and the Lord hath smitten him
by the hand of a woman.   APOCRYPHA

A MOTHER AND HER SEVEN SONS

It came to pass also, that seven brethren with their mother were taken, and compelled by the king against the law to taste swine's flesh, and were tormented with scourges and whips.

But one of them that spake first said thus, What wouldest thou ask or learn of us? we are ready to die, rather than to transgress the laws of our fathers.

Then the king, being in a rage, commanded pans and caldrons to be made hot:

Which forthwith being heated, he commanded to cut out the tongue of him that spake first, and to cut off the utmost parts of his body, the rest of his brethren and his mother looking on.

Now when he was thus maimed in all his members, he commanded him being yet alive to be brought to the fire, and to be fried in the pan: and as the vapour of the pan was for a good space dispersed, they exhorted one another with the mother to die manfully, saying thus,

The Lord God looketh upon us, and in truth hath comfort in us, as Moses in his song, which witnessed to their faces, declared, saying, And he shall be comforted in his servants.

So when the first was dead after this manner, they brought the second to make him a mocking stock: and when they had pulled off the skin of his head with the hair, they asked him, Wilt thou eat, before thou be punished throughout every member of thy body?

But he answered in his own language, and said, No. Wherefore he also received the next torment in order, as the former did.

And when he was at the last gasp, he said, Thou like a fury takest us out of this present life, but the King of the world shall raise us up, who have died for his laws, unto everlasting life.

After him was the third made a mocking stock: and when he was required, he put out his tongue, and that right soon, holding forth his hands manfully,

And said courageously, These I had from heaven; and for

his laws I despise them; and from him I hope to receive them again.

Insomuch that the king, and they that were with him, marvelled at the young man's courage, for that he nothing regarded the pains.

Now when this man was dead also, they tormented and mangled the fourth in like manner.

So when he was ready to die he said thus, It is good, being put to death by men, to look for hope from God to be raised up again by him: as for thee, thou shalt have no resurrection to life.

Afterward they brought the fifth also, and mangled him.

Then looked he unto the king, and said, Thou hast power over men, thou art corruptible, thou doest what thou wilt; yet think not that our nation is forsaken of God;

But abide a while, and behold his great power, how he will torment thee and thy seed.

After him also they brought the sixth, who being ready to die said, Be not deceived without cause: for we suffer these things for ourselves, having sinned against our God: therefore marvellous things are done unto us.

But think not thou, that takest in hand to strive against God, that thou shalt escape unpunished.

But the mother was marvellous above all, and worthy of honourable memory: for when she saw her seven sons slain within the space of one day, she bare it with a good courage, because of the hope that she had in the Lord.

Yea, she exhorted every one of them in her own language, filled with courageous spirits; and stirring up her womanish thoughts with a manly stomach, she said unto them,

Doubtless the Creator of the world, who formed the generation of man, and found out the beginning of all things, will also of his own mercy give you breath and life again, as ye now regard not your own selves for his laws' sake.

Now Antiochus, thinking himself despised, and suspecting it to be a reproachful speech, whilst the youngest was yet alive, did not only exhort him by words, but also assured him with oaths, that he would make him both a rich and a happy man, if he would turn from the laws of his fathers; and that also he would take him for his friend, and trust him with affairs.

But when the young man would in no case hearken unto

him, the king called his mother, and exhorted her that she would counsel the young man to save his life.

And when he had exhorted her with many words, she promised him that she would counsel her son.

But she bowing herself toward him, laughing the cruel tyrant to scorn, spake in her country language on this manner: O my son, have pity upon me that nourished thee, and brought thee up unto this age, and endured the troubles of education.

I beseech thee, my son, look upon heaven and the earth, and all that is therein, and consider that God made them of things that were not; and so was mankind made likewise.

Fear not this tormentor, but, being worthy of thy brethren, take thy death, that I may receive thee again in mercy with thy brethren.

Whiles she was yet speaking these words, the young man said, Whom wait ye for? I will not obey the king's commandment: but I will obey the commandment of the law that was given unto our fathers by Moses.

And thou, that hast been the author of all mischief against the Hebrews, shalt not escape the hands of God.

For we suffer because of our sins,

And though the living Lord be angry with us a little while for our chastening and correction, yet shall he be at one again with his servants.

But thou, O godless man, and of all other most wicked, be not lifted up without a cause, nor puffed up with uncertain hopes, lifting up thy hand against the servants of God:

For thou hast not yet escaped the judgment of Almighty God, who seeth all things.

For our brethren, who now have suffered a short pain, are dead under God's covenant of everlasting life: but thou, through the judgment of God, shalt receive just punishment for thy pride.

But I, as my brethren, offer up my body and life for the laws of our fathers, beseeching God that he would speedily be merciful unto our nation; and that thou by torments and plagues mayest confess, that he alone is God;

And that in me and my brethren the wrath of the Almighty, which is justly brought upon all our nation, may cease.

Then the king, being in a rage, handled him worse than all
the rest, and took it grievously that he was mocked.

So this man died undefiled, and put his whole trust in the
Lord.

Last of all after the sons the mother died.

APOCRYPHA.

DYING HEROES

I AM the mash'd fireman with breast-bone broken,
Tumbling walls buried me in their debris,
Heat and smoke I inspired, I heard the yelling shouts of my
comrades,
I heard the distant click of their picks and shovels,
They have clear'd the beams away, they tenderly lift me
forth.

I lie in the night air in my red shirt, the pervading hush is
for my sake,
Painless after all I lie, exhausted, but not so unhappy,
White and beautiful are the faces around me, the heads are
bared of their fire-caps,
The kneeling crowd fades with the light of the torches.

I am an old artillerist, I tell of my fort's bombardment,
I am there again.

Again the long roll of the drummers,
Again the attacking cannon, mortars,
Again to my listening ears the cannon responsive.
I take part, I see and hear the whole,
The cries, curses, roar, the plaudits for well-aim'd shots,
The ambulanza slowly passing trailing its red drip,
Workmen searching after damages, making indispensable
repairs,
The fall of grenades through the rent roof, the fan-shaped
explosion,
The whizz of limbs, heads, stone, wood, iron, high in the air.

Again gurgles the mouth of my dying general, he furiously
waves with his hand,
He gasps through the clot, *Mind not me—mind—the
entrenchments*.   WALT WHITMAN.

THE GLOVE AND THE LIONS

KING FRANCIS was a hearty king, and loved a royal sport,
And one day as his lions fought, sat looking on the court;
The nobles filled the benches, with the ladies by their side,
And 'mongst them sat the Count de Lorge, with one for whom
    he sighed:
And truly 'twas a gallant thing to see that crowning show,
Valour and love, and a king above, and the royal beasts below.

Ramped and roared the lions, with horrid laughing jaws;
They bit, they glared, gave blows like bears, a wind went
    with their paws;
With wallowing might and stifled roar they rolled on one
    another,
Till all the pit with sand and mane, was in a thunderous
    smother;
The bloody foam above the bars came whizzing through the
    air;
Said Francis then, " Faith, gentlemen, we're better here than
    there."

De Lorge's love o'erheard the King, a beauteous lively dame,
With smiling lips and sharp bright eyes, which always seemed
    the same:
She thought, the Count my lover is brave as brave can be;
He surely would do wondrous things to show his love of me;
King, ladies, lovers, all look on; the occasion is divine;
I'll drop my glove, to prove his love; great glory will be
    mine.

She dropped her glove, to prove his love, then looked at him
    and smiled;
He bowed, and in a moment leaped among the lions wild:
The leap was quick, return was quick, he has regained his
    place,
Then threw the glove, but not with love, right in the lady's
    face.
" By Heav'n!" said Francis, " rightly done!" and he rose
    from where he sat:
" No love," quoth he, " but vanity, sets love a task like that."

LEIGH HUNT.

CORONACH

He is gone on the mountain,
  He is lost to the forest,
Like a summer-dried fountain,
  When our need was the sorest.
The fount reappearing
  From the raindrops shall borrow,
But to us comes no cheering,
  To Duncan no morrow!

The hand of the reaper
  Takes the ears that are hoary;
But the voice of the weeper
  Wails manhood in glory.
The autumn winds rushing
  Waft the leaves that are serest,
But our flower was in flushing
  When blighting was nearest.

Fleet foot on the correi,
  Sage counsel in cumber,
Red hand in the foray,
  How sound is thy slumber!
Like the dew on the mountain,
  Like the foam on the river,
Like the bubble on the fountain,
  Thou art gone, and for ever!

Sir Walter Scott.

BRAVERY

King. You are, I think, assured I love you not.
Ch. Just. I am assured, if I be measured rightly,
Your majesty hath no just case to hate me.
King. No!
How might a prince of my great hopes forget
So great indignities you laid upon me?
What! rate, rebuke, and roughly send to prison

The immediate heir of England! Was this easy?
May this be wash'd in Lethe, and forgotten?

   Ch. Just. I then did use the person of your father,
The image of his power lay then in me:
And, in the administration of his law,
Whiles I was busy for the commonwealth,
Your highness pleased to forget my place,
The majesty and power of law and justice,
The image of the king, whom I presented,
And struck me in my very seat of judgment—
Whereon, as an offender to your father,
I gave bold way to my authority,
And did commit you. If the deed were ill,
Be you contented, wearing now the garland,
To have a son set your decrees at nought;
To pluck down justice from your awful bench;
To trip the course of law, and blunt the sword
That guards the peace and safety of your person:
Nay, more; to spurn at your most royal image,
And mock your workings in a second body.
Question your royal thoughts, make the case yours;
Be now the father, and propose a son:
Hear your own dignity so much profaned,
See your most dreadful laws so loosely slighted,
Behold yourself so by a son disdain'd;
And then imagine me taking your part,
And, in your power soft silencing your son:
After this cold considerance, sentence me;
And as you are a king, speak in your state,
What I have done, that misbecame my place,
My person, or my liege's sovereignty.

   King. You are right, justice, and you weigh this well:
Therefore still bear the balance, and the sword:
And I do wish your honours may increase,
Till you do live to see a son of mine
Offend you and obey you, as I did.
So shall I live to speak my father's words,
Happy am I, that have a man so bold,
That dares do justice on my proper son ;
And not less happy, having such a son,
That would deliver up his greatness so
Into the hands of justice.—You did commit me:

For which, I do commit into your hand
The unstain'd sword that you have used to bear,
With this remembrance,—that you use the same
With the like bold, just, and impartial spirit,
As you have done 'gainst me.   There is my hand;
You shall be as a father to my youth:
My voice shall sound as you do prompt mine ear;
And I will stoop and humble my intents
To your well-practised, wise directions.
                              WILLIAM SHAKESPEARE.

SAMSON AGONISTES

OCCASIONS drew me early to this city;
And, as the gates I entered with sun-rise,
The morning trumpets festival proclaim'd
Through each high street: little I had dispatch'd,
When all abroad was rumour'd that this day
Samson should be brought forth, to show the people
Proof of his mighty strength in feats and games;
I sorrow'd at his captive state, but minded
Not to be absent at that spectacle.
The building was a spacious theatre,
Half round, on two main pillars vaulted high,
With seats where all the lords, and each degree
Of sort, might sit in order to behold;
The other side was open, where the throng,
On banks and scaffolds, under sky might stand;
I, among these, aloof obscurely stood.
The feast and noon grew high, and sacrifice
Had fill'd their hearts with mirth, high cheer, and wine,
When to their sports they turn'd.   Immediately
Was Samson as a public servant brought,
In their state livery clad: before him pipes
And timbrels; on each side went armed guards,
Both horse and foot; before him and behind,
Archers and slingers, cataphracts and spears.
At sight of him the people with a shout
Rifted the air, clamouring their god with praise,
Who had made their dreadful enemy their thrall.

He, patient, but undaunted, where they led him,
Came to the place; and what was set before him,
Which without help of eye might be assay'd,
To heave, pull, draw, or break, he still perform'd
All with incredible, stupendous force,
None daring to appear antagonist.
At length, for intermission's sake, they led him
Between the pillars; he his guide requested
(For so from such as nearer stood we heard),
As over-tired, to let him lean awhile,
With both his arms, on those two massy pillars,
That to the arched roof gave main support.
He, unsuspicious, led him; which, when Samson
Felt in his arms, with head awhile inclined,
And eyes fast fix'd, he stood, as one who pray'd,
Or some great matter in his mind revolved:
At last, with head erect, thus cried aloud:—
" Hitherto, lords, what your commands imposed
I have perform'd, as reason was, obeying,
Not without wonder or delight beheld:
Now, of my own accord, such other trial
I mean to show you of my strength, yet greater,
As with amaze shall strike all who behold."
This utter'd, straining all his nerves, he bow'd:
As with the force of winds and waters pent,
When mountains tremble, those two massy pillars
With horrible convulsion to and fro
He tugg'd, he shook, till down they came, and drew
The whole roof after them with burst of thunder
Upon the heads of all who sat beneath,
Lords, ladies, captains, counsellors, or priests,
Their choice nobility, and flower, not only
Of this, but each Philistian city round,
Met from all parts to solemnise this feast.
Samson, with these immix'd, inevitably
Pull'd down the same destruction on himself.

JOHN MILTON.

ODE ON THE DEATH OF THE DUKE OF WELLINGTON

I

Bury the Great Duke
  With an empire's lamentation,
Let us bury the Great Duke
  To the noise of the mourning of a mighty nation,
Mourning when their leaders fall,
Warriors carry the warrior's pall,
And sorrow darkens hamlet and hall.

II

Where shall we lay the man whom we deplore?
Here, in streaming London's central roar.
Let the sound of those he wrought for,
And the feet of those he fought for,
Echo round his bones for evermore.

III

Lead out the pageant: sad and slow,
As fits an universal woe,
Let the long long procession go,
And let the sorrowing crowd about it grow,
And let the mournful martial music blow;
The last great Englishman is low.

IV

Mourn, for to us he seems the last,
Remembering all his greatness in the Past.
No more in soldier fashion will he greet
With lifted hand the gazer in the street.
O friends, our chief state-oracle is mute:
Mourn for the man of long-enduring blood,
The statesman-warrior, moderate, resolute,
Whole in himself, a common good.
Mourn for the man of amplest influence,
Yet clearest of ambitious crime,
Our greatest yet with least pretence,

Great in council and great in war,
Foremost captain of his time,
Rich in saving common-sense,
And, as the greatest only are,
In his simplicity sublime.
O good gray head which all men knew,
O voice from which their omens all men drew,
O iron nerve to true occasion true,
O fall'n at length that tower of strength
Which stood four-square to all the winds that blew!
Such was he whom we deplore.
The long self-sacrifice of life is o'er.
The great World-victor's victor will be seen no more.

                    v

All is over and done:
Render thanks to the Giver,
England, for thy son.
Let the bell be toll'd.
Render thanks to the Giver,
And render him to the mould.
Under the cross of gold
That shines over city and river,
There he shall rest for ever
Among the wise and the bold.
Let the bell be toll'd:
And a reverent people behold
The towering car, the sable steeds:
Bright let it be with its blazon'd deeds,
Dark in its funeral fold.
Let the bell be toll'd:
And a deeper knell in the heart be knoll'd;
And the sound of the sorrowing anthem roll'd
Thro' the dome of the golden cross;
And the volleying cannon thunder his loss;
He knew their voices of old.
For many a time in many a clime
His captain's ear has heard them boom
Bellowing victory, bellowing doom:
When he with those deep voices wrought,
Guarding realms and kings from shame;
With those deep voices our dead captain taught

The tyrant, and asserts his claim
In that dread sound to the great name,
Which he has worn so pure of blame,
In praise and in dispraise the same,
A man of well-attemper'd frame.
O civic muse, to such a name,
To such a name for ages long,
To such a name,
Preserve a broad approach of fame,
And ever-echoing avenues of song.

VI

Who is he that cometh, like an honour'd guest,
With banner and with music, with soldier and with priest,
With a nation weeping, and breaking on my rest?
Mighty Seaman, this is he,
Was great by land as thou by sea.
Thine island loves thee well, thou famous man,
The greatest sailor since our world began.
Now, to the roll of muffled drums,
To thee the greatest soldier comes;
For this is he
Was great by land as thou by sea;
His foes were thine; he kept us free;
O give him welcome, this is he,
Worthy of our gorgeous rites,
And worthy to be laid by thee;
For this is England's greatest son,
He that gain'd a hundred fights,
Nor ever lost an English gun;
This is he that far away
Against the myriads of Assaye
Clash'd with his fiery few and won;
And underneath another sun,
Warring on a later day,
Round affrighted Lisbon drew
The treble works, the vast designs
Of his labour'd rampart-lines,
Where he greatly stood at bay,
Whence he issued forth anew,
And ever greater and greater grew,
Beating from the wasted vines

Back to France her banded swarms,
Back to France with countless blows,
Till o'er the hills her eagles flew
Beyond the Pyrenean pines,
Follow'd up in valley and glen
With blare of bugle, clamour of men,
Roll of cannon and clash of arms,
And England pouring on her foes.
Such a war had such a close.
Again their ravening eagle rose
In anger, wheel'd on Europe-shadowing wings,
And barking for the thrones of kings;
Till one that sought but Duty's iron crown
On that loud sabbath shook the spoiler down;
A day of onsets of despair!
Dash'd on every rocky square
Their surging charges foam'd themselves away;
Last, the Prussian trumpet blew;
Thro' the long-tormented air
Heaven flash'd a sudden jubilant ray,
And down we swept and charged and overthrew.
So great a soldier taught us there,
What long-enduring hearts could do
In that world earthquake, Waterloo!
Mighty Seaman, tender and true,
And pure as he from taint of craven guile,
O saviour of the silver-coasted isle,
O shaker of the Baltic and the Nile,
If aught of things that here befall
Touch a spirit among things divine,
If love of country move thee there at all,
Be glad, because his bones are laid by thine!
And thro' the centuries let a people's voice
In full acclaim,
A people's voice,
The proof and echo of all human fame,
A people's voice, when they rejoice
At civic revel and pomp and game,
Attest their great commander's claim
With honour, honour, honour, honour to him,
Eternal honour to his name.

LORD TENNYSON.

LAMENT OVER SIR PHILIP SIDNEY

Come to me grief, for ever,
Come to me tears day and night,
Come to me plaint! Ah, helpless,
Just grief; heart's tears! plaint worthy.

Go from me dread to die now,
Go from me care to live now,
Go from me joys all on earth,
Sidney, O Sidney, is dead.

He whom the court adorned,
He whom the country courtes'd,
He who made happy his friends,
He that did good to all men.

Sidney, the hope of land strange,
Sidney, the flower of England,
Sidney, the spirit heroic,
Sidney is dead.   O dead, dead.

ANON.

LAMENT OVER SAUL

The beauty of Israel is slain upon thy high places:
How are the mighty fallen!
Tell it not in Gath,
Publish it not in the streets of Askelon;
Lest the daughters of the Philistines rejoice,
Lest the daughters of the uncircumcised triumph.
Ye mountains of Gilboa, let there be no dew,
Neither let there be rain, upon you, nor fields of offerings:
For there the shield of the mighty is vilely cast away,
The shield of Saul, as though he had not been anointed with
      oil.
From the blood of the slain,
From the fat of the mighty,
The bow of Jonathan turned not back,
And the sword of Saul returned not empty.

Saul and Jonathan
Were lovely and pleasant in their lives,
And in their death they were not divided:
They were swifter than eagles,
They were stronger than lions.
Ye daughters of Israel, weep over Saul,
Who clothed you in scarlet, with other delights,
Who put on ornaments of gold upon your apparel.
How are the mighty fallen in the midst of the battle!
O Jonathan, thou wast slain in thine high places.
I am distressed for thee, my brother Jonathan:
Very pleasant has t thou been unto me:
Thy love to me was wonderful,
Passing the love of women.
How are the mighty fallen,
And the weapons of war perished!

2 SAMUEL I.

A HERO IN PRISON

THIS, this is he; softly awhile,
Let us not break in upon him;
O change beyond report, thought, or belief!
See how he lies at random, carelessly diffus'd,
With languish't head unpropt,
As one past hope, abandon'd,
And by himself given over;
In slavish habit, ill-fitted weeds
O'er-worn and soil'd;
Or do my eyes misrepresent?   Can this be he,
That heroic, that renown'd,
Irresistible Samson?

JOHN MILTON.

A HERO IN DESPAIR

ALL otherwise to me my thoughts portend,
That these dark orbs no more shall treat with light,
Nor th' other light of life continue long,
But yield to double darkness, nigh at hand:

So much I feel my genial spirits droop,
My hopes all flat, Nature within me seems
In all her functions weary of herself,
My race of glory run, and race of shame,
And I shall shortly be with them at rest.

O! that torment should not be confin'd
To the body's wounds and sores,
With maladies innumerable
In heart, head, breast, and reins;
But must secret passage find
To th' inmost mind,
There exercise all his fierce accidents,
And on her purest spirits prey,
As on entrails, joints, and limbs,
With answerable pains, but more intense,
Though void of corporal sense.

JOHN MILTON.

A BRAVE EPITAPH

COME, come, no time for lamentation now,
Nor much more cause; Samson hath quit himself
Like Samson, and heroically hath finish'd
A life heroic, on his enemies
Fully reveng'd, hath left them years of mourning,
And lamentation to the sons of Caphtor,
Through all Philistian bounds; to Israel
Honour hath left, and freedom, let but them
Find courage to lay hold on this occasion;
To himself and father's house eternal fame;
And which is best and happiest yet, all this
With God not parted from him, as was fear'd,
But favouring and assisting to the end.
Nothing is here for tears, nothing to wail
Or knock the breast, no weakness, no contempt,
Dispraise, or blame, nothing but well and fair,
And what may quiet us in a death so noble.

JOHN MILTON.

M

JEPHTHAH'S DAUGHTER

THE daughter of the warrior Gileadite,
   A maiden pure; as when she went along
From Mizpeh's tower'd gate with welcome light,
   With timbrel and with song.

My words leapt forth: " Heaven heads the count of crimes
   With that wild oath."   She render'd answer high:
" Not so; nor once alone, a thousand times
   I would be born and die.

" Single I grew, like some green plant, whose root
   Creeps to the garden water-pipes beneath,
Feeding the flower; but ere my flower to fruit
   Changed, I was ripe for death.

" My God, my land, my father—these did move
   Me from my bliss of life, that Nature gave,
Lower'd softly with a threefold cord of love
   Down to a silent grave.

" And I went mourning, ' No fair Hebrew boy
   Shall smile away my maiden blame among
The Hebrew mothers '—emptied of all joy,
   Leaving the dance and song,

" Leaving the olive-gardens far below,
   Leaving the promise of my bridal bower,
The valleys of grape-loaded vines that glow
   Beneath the battled tower.

" The light white cloud swam over us.   Anon
   We heard the lion roaring from his den;
We saw the large white stars rise one by one,
   Or, from the darken'd glen,

" Saw God divide the night with flying flame,
   And thunder on the everlasting hills.
I heard Him, for He spake, and grief became
   A solemn scorn of ills.

" When the next moon was roll'd into the sky,
 Strength came to me that equall'd my desire.
How beautiful a thing it was to die
 For God and for my sire!

" It comforts me in this one thought to dwell,
 That I subdued me to my father's will;
Because the kiss he gave me, ere I fell,
 Sweetens the spirit still.

" Moreover it is written that my race
 Hew'd Ammon, hip and thigh, from Aroer
On Arnon unto Minneth." Here her face
 Glow'd as I look'd at her.

She lock'd her lips: she left me where I stood:
 " Glory to God," she sang, and past afar,
Thridding the sombre boskage of the wood,
 Toward the morning star.

LORD TENNYSON.

IPHIGENIA

AT length I saw a lady within call,
 Stiller than chisell'd marble, standing there;
A daughter of the gods, divinely tall,
 And most divinely fair.

Her loveliness with shame and with surprise
 Froze my swift speech: she turning on my face
The star-like sorrows of immortal eyes,
 Spoke slowly in her place.

" I had great beauty: ask thou not my name:
 No one can be more wise than destiny.
Many drew swords and died. Where'er I came
 I brought calamity."

" No marvel, sovereign lady: in fair field
 Myself for such a face had boldly died,"
I answer'd free; and turning I appeal'd
 To one that stood beside.

But she, with sick and scornful looks averse,
    To her full height her stately stature draws;
" My youth," she said, " was blasted with a curse:
    This woman was the cause.

" I was cut off from hope in that sad place,
    Which yet to name my spirit loathes and fears:
My father held his hand upon his face;
    I, blinded with my tears,

" Still strove to speak: my voice was thick with sighs
    As in a dream.   Dimly I could descry
The stern black-bearded kings with wolfish eyes,
    Waiting to see me die.

" The high masts flicker'd as they lay afloat;
    The crowds, the temples, waver'd, and the shore;
The bright death quiver'd at the victim's throat;
    Touch'd; and I knew no more."

LORD TENNYSON.

THE ACADEMY AT VENICE

A MODERN daub it was, perchance,
    I know not: but the connoisseur
    From Titian's hues, I dare be sure,
Had never turned one kindly glance,

Where Byron, somewhat drest-up, draws
    His sword, impatient long, and speaks
    Unto a tribe of motley Greeks
His fealty to their good cause.

Not far, assumed to mystic bliss,
    Behold the ecstatic Virgin rise!
    Ah, wherefore vainly, to fond eyes
That melted into tears for this?

Yet if we must live, as would seem,
    These peremptory heats to claim,
    Ah, not for profit, not for fame,
And not for pleasure's giddy dream,

And not for piping empty reeds,
And not for colouring idle dust;
If live we positively must,
God's name be blest for noble deeds.

ARTHUR HUGH CLOUGH.

THE KNIGHT'S LEAP

" So the foemen have fired the gate, men of mine?
    And the water is spent and gone?
Then bring me a cup of red Ahr-wine;
    I never shall drink but this one.

" And reach me my harness, and saddle my horse,
    And lead him me round to the door;
He must take such a leap to-night perforce,
    As horse never took before.

" I have fought my fight, I have lived my life,
    I have drunk my share of wine;
From Trier to Coln there was never a knight
    Led a merrier life than mine.

" I have lived by the saddle for years two score;
    And if I must die on tree,
Then the old saddle-tree, which has borne me of yore,
    Is the properest timber for me.

" So now to show bishop, and burgher, and priest,
    How the Altenahr hawk can die—
If they smoke the old falcon out of his nest,
    He must take to his wings and fly."

He harnessed himself by the clear moonshine,
    And he mounted his horse at the door;
And he drained such a cup of the red Ahr-wine
    As man never drained before.

He spurred the old horse, and he held him tight,
    And he leapt him over the wall,
Out over the cliff, out into the night,
    Three hundred feet of fall.

They found him next morning below in the glen,
   With never a bone in him whole—
A mass, or a prayer, now, good gentlemen,
   For such a bold rider's soul!

CHARLES KINGSLEY.

THE BRAVE WOMEN OF TANN

SATE the heavy burghers
   In their gloomy hall,
Pondering all the dangers
   Likely to befall,—
Ward they yet or yield the strangers
   Their beleaguer'd wall.

" All our trade is ruin'd:
   Saw I this afar,—
Said I not—our markets
   Month-long siege will mar?
Let not our good town embark its
   Fortunes on this war.

" Now our folly takes us:
   War first hath his share,
Famine now; who dreameth
   Bankrupts can repair
Double loss? or likely seemeth
   Victors should despair?

" And our trade is ruin'd:
   Little that remains
Let us save, to hearse us
   From these bloody pains,
Ere the wrathful foe amerce us
   Of our farthest gains! "

Up and speaks young Hermann
   With the flushing cheek—
" Shame were it to render:
   Though the wall be weak "——

Say the old men— " Let us end or
   Certain death we seek ! "

In their gloomy chamber
   Thus their councils wend:—
" Five of our most trusted
   With the morn descend;
Say—So peace may be adjusted
   Chained lives we'll spend.

" Now home to our women!
   They'll be glad to learn
We have weigh'd so gravely
   ' Peace ' hath fill'd the urn:
Though in truth they've borne them bravely
   In this weary turn."

Home unto their women;
   But each burgher found
Scorn in place of smiling:
   For each good-wife frown'd
On this coward reconciling,
   Peace with honour bound.

In their morrow's council
   Woman voices rise:
" Count ye babes and women
   But as merchandise,
To be traffick'd with the foemen,—
   Things of such a price?

" We will man your ramparts;
   Ye, who are not men,
Go hide in your coffers!
   We will call you when "——
Slid home 'mid the crowd of scoffers
   Those five heralds then.

In the morrow's danger
   Women take their share;
Many a sad grey morning
   Found them watching there:
Till we learn'd from their high scorning
   To make light of care.

Chief with our gaunt warders
    Hermann's young Betrothed
Pass'd, like Victory's Splendour,—
    In bright courage clothed:
Fear hid, fearful to offend her,
    Knowing himself loathed.

Blinding red the sunset!
    In that hopeful breast
Stay'd the foeman's arrow.
    So 'twas won.   The rest—
How Despair in strait most narrow
    Smote the Conqueror's crest—

Matters not.   Our women
    Drove him to his den.
'Twas his last invasion;
    We've had peace since then.—
This is why on State occasion
    They precede our men.

WM. JAMES LINTON.

THE KING

Then the King in low deep tones,
And simple words of great authority,
Bound them by so strait vows to his own self,
That when they rose, knighted from kneeling, some
Were pale as at the passing of a ghost,
Some flush'd, and others dazed, as one who wakes
Half-blinded at the coming of a light.

But when he spake and cheer'd his Table Round
With large, divine, and comfortable words,
Beyond my tongue to tell thee—I beheld
From eye to eye thro' all their Order flash
A momentary likeness of the King:
And ere it left their faces, thro' the cross
And those around it and the Crucified,
Down from the casement over Arthur, smote

Flame-colour, vert and azure, in three rays,
One falling upon each of three fair queens,
Who stood in silence near his throne, the friends
Of Arthur, gazing on him, tall, with bright
Sweet faces, who will help him at his need.

And there I saw mage Merlin, whose vast wit
And hundred winters are but as the hands
Of loyal vassals toiling for their liege.

And near him stood the Lady of the Lake,
Who knows a subtler magic than his own—
Clothed in white samite, mystic, wonderful.
She gave the King his huge cross-hilted sword,
Whereby to drive the heathen out: a mist
Of incense curl'd about her, and her face
Wellnigh was hidden in the minster gloom;
But there was heard among the holy hymns
A voice as of the waters, for she dwells
Down in a deep; calm, whatsoever storms
May shake the world, and when the surface rolls,
Hath power to walk the waters like our Lord.

There likewise I beheld Excalibur
Before him at his crowning borne, the sword
That rose from out the bosom of the lake,
And Arthur row'd across and took it—rich
With jewels, elfin Urim, on the hilt,
Bewildering heart and eye—the blade so bright
That men are blinded by it—on one side,
Graven in the oldest tongue of all this world,
" Take me," but turn the blade and ye shall see,
And written in the speech ye speak yourself,
" Cast me away! "   And sad was Arthur's face
Taking it, but old Merlin counsell'd him,
" Take thou and strike! the time to cast away
Is yet far-off."   So this great brand the king
Took, and by this will beat his foemen down.
LORD TENNYSON.

THE IDEAL

THIS is the day, which down the void abysm
At the Earth-born's spell yawns for Heaven's despotism,
　　And Conquest is dragged captive through the deep:
Love, from its awful throne of patient power
In the wise heart, from the last giddy hour
　　Of dread endurance, from the slippery, steep,
And narrow verge of crag-like agony, springs
And folds over the world its healing wings.

Gentleness, Virtue, Wisdom, and Endurance,
These are the seals of that most firm assurance
　　Which bars the pit over Destruction's strength;
And if, with infirm hand, Eternity,
Mother of many acts and hours, should free
　　The serpent that would clasp her with his length;
These are the spells by which to reassume
An empire o'er the disentangled doom.

To suffer woes which Hope thinks infinite;
To forgive wrongs darker than death or night;
　　To defy power, which seems omnipotent;
To love, and bear; to hope till Hope creates
From its own wreck the thing it contemplates;
　　Neither to change, nor falter, nor repent;
This, like thy glory, Titan, is to be
Good, great and joyous, beautiful and free;
This is alone Life, Joy, Empire, and Victory.

P. B. SHELLEY.

PROMETHEUS

WHO reigns? There was the Heaven and Earth at first,
And Light and Love; then Saturn, from whose throne
Time fell, an envious shadow: such the state
Of the earth's primal spirits beneath his sway,
As the calm joy of flowers and living leaves
Before the wind or sun has withered them
And semivital worms; but he refused

The birthright of their being, knowledge, power,
The skill which wields the elements, the thought
Which pierces this dim universe like light,
Self-empire, and the majesty of love;
For thirst of which they fainted.   Then Prometheus
Gave wisdom, which is strength, to Jupiter,
And with this law alone, " Let man be free,"
Clothed him with the dominion of wide Heaven.
To know nor faith, nor love, nor law; to be
Omnipotent but friendless is to reign;
And Jove now reigned; for on the race of man
First famine, and then toil, and then disease,
Strife, wounds, and ghastly death unseen before,
Fell; and the unseasonable seasons drove
With alternating shafts of frost and fire,
Their shelterless, pale tribes to mountain caves:
And in their desert hearts fierce wants he sent,
And mad disquietudes, and shadows idle
Of unreal good, which levied mutual war,
So ruining the lair wherein they raged.
Prometheus saw, and waked the legioned hopes
Which sleep within folded Elysian flowers,
Nepenthe, Moly, Amaranth, fadeless blooms,
That they might hide with thin and rainbow wings
The shape of Death; and Love he sent to bind
The disunited tendrils of that vine
Which bears the wine of life, the human heart;
And he tamed fire which, like some beast of prey,
Most terrible, but lovely, played beneath
The frown of man; and tortured to his will
Iron and gold, the slaves and signs of power,
And gems and poisons, and all subtlest forms
Hidden beneath the mountains and the waves.
He gave man speech, and speech created thought,
Which is the measure of the universe;
And Science struck the thrones of earth and heaven,
Which shook, but fell not; and the harmonious mind
Poured itself forth in all-prophetic song;
And music lifted up the listening spirit
Until it walked, exempt from mortal care,
Godlike, o'er the clear billows of sweet sound;
And human hands first mimicked and then mocked,

With moulded limbs more lovely than its own,
The human form, till marble grew divine;
And mothers, gazing, drank the love men see
Reflected in their race, behold, and perish.
He told the hidden power of herbs and springs,
And Disease drank and slept.   Death grew like sleep.
He taught the implicated orbits woven
Of the wide-wandering stars; and how the sun
Changes his lair, and by what secret spell
The pale moon is transformed, when her broad eye
Gazes not on the interlunar sea:
He taught to rule, as life directs the limbs,
The tempest-wingèd chariots of the Ocean,
And the Celt knew the Indian.   Cities then
Were built, and through their snow-like columns flowed
The warm winds, and the azure aether shone,
And the blue sea and shadowy hills were seen.
Such, the alleviations of his state,
Prometheus gave to man, for which he hangs
Withering in destined pain: but who rains down
Evil, the immedicable plague, which, while
Man looks on his creation like a God
And sees that it is glorious, drives him on,
The wreck of his own will, the scorn of earth,
The outcast, the abandoned, the alone?

                                        P. B. SHELLEY.

CHILDE ROLAND

I

My first thought was, he lied in every word,
    That hoary cripple, with malicious eye
    Askance to watch the working of his lie
On mine, and mouth scarce able to afford
Suppression of the glee that pursed and scored
    Its edge at one more victim gained thereby.

II

What else should he be set for, with his staff?
    What, save to waylay with his lies, ensnare
    All travellers that might find him posted there,

And ask the road?   I guessed what skull-like laugh
Would break, what crutch 'gin write my epitaph
  For pastime in the dusty thoroughfare,

III

If at his counsel I should turn aside
  Into that ominous tract which, all agree,
  Hides the Dark Tower.   Yet acquiescingly
I did turn as he pointed; neither pride
Nor hope rekindling at the end descried,
  So much as gladness that some end should be.

IV

For, what with my whole world-wide wandering,
  What with my search drawn out thro' years, my hope
  Dwindled into a ghost not fit to cope
With that obstreperous joy success would bring,—
I hardly tried now to rebuke the spring
  My heart made, finding failure in its scope.

V

As when a sick man very near to death
  Seems dead indeed, and feels begin and end
  The tears and takes the farewell of each friend,
And hears one bid the other go, draw breath
Freelier outside (" since all is o'er," he saith,
  " And the blow fall'n no grieving can amend "),

VI

While some discuss if near the other graves
  Be room enough for this, and when a day
  Suits best for carrying the corpse away,
With care about the banners, scarves and staves,—
And still the man hears all, and only craves
  He may not shame such tender love and stay.

VII

Thus, I had so long suffered in this quest,
  Heard failure prophesied so oft, been writ
  So many times among " The Band "—to wit,
The knights who to the Dark Tower's search addressed
Their steps—that just to fail as they, seemed best,
  And all the doubt was now—should I be fit.

VIII

So, quiet as despair, I turned from him,
　　That hateful cripple, out of his highway
　　Into the path he pointed.　All the day
Had been a dreary one at best, and dim
Was settling to its close, yet shot one grim
　　Red leer to see the plain catch its estray.

IX

For mark! no sooner was I fairly found
　　Pledged to the plain, after a pace or two,
　　Than pausing to throw backward a last view
To the safe road, 'twas gone! grey plain all round!
Nothing but plain to the horizon's bound.
　　I might go on; nought else remained to do.

X

So on I went.　I think I never saw
　　Such starved ignoble nature; nothing throve:
　　For flowers—as well expect a cedar grove!
But cockle, spurge, according to their law
Might propagate their kind, with none to awe,
　　You'd think: a burr had been a treasure-trove.

XI

No! penury, inertness, and grimace,
　　In some strange sort, were the land's portion.　"See
　　Or shut your eyes"—said Nature peevishly—
"It nothing skills: I cannot help my case:
The Judgment's fire alone can cure this place,
　　Calcine its clods and set my prisoners free."

XII

If there pushed any ragged thistle-stalk
　　Above its mates, the head was chopped—the bents
　　Were jealous else.　What made those holes and rents
In the dock's harsh swarth leaves—bruised as to baulk
All hope of greenness? 'tis a brute must walk
　　Pushing their life out, with a brute's intents.

XIII

As for the grass, it grew as scant as hair
  In leprosy—thin dry blades pricked the mud
  Which underneath looked kneaded up with blood.
One stiff blind horse, his every bone a-stare,
Stood stupefied, however he came there—
  Thrust out past service from the devil's stud!

XIV

Alive? he might be dead for all I know,
  With that red gaunt and colloped neck a-strain,
  And shut eyes underneath the rusty mane.
Seldom went such grotesqueness with such woe:
I never saw a brute I hated so—
  He must be wicked to deserve such pain.

XV

I shut my eyes and turned them on my heart.
  As a man calls for wine before he fights,
  I asked one draught of earlier, happier sights
Ere fitly I could hope to play my part.
Think first, fight afterwards—the soldier's art:
  One taste of the old times sets all to rights!

XVI

Not it! I fancied Cuthbert's reddening face
  Beneath its garniture of curly gold,
  Dear fellow, till I almost felt him fold
An arm in mine to fix me to the place,
That way he used. Alas! one night's disgrace!
  Out went my heart's new fire and left it cold.

XVII

Giles, then, the soul of honour—there he stands
  Frank as ten years ago when knighted first.
  What honest men should dare (he said) he durst.
Good—but the scene shifts—faugh! what hangman's hands
Pin to his breast a parchment? his own bands
  Read it. Poor traitor, spit upon and curst!

XVIII

Better this present than a past like that—
  Back therefore to my darkening path again.
  No sound, no sight as far as eye could strain.
Will the night send a howlet or a bat?
I asked: when something on the dismal flat
  Came to arrest my thoughts and change their train.

XIX

A sudden little river crossed my path
  As unexpected as a serpent comes.
  No sluggish tide congenial to the glooms—
This, as it forthed by, might have been a bath
For the fiend's glowing hoof—to see the wrath
  Of its black eddy bespate with flakes and spumes.

XX

So petty yet so spiteful! all along,
  Low scrubby alders kneeled down over it;
  Drenched willows flung them headlong in a fit
Of mute despair, a suicidal throng:
The river which had done them all the wrong,
  Whate'er that was, rolled by, deterred no whit.

XXI

Which, while I forded,—good saints, how I feared
  To set my foot upon a dead man's cheek,
  Each step, or feel the spear I thrust to seek
For hollows, tangled in his hair or beard!
—It may have been a water-rat I speared,
  But, ugh! it sounded like a baby's shriek.

XXII

Glad was I when I reached the other bank.
  Now for a better country. Vain presage!
  Who were the strugglers, what war did they wage
Whose savage trample thus could pad the dank
Soil to a plash? toads in a poisoned tank,
  Or wild cats in a red-hot iron cage—

XXIII

The fight must so have seemed in that fell cirque.
  What kept them there, with all the plain to choose?
  No foot-print leading to that horrid mews,
None out of it: mad brewage set to work
Their brains, no doubt, like galley-slaves the Turk
  Pits for his pastime, Christians against Jews.

XXIV

And more than that—a furlong on—why, there!
  What bad use was that engine for, that wheel,
  Or brake, not wheel—that harrow fit to reel
Men's bodies out like silk? with all the air
Of Tophet's tool, on earth left unaware,
  Or brought to sharpen its rusty teeth of steel.

XXV

Then came a bit of stubbed ground, once a wood,
  Next a marsh, it would seem, and now mere earth
  Desperate and done with; (so a fool finds mirth,
Makes a thing and then mars it, till his mood
Changes and off he goes!) within a rood
  Bog, clay and rubble, sand and stark black dearth.

XXVI

Now blotches rankling, coloured gay and grim,
  Now patches where some leanness of the soil's
  Broke into moss or substances like boils;
Then came some palsied oak, a cleft in him
Like a distorted mouth that splits its rim
  Gaping at death, and dies while it recoils.

XXVII

And just as far as ever from the end!
  Nought in the distance but the evening, nought
  To point my footstep further! At the thought,
A great black bird, Apollyon's bosom-friend,
Sailed past, nor beat his wide wing dragon-penned
  That brushed my cap—perchance the guide I sought.

XXVIII

For looking up, aware I somehow grew,
   'Spite of the dusk, the plain had given place
    All round to mountains—with such name to grace
Mere ugly heights and heaps now stol'n in view.
How thus they had surprised me,—solve it, you!
    How to get from them was no plainer case.

XXIX

Yet half I seemed to recognise some trick
   Of mischief happened to me, God knows when—
    In a bad dream perhaps. Here ended, then,
Progress this way. When, in the very nick
Of giving up, one time more, came a click
    As when a trap shuts—you're inside the den!

XXX

Burningly it came on me all at once,
   This was the place! those two hills on the right
    Crouched like two bulls locked horn in horn in fight—
While to the left, a tall scalped mountain . . . Dunce,
Fool, to be dozing at the very nonce,
    After a life spent training for the sight!

XXXI

What in the midst lay but the Tower itself?
   The round squat turret, blind as the fool's heart,
    Built of brown stone, without a counterpart
In the whole world. The tempest's mocking elf
Points to the shipman thus the unseen shelf
    He strikes on, only when the timbers start.

XXXII

Not see? because of night perhaps?—Why, day
   Came back again for that! before it left,
    The dying sunset kindled through a cleft:
The hills, like giants at a hunting, lay—
Chin upon hand, to see the game at bay,—
    " Now stab and end the creature—to the heft!"

XXXIII

Not hear? when noise was everywhere? it tolled
  Increasing like a bell.   Names in my ears,
  Of all the lost adventurers my peers,—
How such a one was strong, and such was bold,
And such was fortunate, yet each of old
  Lost, lost! one moment knelled the woe of years.

XXXIV

There they stood, ranged along the hill-sides—met
  To view the last of me, a living frame
  For one more picture! in a sheet of flame
I saw them and I knew them all.   And yet
Dauntless the slug-horn to my lips I set
  And blew.   "*Childe Roland to the Dark Tower came.*"
                     ROBERT BROWNING.

MARY QUEEN OF SCOTS

Now Nature hangs her mantle green
  On every blooming tree,
And spreads her sheets o' daisies white
  Out o'er the grassy lea:
Now Phœbus cheers the crystal streams,
  And glads the azure skies;
But nought can glad the weary wight
  That fast in durance lies.

Now lav'rocks wake the merry morn,
  Aloft on dewy wing;
The merle, in his noontide bower,
  Makes woodland echoes ring;
The mavis wild, wi' mony a note,
  Sings drowsy day to rest:
In love and freedom they rejoice,
  Wi' care nor thrall opprest.

Now blooms the lily by the bank,
  The primrose down the brae;
The hawthorn's budding in the glen,
  And milk-white is the slae;

The meanest hind in fair Scotland
　　May rove their sweets amang;
But I, the queen of a' Scotland,
　　Maun lie in prison strang!

I was the queen o' bonny France,
　　Where happy I hae been;
Fu' lightly rase I in the morn,
　　As blithe lay down at e'en:
And I'm the sovereign of Scotland,
　　And mony a traitor there;
Yet here I lie in foreign bands,
　　And never-ending care.

But as for thee, thou false woman!—
　　My sister and my fae,
Grim Vengeance yet shall whet a sword
　　That through thy soul shall gae!
The weeping blood in woman's breast
　　Was never known to thee;
Nor the balm that draps on wounds of woe
　　Frae woman's pitying ee.

My son! my son! may kinder stars
　　Upon thy fortune shine!
And may those pleasures gild thy reign,
　　That ne'er wad blink on mine!
God keep thee frae thy mother's faes,
　　Or turn their hearts to thee:
And where thou meet'st thy mother's friend,
　　Remember him for me!

Oh! soon to me may summer suns
　　Nae mair light up the morn!
Nae mair to me the autumn winds
　　Wave o'er the yellow corn!
And in the narrow house o' death
　　Let winter round me rave;
And the next flowers that deck the spring
　　Bloom on my peaceful grave!

ROBERT BURNS.

PORTRAITS AND CHARACTER

TO THE QUEEN

THESE to His Memory—since he held them dear,
Perchance as finding there unconsciously
Some image of himself—I dedicate,
I dedicate, I consecrate with tears—
These Idylls.

        And indeed He seems to me
Scarce other than my king's ideal knight,
" Who reverenced his conscience as his king;
Whose glory was, redressing human wrong;
Who spake no slander, no, nor listen'd to it;
Who loved one only and who clave to her—"
Her—over all whose realms to their last isle,
Commingled with the gloom of imminent war,
The shadow of His loss drew like eclipse,
Darkening the world.   We have lost him: he is gone:
We know him now: all narrow jealousies
Are silent; and we see him as he moved,
How modest, kindly, all-accomplish'd, wise,
With what sublime repression of himself,
And in what limits, and how tenderly;
Not swaying to this faction or to that;
Not making his high place the lawless perch
Of wing'd ambitions, nor a vantage-ground
For pleasure; but thro' all this tract of years
Wearing the white flower of a blameless life,
Before a thousand peering littlenesses,
In that fierce light which beats upon a throne,
And blackens every blot: for where is he,
Who dares foreshadow for an only son
A lovelier life, a more unstain'd, than his?
Or how should England dreaming of *his* sons
Hope more for these than some inheritance
Of such a life, a heart, a mind as thine,
Thou noble Father of her Kings to be,
Laborious for her people and her poor—

Voice in the rich dawn of an ampler day—
Far-sighted summoner of War and Waste
To fruitful strifes and rivalries of peace—
Sweet nature gilded by the gracious gleam
Of letters, dear to Science, dear to Art,
Dear to thy land and ours, a Prince indeed,
Beyond all titles, and a household name,
Hereafter, thro' all times, Albert the Good.

Break not, O woman's heart, but still endure,
Break not, for thou art Royal, but endure,
Remembering all the beauty of that star
Which shone so close beside Thee that ye made
One light together, but has past and leaves
The Crown a lonely splendour.

　　　　　　　　May all love,
His love, unseen but felt, o'ershadow Thee,
The love of all thy sons encompass Thee,
The love of all Thy daughters cherish Thee,
The love of all Thy people comfort Thee,
Till God's love set Thee at his side again!

　　　　　　　　　　　　LORD TENNYSON.

THE UPRIGHT LIFE

THE man of life upright,
　　Whose guiltless heart is free
From all dishonest deeds,
　　Or thought of vanity;

The man whose silent days
　　In harmless joys are spent,
Whom hopes cannot delude
　　Nor sorrow discontent:

That man needs neither towers
　　Nor armour for defence,
Nor secret vaults to fly
　　From thunder's violence:

He only can behold
   With unaffrighted eyes
The horrors of the deep
   And terrors of the skies.

Thus scorning all the cares
   That fate or fortune brings,
He makes the heaven his book,
   His wisdom heavenly things;

Good thoughts his only friends,
   His wealth a well-spent age,
The earth his sober inn
   And quiet pilgrimage.

THOMAS CAMPION.

MY MIND TO ME A KINGDOM IS

My mind to me a kingdom is,
   Such present joys therein I find,
That it excels all other bliss
   That earth affords or grows by kind:
Though much I want which most would have
Yet still my mind forbids to crave.

No princely pomp, no wealthy store,
   No force to win the victory,
No wily wit to salve a sore,
   No shape to feed a loving eye;
To none of these I yield as thrall,
For why? my mind doth serve for all.

I see how plenty surfeits oft,
   And hasty climbers soon do fall;
I see that those which are aloft
   Mishap doth threaten most of all;
They get with toil, they keep with fear:
Such cares my mind could never bear.

Content to live, this is my stay;
   I seek no more than may suffice;

I press to bear no haughty sway;
   Look, what I lack my mind supplies:
Lo! thus I triumph like a king,
Content with that my mind doth bring.

Some have too much, yet still do crave;
   I little have, and seek no more.
They are but poor, though much they have,
   And I am rich with little store;
They poor, I rich; they beg, I give;
They lack, I leave; they pine, I live.

I laugh not at another's loss;
   I grudge not at another's gain;
No worldly waves my mind can toss;
   My state at one doth still remain:
I fear no foe, I fawn no friend;
I loathe not life, nor dread my end.

Some weigh their pleasure by their lust,
   Their wisdom by their rage of will;
Their treasure is their only trust;
   A cloaked craft their store of skill:
But all the pleasure that I find
Is to maintain a quiet mind.

My wealth is health and perfect ease:
   My conscience clear my chief defence;
I neither seek by bribes to please,
   Nor by deceit to breed offence:
Thus do I live; thus will I die;
Would all did so as well as I!

SIR EDWARD DYER.

HOW HAPPY IS HE BORN

How happy is he born and taught
That serveth not another's will;
Whose armour is his honest thought
And simple truth his utmost skill;

Whose passions not his masters are,
Whose soul is still prepared for death,
Untied unto the world by care
Of public fame, or private breath;

Who envies none that chance doth raise
Nor vice; who never understood
How deepest wounds are given by praise;
Nor rules of state, but rules of good:

Who hath his life from rumours freed,
Whose conscience is his strong retreat;
Whose state can neither flatterers feed,
Nor ruin make oppressors great;

Who God doth late and early pray
More of His grace than gifts to lend;
And entertains the harmless day
With a religious book or friend.

This man is freed from servile bands
Of hope to rise, or fear to fall:
Lord of himself, though not of lands;
And, having nothing, yet hath all.

SIR HENRY WOTTON.

EPISTLE TO THE LADY MARGARET

HE that of such a height hath built his mind,
And rear'd the dwelling of his thoughts so strong,
As neither fear nor hope can shake the frame
Of his resolved pow'rs; nor all the wind
Of vanity or malice pierce to wrong
His settled peace, or to disturb the same:
What a fair seat hath he, from whence he may
The boundless wastes and wilds of man survey?
  And with how free an eye doth he look down
Upon these lower regions of turmoil?
Where all the storms of passions mainly beat
On flesh and blood: where honour, pow'r, renown
Are only gay afflictions, golden toil?
Where greatness stands upon as feeble feet

As frailty doth; and only great doth seem
To little minds, who do it so esteem.
    He looks upon the mightiest monarch's wars
But only as on stately robberies;
Where evermore the fortune that prevails
Must be the right: the ill-succeeding mars
The fairest and the best-fac'd enterprise.
Great pirate Pompey lesser pirates quails:
Justice, he sees (as if seduced), still
Conspires with pow'r, whose cause must not be ill.
    He sees the face of Right t' appear as manifold
As are the passions of uncertain man;
Who puts it in all colours, all attires,
To serve his ends, and make his courses hold.
He sees, that let deceit work what it can,
Plot and contrive base ways to high desires,
That the all-guiding Providence doth yet,
All disappoint, and mocks this smoke of wit.
    Nor is he mov'd with all the thunder-cracks
Of tyrants' threats, or with the surly brow
Of pow'r, that proudly sits on others' crimes;
Charg'd with more crying sins than those he checks.
The storms of sad confusion, that may grow
Up in the present for the coming times,
Appal not him, that hath no side at all,
But of himself, and knows the worst can fall.
    Altho' his heart, so near allied to earth,
Cannot but pity the perplexed state
Of troublous and distress'd mortality,
That thus make way unto the ugly birth
Of their own sorrows, and do still beget
Affliction upon imbecility:
Yet seeing thus the course of things must run,
He looks thereon not strange, but as fore-done.
    And whilst distraught ambition compasses,
And is encompass'd; whilst as craft deceives,
And is deceiv'd; whilst man doth ransack man,
And builds on blood, and rises by distress;
And th' inheritance of desolation leaves
To great-expecting hopes: he looks thereon,
As from the shore of peace, with unwet eye,
And bears no venture in impiety.   SAMUEL DANIEL.

FOR WHAT IS LIFE?

For what is life, if measured by the space
    Not by the act?
Or masked man, if valued by his face,
    Above his fact?
    Here's one outlived his peers,
    And told forth fourscore years;
He vexed time, and busied the whole state;
    Troubled both foes and friends;
    But ever to no ends:
    What did this stirrer, but die late?
How well at twenty had he fallen or stood!
For three of his fourscore, he did no good.

    It is not growing like a tree
    In bulk, doth make men better be;
Or standing long an oak, three hundred year,
To fall a log at last, dry, bald, and sear:
    A lily of a day
    Is fairer far in May
    Although it fall and die that night;
    It was the plant, and flower of light.
In small proportions we just beauties see;
And in short measures, life may perfect be.

Ben Jonson.

THE KNIGHT'S TOMB

Where is the grave of Sir Arthur O'Kellyn?
Where may the grave of that good man be?—
By the side of a spring, on the breast of Helvellyn,
Under the twigs of a young birch tree!
The oak that in summer was sweet to hear,
And rustled its leaves in the fall of the year,
And whistled and roar'd in the winter alone,
Is gone,—and the birch in its stead is grown.—
The Knight's bones are dust,
And his good sword rust;—
His soul is with the saints, I trust.

Sir Walter Scott.

THE HAPPY WARRIOR

WHO is the happy warrior? Who is he
Whom every man in arms should wish to be?
It is the generous spirit, who, when brought
Among the tasks of real life, hath wrought
Upon the plan that pleased his childish thought:
Whose high endeavours are an inward light
That make the path before him always bright;
Who, with a natural instinct to discern
What knowledge can perform, is diligent to learn;
Abides by this resolve, and stops not there,
But makes his moral being his prime care;
Who doom'd to go in company with pain,
And fear, and bloodshed, miserable train!
Turns his necessity to glorious gain;
In faith of these doth exercise a power
Which is our human nature's highest dower;
Controls them and subdues, transmutes, bereaves
Of their bad influence, and their good receives;
By objects which might force the soul to abate
Her feeling, render'd more compassionate;
Is placable—because occasions rise
So often that demand such sacrifice;
More skilful in self-knowledge, even more pure,
As tempted more; more able to endure,
As more exposed to suffering and distress;
Thence, also, more alive to tenderness.
'Tis he whose law is reason; who depends
Upon that law as on the best of friends;
Whence, in a state where men are tempted still
To evil for a guard against worse ill,
And what in quality or act is best
Doth seldom on a right foundation rest,
He fixes good on good alone, and owes
To virtue every triumph that he knows;
Who, if he rise to station of command,
Rises by open means; and there will stand
On honourable terms, or else retire,
And in himself possess his own desire;

Who comprehends his trust, and to the same
Keeps faithful with a singleness of aim;
And therefore does not stoop, nor lie in wait
For wealth, or honours, or for worldly state;
Whom they must follow; on whose head must fall,
Like showers of manna, if they come at all;
Whose powers shed round him in the common strife,
Or mild concerns of ordinary life,
A constant influence, a peculiar grace;
But who, if he be call'd upon to face
Some awful moment to which Heaven has joined
Great issues, good or bad for human kind,
Is happy as a lover; and attired
With sudden brightness, like a man inspired;
And through the heat of conflict keeps the law
In calmness made, and sees what he foresaw;
Or if an unexpected call succeed,
Come when it will, is equal to the need:
He who, though thus endued as with a sense
And faculty for storm and turbulence,
Is yet a soul whose master bias leans
To homefelt pleasures and to gentle scenes,
Sweet images! which, wheresoe'er he be,
Are at his heart; and such fidelity
It is his darling passion to approve;
More brave for this, that he hath much to love.
'Tis, finally, the man, who, lifted high,
Conspicuous object in a nation's eye,
Or left unthought of in obscurity,—
Who, with a toward or untoward lot,
Prosperous or adverse, to his wish or not,
Plays, in the many games of life, that one
Where what he most doth value must be won;
Whom neither shape of danger can dismay,
Nor thought of tender happiness betray;
Who, not content that former worth stand fast,
Looks forward, persevering to the last,
From well to better, daily self-surpass'd:
Who, whether praise of him must walk the earth
For ever, and to noble deeds give birth,
Or he must go to dust without his fame,
And leave a dead, unprofitable name,

Finds comfort in himself and in his cause;
And, while the mortal mist is gathering, draws
His breath in confidence of Heaven's applause:
This is the happy warrior; this is he
Whom every man in arms should wish to be.

WILLIAM WORDSWORTH.

DOST THOU LOOK BACK?

Dost thou look back on what hath been,
    As some divinely gifted man,
    Whose life in low estate began
And on a simple village green;

Who breaks his birth's invidious bar,
    And grasps the skirts of happy chance,
    And breasts the blows of circumstance,
And grapples with his evil star;

Who makes by force his merit known
    And lives to clutch the golden keys,
    To mould a mighty state's decrees,
And shape the whisper of the throne;

And moving up from high to higher,
    Becomes on Fortune's crowning slope
    The pillar of a people's hope,
The centre of a world's desire;

Yet feels, as in a pensive dream,
    When all his active powers are still,
    A distant dearness in the hill,
A secret sweetness in the stream,

The limit of his narrower fate,
    While yet beside its vocal springs
    He play'd at counsellors and kings,
With one that was his earliest mate;

Who ploughs with pain his native lea
    And reaps the labour of his hands,
    Or in the furrow musing stands;
" Does my old friend remember me? "

LORD TENNYSON.

DR. LEVETT

CONDEMNED to Hope's delusive mine,
   As on we toil from day to day,
By sudden blast or slow decline
   Our social comforts drop away.

Well tried through many a varying year,
   See Levett to the grave descend:
Officious, innocent, sincere,
   Of every friendless name the friend.

Yet still he fills affection's eye,
   Obscurely wise and coarsely kind;
Nor, lettered arrogance, deny
   Thy praise to merit unrefined.

When fainting Nature called for aid,
   And hovering death prepared the blow,
His vigorous remedy displayed
   The power of art without the show.

In misery's darkest caverns known,
   His ready help was ever nigh,
Where hopeless anguish poured his groan,
   And lonely want retired to die.

No summons mocked by chill delay,
   No petty gains disdained by pride:
The modest wants of every day
   The toil of every day supplied.

His virtues walked their narrow round,
   Nor made a pause, nor left a void;
And sure the eternal Master found
   His single talent well employed.

The busy day, the peaceful night,
   Unfelt, uncounted, glided by;

His frame was firm, his powers were bright,
    Though now his eightieth year was nigh.

Then, with no throbs of fiery pain,
    No cold gradations of decay,
Death broke at once the vital chain,
    And freed his soul the nearest way.
                            SAMUEL JOHNSON.

A MAN

THIS was the noblest Roman of them all:
All the conspirators, save only he,
Did that they did in envy of great Cæsar,
He, only, in a general honest thought,
And common good to all, made one of them.
His life was gentle; and the elements
So mix'd in him, that Nature might stand up,
And say to all the world, *This was a man!*
                            WILLIAM SHAKESPEARE.

A FAREWELL

Cas. Now, most noble Brutus,
The gods to-day stand friendly; that we may,
Lovers, in peace, lead on our days to age!
But, since the affairs of men rest still uncertain,
Let's reason with the worst that may befall.
If we do lose this battle, then is this
The very last time we shall speak together:
What are you then determined to do?
    Bru. Even by the rule of that philosophy,
By which I did blame Cato for the death
Which he did give himself:—I know not how,
But I do find it cowardly and vile,
For fear of what might fall, so to prevent
The time of life:—arming myself with patience,
To stay the providence of some high powers,
That govern us below.

Cas. Then, if we lose this battle,
You are contented to be led in triumph
Through the streets of Rome?

Bru. No, Cassius, no: think not, thou noble Roman,
That ever Brutus will go bound to Rome;
He bears too great a mind. But this same day
Must end that work, the ides of March began;
And whether we shall meet again, I know not.
Therefore our everlasting farewell take:—
For ever, and for ever, farewell, Cassius!
If we do meet again, why we shall smile;
If not, why then this parting was well made.

Cas. For ever, and for ever, farewell, Brutus!
If we do meet again, we'll smile indeed;
If not, 'tis true, this parting was well made.

Bru. Why then, lead on.—O, that a man might know
The end of this day's business, ere it come!
But it sufficeth, that the day will end,
And then the end is known.—Come, ho! away!

WILLIAM SHAKESPEARE.

JULIUS CÆSAR

Ant. O mighty Cæsar! Dost thou lie so low?
Are all thy conquests, glories, triumphs, spoils,
Shrunk to this little measure?—Fare thee well.—
I know not, gentlemen, what you intend,
Who else must be let blood, who else is rank:
If I myself, there is no hour so fit
As Cæsar's death hour; nor no instrument
Of half that worth as those your swords, made rich
With the most noble blood of all this world.
I do beseech ye, if ye bear me hard,
Now, whilst your purple hands do reek and smoke,
Fulfil your pleasure. Live a thousand years,
I shall not find myself so apt to die:
No place will please me so, no mean of death,
As here by Cæsar, and by you cut off,
The choice and master spirits of this age.

Bru. O Antony! beg not your death of us.

Though now we must appear bloody and cruel,
As, by our hands, and this our present act,
You see we do; yet see you but our hands,
And this the bleeding business they have done:
Our hearts you see not, they are pitiful;
And pity to the general wrong of Rome
(As fire drives out fire, so pity, pity,)
Hath done this deed on Cæsar. For your part,
To you our swords have leaden points, Mark Antony:
Our arms, in strength of malice, and our hearts,
Of brother's temper, do receive you in
With all kind love, good thoughts, and reverence.

   Cas. Your voice shall be as strong as any man's
In the disposing of new dignities.

   Bru. Only be patient, till we have appeased
The multitude, beside themselves with fear,
And then we will deliver you the cause,
Why I, that did love Cæsar when I struck him,
Have thus proceeded.

   Ant. I doubt not of your wisdom.
Let each man render me his bloody hand:
First, Marcus Brutus, will I shake with you;—
Next, Caius Cassius, do I take your hand;—
Now, Decius Brutus, yours;—now yours, Metellus;
Yours, Cinna;—and, my valiant Casca, yours;—
Though last, not least in love, yours, good Trebonius.
Gentlemen all,—alas! what shall I say?
My credit now stands on such slippery ground,
That one of two bad ways you must conceit me,
Either a coward or a flatterer.—
That I did love thee, Cæsar, O, 'tis true:
If then thy spirit look upon us now,
Shall it not grieve thee, dearer than thy death,
To see thy Antony making his peace,
Shaking the bloody fingers of thy foes,
Most noble! in the presence of thy corse?
Had I as many eyes as thou hast wounds,
Weeping as fast as they stream forth thy blood,
It would become me better, than to close
In terms of friendship with thine enemies.
Pardon me, Julius!—Here wast thou bay'd, brave hart:
Here didst thou fall; and here thy hunters stand,

Sign'd in thy spoil, and crimson'd in thy lethe.
O world! thou wast the forest to this hart;
And this, indeed, O world, the heart of thee.—
How like a deer, stricken by many princes,
Dost thou here lie!

    Cas. Mark Antony.

    Ant. Pardon me, Caius Cassius:
The enemies of Cæsar shall say this;
Then, in a friend, it is cold modesty.

    Cas. I blame you not for praising Cæsar so:
But what compact mean you to have with us?
Will you be prick'd in number of our friends;
Or shall we on, and not depend on you?

    Ant. Therefore I took your hands; but was, indeed,
Sway'd from the point, by looking down on Cæsar.
Friends am I with you all, and love you all:
Upon this hope, that you shall give me reasons,
Why, and wherein, Cæsar was dangerous.

    Bru. Or else were this a savage spectacle;
Our reasons are so full of good regard,
That were you, Antony, the son of Cæsar,
You should be satisfied.

    Ant. That's all I seek:
And am moreover suitor, that I may
Produce his body to the market-place;
And in the pulpit, as becomes a friend,
Speak in the order of his funeral.

    Bru. You shall, Mark Antony.

    Cas. Brutus, a word with you.—
You know not what you do; Do not consent   (*Aside.*)
That Antony speak in his funeral:
Know you how much the people may be moved
By that which he will utter?

    Bru. By your pardon;—
I will myself into the pulpit first,
And shew the reason of our Cæsar's death:
What Antony shall speak, I will protest
He speaks by leave and by permission;
And that we are contented, Cæsar shall
Have all true rites, and lawful ceremonies.
It shall advantage more than do us wrong.

    Cas. I know not what may fall; I like it not.

Bru. Mark Antony, here, take you Cæsar's body.
You shall not in your funeral speech blame us,
But speak all good you can devise of Cæsar;
And say, you do't by our permission;
Else shall you not have any hand at all
About his funeral: And you shall speak
In the same pulpit whereto I am going,
After my speech is ended.

   Ant. Be it so;
I do desire no more.
Bru. Prepare the body then, and follow us.

                         [*Exeunt all but Antony.*

   Ant. O pardon me, thou piece of bleeding earth,
That I am meek and gentle with these butchers!
Thou art the ruins of the noblest man
That ever lived in the tide of times.
Wo to the hand that sheds this costly blood!
Over thy wounds now do I prophesy,—
Which, like dumb mouths, do ope their ruby lips,
To beg the voice and utterance of my tongue;—
A curse shall light upon the limbs of men;
Domestic fury, and fierce civil strife,
Shall cumber all the parts of Italy:
Blood and destruction shall be so in use,
And dreadful objects so familiar,
That mothers shall but smile, when they behold
Their infants quarter'd with the hands of war;
All pity choked with custom of fell deeds:
And Cæsar's spirit, raging for revenge,
With Ate by his side, come hot from hell,
Shall in these confines, with a monarch's voice,
Cry *Havoc*, and let slip the dogs of war;
That this foul deed shall smell above the earth
With carrion men, groaning for burial.

Enter a Servant.

You serve Octavius Cæsar, do you not?
   Serv. I do, Mark Antony.
   Ant. Cæsar did write for him to come to Rome.
   Serv. He did receive his letters, and is coming:
And bid me say to you by word of mouth,—
O Cæsar!—   (*Seeing the body.*)

Ant. Thy heart is big, get thee apart and weep.
Passion, I see, is catching; for mine eyes,
Seeing those beads of sorrow stand in thine,
Began to water. Is thy master coming?

Serv. He lies to-night within seven leagues of Rome.

Ant. Post back with speed, and tell him what hath chanced.
Here is a mourning Rome, a dangerous Rome,
No Rome of safety for Octavius yet;
Hie hence, and tell him so. Yet, stay a while;
Thou shalt not back, till I have borne this corse
Into the market-place: there shall I try,
In my oration, how the people take
The cruel issue of these bloody men;
According to the which thou shalt discourse
To young Octavius of the state of things.
Lend me your hand.   *[Exeunt with Cæsar's body.*

SCENE II.—*The same. The Forum.*

Enter BRUTUS *and* CASSIUS, *and a throng of Citizens.*

Cit. We will be satisfied; let us be satisfied.

Bru. Then follow me, and give me audience, friends.—
Cassius, go you into the other street,
And part the numbers.—
Those that will hear me speak, let them stay here;
Those that will follow Cassius, go with him;
And public reasons shall be rendered
Of Cæsar's death.

1 Cit. I will hear Brutus speak.

2 Cit. I will hear Cassius; and compare their reasons,
When severally we hear them rendered.
    [Exit Cassius, with some of the Citizens, Brutus
      goes into the Rostrum.

3 Cit. The noble Brutus is ascended: Silence!

Bru. Be patient till the last.
Romans, countrymen, and lovers! hear me for my cause;
and be silent, that you may hear: believe me for mine honour;
and have respect to mine honour, that you may believe:
censure me in your wisdom; and awake your senses, that you
may the better judge. If there be any in this assembly, any
dear friend of Cæsar's, to him I say, that Brutus' love to
Cæsar was no less than his. If then that friend demand why

Brutus rose against Cæsar this is my answer,—Not that I
loved Cæsar less, but that I loved Rome more. Had you
rather Cæsar were living, and die all slaves; or that Cæsar
were dead, to live all free men? As Cæsar loved me, I weep
for him; as he was fortunate, I rejoice at it; as he was valiant,
I honour him: but, as he was ambitious, I slew him: There is
tears, for his love; joy, for his fortune; honour, for his
valour; and death, for his ambition. Who is here so base
that would be a bondman? If any, speak; for him have I
offended. Who is here so rude, that would not be a Roman?
If any, speak; for him have I offended. Who is here so vile,
that will not love his country? If any, speak; for him have
I offended. I pause for a reply.

    Cit. None, Brutus, none.   (*Several speaking at once.*)

    Bru. Then none have I offended. I have done no more
to Cæsar, than you should do to Brutus. The question of
his death is enrolled in the Capitol, his glory not extenuated,
wherein he was worthy; nor his offences enforced, for which
he suffered death.

Enter ANTONY *and others, with Cæsar's body.*

Here comes his body, mourned by Mark Antony, who,
though he had no hand in his death, shall receive the benefit
of his dying, a place in the commonwealth: As which of you
shall not? With this I depart; That, as I slew my best lover
for the good of Rome, I have the same dagger for myself,
when it shall please my country to need my death.

    Cit. Live, Brutus, live! live!

    1 *Cit.* Bring him with triumph home unto his house.

    2 *Cit.* Give him a statue with his ancestors.

    3 *Cit.* Let him be Cæsar.

    4 *Cit.* Cæsar's better parts

Shall now be crown'd in Brutus.

    1 *Cit.* We'll bring him to his home with shouts and
clamours.

    Bru. My countrymen.

    2 *Cit.* Peace; silence! Brutus speaks.

    1 *Cit.* Peace, ho!

    Bru. Good countrymen, let me depart alone,
And, for my sake, stay here with Antony:
Do grace to Cæsar's corpse, and grace his speech
Tending to Cæsar's glories; which Mark Antony,

By our permission, is allow'd to make.
I do entreat you, not a man depart,
Save I alone, till Antony have spoke.   *[Exit.*

  1 *Cit.* Stay, ho! and let us hear Mark Antony.
  3 *Cit.* Let him go up into the public chair;
We'll hear him:—Noble Antony, go up.
  Ant. For Brutus' sake, I am beholden to you.
  4 *Cit.* What does he say of Brutus?
  3 *Cit.* He says, for Brutus' sake,
He finds himself beholden to us all.
  4 *Cit.* 'Twere best he speak no harm of Brutus here.
  1 *Cit.* This Cæsar was a tyrant.
  3 *Cit.* Nay, that's certain:
We are bless'd that Rome is rid of him.
  2 *Cit.* Peace; let us hear what Antony can say.
  Ant. You gentle Romans,—
  Cit. Peace, ho! let us hear him.
  Ant. Friends, Romans, countrymen, lend me your ears;
I come to bury Cæsar, not to praise him.
The evil that men do lives after them;
The good is oft interred with their bones;
So let it be with Cæsar.   The noble Brutus
Hath told you Cæsar was ambitious:
If it were so, it was a grievous fault;
And grievously hath Cæsar answer'd it.
Here, under leave of Brutus, and the rest,
(For Brutus is an honourable man;
So are they all, all honourable men:)
Come I to speak in Cæsar's funeral.
He was my friend, faithful and just to me:
But Brutus says he was ambitious;
And Brutus is an honourable man.
He hath brought many captives home to Rome,
Whose ransoms did the general coffers fill:
Did this in Cæsar seem ambitious?
When that the poor have cried, Cæsar hath wept;
Ambition should be made of sterner stuff:
Yet Brutus says he was ambitious;
And Brutus is an honourable man.
You all did see that on the Lupercal
I thrice presented him a kingly crown,
Which he did thrice refuse.   Was this ambition?

Yet Brutus says he was ambitious;
And, sure, he is an honourable man.
I speak not to disprove what Brutus spoke,
But here I am to speak what I do know.
You all did love him once, not without cause;
What cause withholds you then to mourn for him?
O judgment, thou art fled to brutish beasts,
And men have lost their reason!—Bear with me;
My heart is in the coffin there with Cæsar,
And I must pause, till it come back to me.

 1 *Cit.* Methinks there is much reason in his sayings.

 2 *Cit.* If thou consider rightly of the matter,
Cæsar has had great wrong.

 3 *Cit.*   Has he, masters?
I fear, there will a worse come in his place.

 4 *Cit.* Mark'd ye his words? he would not take the crown;
Therefore, 'tis certain, he was not ambitious.

 1 *Cit.* If it be found so, some will dear abide it.

 2 *Cit.* Poor soul! his eyes are red as fire with weeping.

 3 *Cit.* There's not a nobler man in Rome than Antony.

 4 *Cit.* Now mark him, he begins again to speak.

 Ant. But yesterday the word of Cæsar might
Have stood against the world: now lies he there,
And none so poor to do him reverence.
O masters! if I were disposed to stir
Your hearts and minds to mutiny and rage,
I should do Brutus wrong, and Cassius wrong,
Who, you all know, are honourable men:
I will not do them wrong; I rather choose
To wrong the dead, to wrong myself, and you,
Than I will wrong such honourable men.
But here's a parchment, with the seal of Cæsar,
I found it in his closet, 'tis his will:
Let but the commons hear this testament,
(Which, pardon me, I do not mean to read,)
And they would go and kiss dead Cæsar's wounds,
And dip their napkins in his sacred blood;
Yea, beg a hair of him for memory,
And, dying, mention it within their wills,
Bequeathing it, as a rich legacy,
Unto their issue.

 4 *Cit.* We'll hear the will: Read it, Mark Antony.

Cit. The will, the will; we will hear Cæsar's will.

Ant. Have patience, gentle friends, I must not read it;
It is not meet you know how Cæsar loved you.
You are not wood, you are not stones, but men;
And, being men, hearing the will of Cæsar,
It will inflame you, it will make you mad:
'Tis good you know not that you are his heirs,
For if you should, O, what would come of it!

4 *Cit.* Read the will; we will hear it, Antony:
You shall read us the will; Cæsar's will.

Ant. Will you be patient? Will you stay a while?
I have o'ershot myself, to tell you of it.
I fear, I wrong the honourable men,
Whose daggers have stabb'd Cæsar: I do fear it.

4 *Cit.* They were traitors: Honourable men!

Cit. The will! the testament!

2 *Cit.* They are villains, murderers: The will! read the
will!

Ant. You will compel me then to read the will?
Then make a ring about the corpse of Cæsar,
And let me shew you him that made the will.
Shall I descend? And will you give me leave?

Cit. Come down.

2 *Cit.* Descend.   (*He comes down from the pulpit.*)

3 *Cit.* You shall have leave.

4 *Cit.* A ring; stand round.

1 *Cit.* Stand from the hearse, stand from the body.

2 *Cit.* Room for Antony;—most noble Antony.

Ant. Nay, press not so upon me, stand far off.

Cit. Stand back! room! bear back!

Ant. If you have tears, prepare to shed them now.
You all do know this mantle: I remember
The first time ever Cæsar put it on;
'Twas on a summer's evening, in his tent;
That day he overcame the Nervii:—
Look! In this place ran Cassius' dagger through:
See, what a rent the envious Casca made:
Through this, the well-beloved Brutus stabb'd;
And, as he pluck'd his cursed steel away,
Mark how the blood of Cæsar follow'd it;
As rushing out of doors, to be resolved
If Brutus so unkindly knock'd, or no;

For Brutus, as you know, was Cæsar's angel:
Judge, O you gods, how dearly Cæsar loved him!
This was the most unkindest cut of all:
For when the noble Cæsar saw him stab,
Ingratitude, more strong than traitors' arms,
Quite vanquish'd him: then burst his mighty heart;
And, in his mantle muffling up his face,
Even at the base of Pompey's statua,
Which all the while ran blood, great Cæsar fell.
O, what a fall was there, my countrymen!
Then I, and you, and all of us fell down,
Whilst bloody treason flourish'd over us.
O, now you weep; and, I perceive, you feel
The dint of pity: these are gracious drops.
Kind souls, what, weep you, when you but behold
Our Cæsar's vesture wounded? Look you here,
Here is himself, marr'd, as you see, with traitors.

   1 *Cit.* O piteous spectacle!

   2 *Cit.* O noble Cæsar!

   3 *Cit.* O woful day!

   4 *Cit.* O traitors, villains!

   1 *Cit.* O, most bloody sight!

   2 *Cit.* We will be revenged; revenge; about,—seek,—
     burn,—fire,—kill,—slay!—let not a traitor live.

   Ant. Stay, countrymen.

   1 *Cit.* Peace there:—Hear the noble Antony.

   2 *Cit.* We'll hear him, we'll follow him, we'll die with him.

   Ant. Good friends, sweet friends, let me not stir you up
To such a sudden flood of mutiny.
They, that have done this deed, are honourable;
What private griefs they have, alas, I know not,
That made them do it; they are wise and honourable,
And will, no doubt, with reasons answer you.
I come not, friends, to steal away your hearts;
I am no orator, as Brutus is:
But, as you know me all, a plain blunt man,
That love my friend: and that they know full well
That gave me public leave to speak of him.
For I have neither wit, nor words, nor worth,
Action, nor utterance, nor the power of speech,
To stir men's blood: I only speak right on;
I tell you that, which you yourselves do know;

Shew you sweet Cæsar's wounds, poor, poor dumb mouths,
And bid them speak for me: But were I Brutus,
And Brutus Antony, there were an Antony
Would ruffle up your spirits, and put a tongue
In every wound of Cæsar, that should move
The stones of Rome to rise and mutiny.

Cit. We'll mutiny.

1 *Cit.* We'll burn the house of Brutus.

3 *Cit.* Away then, come, seek the conspirators.

Ant. Yet hear me, countrymen; yet hear me speak.

Cit. Peace, oh! hear Antony, most noble Antony.

Ant. Why, friends, you go to do you know not what:
Wherein hath Cæsar thus deserved your loves?
Alas! you know not:—I must tell you then:—
You have forgot the will I told you of.

Cit. Most true;—the will;—let's stay, and hear the will.

Ant. Here is the will, and under Cæsar's seal.
To every Roman citizen he gives,
To every several man, seventy-five drachmas.

2 *Cit.* Most noble Cæsar!—we'll revenge his death.

3 *Cit.* O royal Cæsar!

Ant. Hear me with patience.

Cit. Peace, ho!

Ant. Moreover, he hath left you all his walks,
His private arbours, and new-planted orchards,
On this side Tiber; he hath left them you,
And to your heirs for ever; common pleasures,
To walk abroad, and recreate yourselves.
Here was a Cæsar: When comes such another?

1 *Cit.* Never, never:—Come away, away:
We'll burn his body in the holy place,
And with the brands fire the traitors' houses.
Take up the body.

2 *Cit.* Go, fetch fire.

3 *Cit.* Pluck down benches.

4 *Cit.* Pluck down forms, windows, any thing.

[*Exeunt Citizens with the body.*

Ant. Now let it work: Mischief, thou art afoot,
Take thou what course thou wilt!

WILLIAM SHAKESPEARE.

HOTSPUR

Enter KING HENRY, NORTHUMBERLAND, WORCESTER, HOT-
SPUR, SIR WALTER BLUNT, *and others.*

K. Hen. My blood hath been too cold and temperate,
Unapt to stir at these indignities,
And you have found me; for, accordingly,
You tread upon my patience; but, be sure,
I will from henceforth rather be myself,
Mighty, and to be fear'd, than my condition
Which hath been smooth as oil, soft as young down,
And therefore lost that title of respect,
Which the proud soul ne'er pays, but to the proud.

Wor. Our house, my sovereign liege, little deserves
The scourge of greatness to be used on it:
And that same greatness too, which our own hands
Have holp to make so portly.

North. My lord,—

K. Hen. Worcester, get thee gone, for I see danger
And disobedience in thine eye: O, sir,
Your presence is too bold and peremptory,
And majesty might never yet endure
The moody frontier of a servant brow.
You have good leave to leave us; when we need
Your use and counsel, we shall send for you.—

                                      [*Exit Worcester.*
You were about to speak.   (*To North.*)

North. Yea, my good lord,
Those prisoners in your highness' name demanded,
Which Harry Percy here at Holmedon took,
Were, as he says, not with such strength denied
As is deliver'd to your majesty:
Either envy, therefore, or misprision
Is guilty of this fault, and not my son.

Hot. My liege, I did deny no prisoners.
But, I remember, when the fight was done,
When I was dry with rage, and extreme toil,
Breathless and faint, leaning upon my sword,
Came there a certain lord, neat, trimly dress'd,
Fresh as a bridegroom; and his chin, new reap'd,

Hotspur

Shew'd like a stubble-land at harvest-home;
He was perfumed like a milliner;
And 'twixt his finger and his thumb he held
A pouncet-box, which ever and anon
He gave his nose, and took 't away again;—
Who, therewith angry, when it next came there,
Took it in snuff:—and still he smil'd, and talk'd:
And, as the soldiers bore dead bodies by,
He call'd them—untaught knaves, unmannerly,
To bring a slovenly unhandsome corse
Betwixt the wind and his nobility.
With many holyday and lady terms
He question'd me; among the rest demanded
My prisoners, in your majesty's behalf.
I then, all smarting, with my wounds being cold,
To be so pester'd with a popinjay,
Out of my grief and my impatience,
Answer'd neglectingly, I know not what;
He should, or he should not; for he made me mad,
To see him shine so brisk, and smell so sweet,
And talk so like a waiting gentlewoman,
Of guns, and drums, and wounds, (God save the mark!)
And telling me, the sovereign'st thing on earth
Was parmaceti, for an inward bruise;
And that it was great pity, so it was,
That villainous saltpetre should be digg'd
Out of the bowels of the harmless earth,
Which many a good tall fellow had destroy'd
So cowardly; and, but for these vile guns,
He would himself have been a soldier.
This bald disjointed chat of his, my lord,
I answer'd indirectly, as I said;
And, I beseech you, let not his report
Come current for an accusation
Betwixt my love and your high majesty.
   Blunt. The circumstance consider'd, good my lord,
Whatever Harry Percy then had said,
To such a person, and in such a place,
At such a time, with all the rest retold,
May reasonably die, and never rise
To do him wrong, or any way impeach
What then he said, so he unsay it now.

K. Hen. Why, yet he doth deny his prisoners;
But with proviso, and exception,—
That we, at our own charge, shall ransom straight
His brother-in-law, the foolish Mortimer;
Who, on my soul, hath wilfully betray'd
The lives of those, that he did leave to fight
Against the great magician, damn'd Glendower;
Whose daughter, as we hear, the earl of March
Hath lately married. Shall our coffers then
Be emptied, to redeem a traitor home?
Shall we buy treason? and indent with fears,
When they have lost and forfeited themselves?
No, on the barren mountains let him starve;
For I shall never hold that man my friend,
Whose tongue shall ask me for one penny cost
To ransome home revolted Mortimer.

  Hot. Revolted Mortimer!
He never did fall off, my sovereign liege,
But by the chance of war:—To prove that true,
Needs no more but one tongue for all those wounds,
Those mouthed wounds, which valiantly he took,
When on the gentle Severn's sedgy bank,
In single opposition, hand to hand,
He did confound the best part of an hour
In changing hardiment with great Glendower:
Three times they breathed, and three times did they drink,
Upon agreement, of swift Severn's flood:
Who, then, affrighted with their bloody looks,
Ran fearfully among the trembling reeds,
And hid his crisp head in the hollow bank
Blood-stained with these valiant combatants.
Never did base and rotten policy
Colour her working with such deadly wounds;
Nor never could the noble Mortimer
Receive so many, and all willingly:
Then let him not be slander'd with revolt.

  K. Hen. Thou dost belie him, Percy, thou dost belie him,
He never did encounter with Glendower;
I tell thee,
He durst as well have met the devil alone,
As Owen Glendower for an enemy.
Art not ashamed? But, sirrah, henceforth

Let me not hear you speak of Mortimer:
Send me your prisoners with the speediest means
Or you shall hear in such a kind from me
As will displease you.—My lord Northumberland,
We license your departure with your son:—
Send us your prisoners, or you'll hear of it.

                [Exeunt King Henry, Blunt, and Train.

  Hot. And if the devil come and roar for them,
I will not send them:—I will after straight,
And tell him so; for I will ease my heart,
Although it be with hazard of my head.

  North. What, drunk with choler? stay, and pause awhile;
Here comes your uncle.

          Re-enter WORCESTER.

  Hot. Speak of Mortimer!
Zounds, I will speak of him; and let my soul
Want mercy, if I do not join with him:
Yea, on his part, I'll empty all these veins,
And shed my dear blood drop by drop i' the dust,
But I will lift the down-trod Mortimer
As high i' the air as this unthankful king,
As this ingrate and canker'd Bolingbroke.

  North. Brother, the king hath made your nephew mad.

                  (To Worcester.)

  Wor. Who struck this heat up after I was gone?

  Hot. He will, forsooth, have all my prisoners;
And when I urged the ransom once again
Of my wife's brother, then his cheek look'd pale;
And on my face he turned an eye of death,
Trembling even at the name of Mortimer.

  Wor. I cannot blame him: Was he not proclaim'd,
By Richard that dead is, the next of blood?

  North. He was; I heard the proclamation:
And then it was, when the unhappy king
(Whose wrongs in us God pardon!) did set forth
Upon his Irish expedition;
From whence he, intercepted, did return
To be deposed, and shortly murdered.

  Wor. And for whose death, we in the world's wide mouth
Live scandalised, and foully spoken of.

  Hot. But, soft, I pray you: Did King Richard then

Proclaim my brother Edmund Mortimer
Heir to the crown?

 North. He did; myself did hear it.

 Hot. Nay, then I cannot blame his cousin king
That wish'd him on the barren mountains starved.
But shall it be, that you,—that set the crown
Upon the head of this forgetful man;
And, for his sake, wear the detested blot
Of murd'rous subornation,—shall it be,
That you a world of curses undergo;
Being the agents, or base second means,
The cords, the ladder, or the hangman rather?—
O, pardon me, that I descend so low,
To shew the line, and the predicament,
Wherein you range under this subtle king.
Shall it, for shame, be spoken in these days,
Or fill up chronicles in time to come,
That men of your nobility and power
Did 'gage them both in an unjust behalf,—
As both of you, God pardon it! have done,—
To put down Richard, that sweet lovely rose,
And plant this thorn, this canker, Bolingbroke?
And shall it, in more shame, be farther spoken,
That you are fool'd, discarded, and shook off
By him, for whom these shames ye underwent?
No; yet time serves, wherein you may redeem
Your banish'd honours, and restore yourselves
Into the good thoughts of the world again:
Revenge the jeering, and disdain'd contempt
Of this proud king; who studies, day and night,
To answer all the debt he owes to you,
Even with the bloody payments of your deaths.
Therefore, I say,——

 Wor. Peace, cousin, say no more:
And now I will unclasp a secret book,
And to your quick-conceiving discontents
I'll read you matter deep and dangerous;
As full of peril, and advent'rous spirit,
As to o'erwalk a current, roaring loud,
On the unstedfast footing of a spear.

 Hot. If he fall in, good-night:—or sink or swim:—
Send danger from the east unto the west,

So honour cross it from the north to south,
And let them grapple.—O! the blood more stirs,
To rouse a lion, than to start a hare,
  North. Imagination of some great exploit
Drives him beyond the bounds of patience.
  Hot. By Heaven, methinks, it were an easy leap,
To pluck bright honour from the pale-faced moon:
Or dive into the bottom of the deep,
Where fathom-line could never touch the ground,
And pluck up drowned honour by the locks;
So he, that doth redeem her hence, might wear,
Without corrival, all her dignities:
But out upon this half-faced fellowship!
  Wor. He apprehends a world of figures here,
But not the form of what he should attend.—
Good cousin, give me audience for a while.
  Hot. I cry you mercy.
  Wor. Those same noble Scots,
That are your prisoners,—
  Hot. I'll keep them all;
By Heaven, he shall not have a Scot of them;
No, if a Scot would save his soul, he shall not:
I'll keep them, by this hand.
  Wor. You start away,
And lend no ear unto my purposes.—
Those prisoners you shall keep.
  Hot. Nay, I will; that's flat.
He said, he would not ransom Mortimer;
Forbad my tongue to speak of Mortimer;
But I will find him, when he lies asleep,
And in his ear I'll holla—Mortimer!
Nay,
I'll have a starling shall be taught to speak
Nothing but Mortimer, and give it him,
To keep his anger still in motion.
  Wor. Hear you,
Cousin, a word.
  Hot. All studies here I solemnly defy,
Save how to gall and pinch this Bolingbroke:
And that same sword-and-buckler prince of Wales–
But that I think his father loves him not,
And would be glad he met with some mischance,

I'd have him poison'd with a pot of ale.

Wor. Farewell, kinsman! I will talk to you,
When you are better temper'd to attend.

North. Why, what a wasp-stung and impatient fool
Art thou, to break into this woman's mood;
Tying thine ear to no tongue but thine own?

Hot. Why, look you, I am whipp'd and scourged with rods,
Nettled, and stung with pismires, when I hear
Of this vile politician Bolingbroke.
In Richard's time,—What do you call the place?—
A plague upon 't—it is in Gloucestershire;
'Twas where the mad-cap duke his uncle kept;
His uncle York:—Where I first bow'd my knee
Unto this king of smiles, this Bolingbroke,
When you and he came back from Ravenspurg.

North. At Berkley Castle.

Hot. You say true;—
Why, what a candy deal of courtesy
This fawning greyhound then did proffer me!
Look,—*when his infant fortune came to age,*
And,—*gentle Harry Percy,*—and *kind cousin,*—
O, the devil take such cozeners! God forgive me!—
Good uncle, tell your tale, for I have done.

Wor. Nay, if you have not, to't again;
We'll stay your leisure.

Hot. I have done, i' faith.

WILLIAM SHAKESPEARE.

TRAITORS

Cam. I do confess my fault;
And do submit me to your highness' mercy.

Grey.
Scroop. } To which we all appeal.

K. Hen. The mercy that was quick in us but late,
By your own counsel is suppress'd and kill'd:
You must not dare, for shame, to talk of mercy;
For your own reasons turn into your bosoms,
As dogs upon their masters, worrying you.
See you, my princes and my noble peers,

These English monsters! My Lord of Cambridge here,
You know how apt our love was to accord
To furnish him with all appertiments
Belonging to his honour; and this man
Hath, for a few light crowns, lightly conspired,
And sworn unto the practices of France,
To kill us here in Hampton: to the which
This knight, no less for bounty bound to us
Than Cambridge is, hath likewise sworn. But, O,
What shall I say to thee, Lord Scroop? thou cruel,
Ingrateful, savage and unhuman creature!
Thou that didst bear the key of all my counsels,
That knew'st the very bottom of my soul,
That almost mightst have coin'd me into gold,
Wouldst thou have practised on me for thy use!
May it be possible, that foreign hire
Could out of thee extract one spark of evil
That might annoy my finger? 't is so strange,
That, though the truth of it stands off as gross
As black and white, my eye will scarcely see it.
Treason and murder ever kept together,
As two yoke-devils sworn to either's purpose,
Working so grossly in a natural cause,
That admiration did not hoop at them:
But thou, 'gainst all proportion, didst bring in
Wonder to wait on treason and on murder:
And whatsoever cunning fiend it was
That wrought upon thee so preposterously
Hath got the voice in hell for excellence:
All other devils that suggest by treasons
Do botch and bungle up damnation
With patches, colours, and with forms being fetch'd
From glistering semblances of piety;
But he that temper'd thee bade thee stand up,
Gave thee no instance why thou shouldst do treason,
Unless to dub thee with the name of traitor.
If that same demon that hath gull'd thee thus
Should with his lion gait walk the whole world,
He might return to vasty Tartar back,
And tell the legions " I can never win
A soul so easy as that Englishman's."
O, how hast thou with jealously infected

The sweetness of affiance!　Show men dutiful?
Why, so didst thou: seem they grave and learned?
Why, so didst thou: come they of noble family?
Why, so didst thou: seem they religious?
Why, so didst thou: or are they spare in diet,
Free from gross passion or of mirth or anger,
Constant in spirit, not swerving with the blood,
Garnish'd and deck'd in modest complement,
Not working with the eye without the ear,
And but in purged judgment trusting neither?
Such and so finely boulted didst thou seem:
And thus thy fall hath left a kind of blot,
To mark the full-fraught man and best indued
With some suspicion.　I will weep for thee;
For this revolt of thine, methinks, is like
Another fall of man.　Their faults are open:
Arrest them to the answer of the law;
And God acquit them of their practices!

WILLIAM SHAKESPEARE.

AFTER THE BATTLE

K. Hen.　　　　　　　　　I tell thee truly, herald,
I know not if the day be ours or no;
For yet a many of your horsemen peer
And gallop o'er the field.
Mont.　　　　　　　　The day is yours.
K. Hen. Praised be God, and not our strength, for it!
What is this castle call'd that stands hard by?

Mont. They call it Agincourt.

K. Hen. Then call we this the field of Agincourt,
Fought on the day of Crispin Crispianus.

Flu. Your grandfather of famous memory, an't please
your majesty, and your great-uncle Edward the Plack Prince
of Wales, as I have read in the chronicles, fought a most
prave pattle here in France.

K. Hen. They did, Fluellen.

Flu. Your majesty says very true: if your majesties is
remembered of it, the Welshmen did goot service in a garden
where leeks did grow, wearing leeks in their Monmouth caps;
which, your majesty know, to this hour is an honourable

padge of the service; and I do pelieve your majesty takes no scorn to wear the leek upon Saint Tavy's day.

K. Hen. I wear it for a memorable honour
For I am Welsh, you know, good countryman.

Flu. All the water in Wye cannot wash your majesty's Welsh ploot out of your pody, I can tell you that: God pless it and preserve it, as long as it pleases his grace, and his majesty too!

K. Hen. Thanks, good my countryman.

Flu. By Cheshu, I am your majesty's countryman, I care not who know it; I will confess it to all the 'orld: I need not to pe ashamed of your majesty, praised pe Got, so long as your majesty is an honest man.

K. Hen. God keep me so! Our heralds go with him:
Bring me just notice of the numbers dead
On both our parts. Call yonder fellow hither.

> [*Points to Williams. Exeunt Heralds with Montjoy.*

Exe. Soldier, you must come to the king.

K. Hen. Soldier, why wearest thou that glove in thy cap?

Will. An 't please your majesty, 't is the gage of one that I should fight withal, if he be alive.

K. Hen. An Englishman?

Will. An 't please your majesty, a rascal that swaggered with me last night; who, if alive and ever dare to challenge this glove, I have sworn to take him a box o' th' ear; or if I can see my glove in his cap, which he swore, as he was a soldier, he would wear if alive, I will strike it out soundly.

K. Hen. What think you, Captain Fluellen? is it fit this soldier keep his oath?

Flu. He is a craven and a villain else, an 't please your majesty, in my conscience.

K. Hen. It may be his enemy is a gentleman of great sort, quite from the answer of his degree.

Flu. Though he pe as goot a gentleman as the tevil is, as Lucifer and Pelzebub himself, it is necessary, look your grace, that he keep his vow and his oath: if he pe perjured, see you now, his reputation is as arrant a villain and a Jack-sauce, as ever his plack shoe trod upon Got's ground and his earth, in my conscience, la!

K. Hen. Then keep thy vow, sirrah, when thou meetest the fellow.

Will. So I will, my liege, as I live.

K. Hen. Who servest thou under?

Will. Under Captain Gower, my liege.

Flu. Gower is a goot captain, and is goot knowledge and literatured in the wars.

K. Hen. Call him hither to me, soldier.

Will. I will, my liege.   [*Exit.*

K. Hen. Here, Fluellen; wear thou this favour for me and stick it in thy cap: when Alençon and myself were down together, I plucked this glove from his helm: if any man challenge this, he is a friend to Alençon, and an enemy to our person; if thou encounter any such, apprehend him, an thou dost me love.

Flu. Your grace does me as great honours as can pe desired in the hearts of his subjects: I would fain see the man, that has but two legs, that shall find himself aggriefed at this glove, that is all; but I would fain see it once, an please Got of his grace that I might see.

K. Hen. Knowest thou Gower?

Flu. He is my dear friend, an please you.

K. Hen. Pray thee, go seek him, and bring him to my tent.

Flu. I will fetch him.   [*Exit.*

K. Hen. My Lord of Warwick, and my brother Gloucester,
Follow Fluellen closely at the heels:
The glove which I have given him for a favour
May haply purchase him a box o' th' ear;
It is the soldier's; I by bargain should
Wear it myself.   Follow, good cousin Warwick:
If that the soldier strike him, as I judge
By his blunt bearing he will keep his word,
Some sudden mischief may arise of it;
For I do know Fluellen valiant
And, touched with choler, hot as gunpowder,
And quickly will return an injury:
Follow, and see there be no harm between them.—
Go you with me, uncle of Exeter.   [*Exeunt.*

SCENE VIII.   *Before* KING HENRY'S *pavilion.*

Enter GOWER *and* WILLIAMS.

Will. I warrant it is to knight you, captain.

Enter FLUELLEN.

Flu. Got's will and his pleasure, captain, I peseech you now, come apace to the king: there is more goot toward you peradventure than is in your knowledge to dream of.

Will. Sir, know you this glove?

Flu. Know the glove! I know the glove is a glove!

Will. I know this; and thus I challenge it. [*Strikes him.*

Flu. 'Sblood! an arrant traitor as any is in the universal world, or in France, or in England!

Gow. How now, sir! you villain!

Will. Do you think I'll be forsworn?

Flu. Stand away, Captain Gower; I will give treason his payment into plows, I warrant you.

Will. I am no traitor.

Flu. That's a lie in thy throat.—I charge you in his majesty's name, apprehend him: he's a friend of the Duke Alençon's.

Enter WARWICK *and* GLOUCESTER.

War. How now, how now! what's the matter?

Flu. My Lord of Warwick, here is—praised pe Got for it! —a most contagious treason come to light, look you, as you shall desire in a summer's day. Here is his majesty.

Enter KING HENRY *and* EXETER.

K. Hen. How now! what's the matter?

Flu. My liege, here is a villain and a traitor, that, look your grace, has struck the glove which your majesty is take out of the helmet of Alençon.

Will. My liege, this was my glove; here is the fellow of it; and he that I gave it to in change promised to wear it in his cap; I promised to strike him, if he did: I met this man with my glove in his cap, and I have been as good as my word.

Flu. Your majesty hear now, saving your majesty's manhood, what an arrant, rascally, peggarly, lousy knave it is: I hope your majesty is pear me testimony and witness, and will avouchment, that this is the glove of Alençon, that your majesty is give me; in your conscience, now?

K. Hen. Give me thy glove, soldier: look, here is the fellow of it.

'Twas I, indeed, thou promised'st to strike;
And thou hast given me most bitter terms.

Flu. And please your majesty, let his neck answer for it, if there is any martial law in the world.

K. Hen. How canst thou make me satisfaction?

Will. All offences, my lord, come from the heart: never came any from mine that might offend your majesty.

K. Hen. It was ourself thou didst abuse.

Will. Your majesty came not like yourself: you appeared to me but as a common man; witness the night, your garments, your lowliness; and what your highness suffered under that shape, I beseech you take it for your own fault and not mine: for had you been as I took you for, I made no offence; therefore, I beseech your highness, pardon me.

K. Hen. Here, uncle Exeter, fill this glove with crowns,
And give it to this fellow.—Keep it, fellow;
And wear it for an honour in thy cap
Till I do challenge it. Give him the crowns:
And, captain, you must needs be friends with him.

Flu. Py this day and this light, the fellow has mettle enough in his pelly. Hold, there is twelve pence for you; and I pray you to serve Got, and keep you out of prawls, and prabbles, and quarrels, and dissensions, and, I warrant you, it is the petter for you.

Will. I will none of your money.

Flu. It is with a goot will; I can tell you, it will serve you to mend your shoes: come, wherefore should you be so pashful? your shoes is not so goot: 't is a goot silling, I warrant you, or I will change it.

William Shakespeare.

COLUMBUS

The cordage creaks and rattles in the wind,
With freaks of sudden hush; the reeling sea
Now thumps like solid rock beneath the stern,
Now leaps with clumsy wrath, strikes short, and, falling
Crumbled to whispery foam, slips rustling down
The broad backs of the waves, which jostle and crowd
To fling themselves upon that unknown shore,

Their used familiar since the dawn of time,
Whither this foredoomed life is guided on
To sway on triumph's hushed, aspiring poise
One glittering moment, then to break fulfilled.

How lonely is the sea's perpetual swing,
The melancholy wash of endless waves,
The sigh of some grim monster undescried,
Fear-painted on the canvas of the dark,
Shifting on his uneasy pillow of brine!
Yet night brings more conpanions than the day
To this drear waste; new constellations burn,
And fairer stars, with whose calm height my soul
Finds nearer sympathy than with my herd
Of earthen souls, whose vision's scanty ring
Makes me its prisoner, to beat my wings
Against the cold bars of their unbelief,
Knowing in vain my own free heaven beyond.

I know not when this hope enthralled me first;
But from my boyhood up I loved to hear
The tall pine-forests of the Apennine
Murmur their hoary legends of the sea,
Which hearing, I in vision clear beheld
The sudden dark of tropic night shut down
O'er the huge whisper of great watery wastes,
The while a pair of herons trailingly
Flapped inland, where some league-wide river hurled
The yellow spoil of unconjectured realms
Far through a gulf's green silence, never scarred
By any but the North wind's hurrying keels.
And not the pines alone; all sights and sounds
To my world-seeking heart paid fealty,
And catered for it as the Cretan bees
Brought honey to the baby Jupiter,
Who in his soft hand crushed a violet,
Godlike foremusing the rough thunder's gripe;
Then did I entertain the poet's song,
My great Idea's guest, and, passing o'er
That iron bridge the Tuscan built to hell,
I heard Ulysses tell of mountain-chains
Whose adamantine links, his manacles,

The western main shook growling, and still gnawed;
I brooded on the wise Athenian's tale
Of happy Atlantis, and heard Björne's keel
Crunch the grey pebbles of the Vinland shore:
For I believed the poets; it is they
Who utter wisdom from the central deep,
And, listening to the inner flow of things,
Speak to the age out of eternity.

Thus ever seems it when my soul can hear
The voice that errs not; then my triumph gleams,
O'er the blank ocean beckoning, and all night
My heart flies on before me as I sail;
Far on I see my lifelong enterprise,
Which rose like Ganges 'mid the freezing snows
Of a world's sordidness, sweep broadening down,
And gathering to itself a thousand streams,
Grow sacred ere it mingle with the sea;
I see the ungated wall of Chaos old,
With blocks Cyclopean hewn of solid night,
Fade like a wreath of unreturning mist
Before the irreversible feet of light;—
And lo, with what clear omen in the east
On day's grey threshold stands the eager dawn,
Like young Leander rosy from the sea
Glowing at Hero's lattice!
               One day more
These muttering shoalbrains leave the helm to me:
God, let me not in their dull ooze be stranded;
Let not this one frail bark, to hollow which
I have dug out the pith and sinewy heart
Of my aspiring life's fair trunk, be so
Cast up to warp and blacken in the sun,
Just as the opposing wind 'gins whistle off
His cheek-swollen mates, and from the leaning mast
Fortune's full sail strains forward!
                 One poor day!—
Remember whose and not how short it is!
It is God's day, it is Columbus's.
A lavish day! One day, with life and heart,
Is more than time enough to find a world.
                       J. R. Lowell.

KOSSUTH

A RACE of nobles may die out,
A royal line may leave no heir;
Wise Nature sets no guards about
Her pewter plate and wooden ware.

But they fail not, the kinglier breed,
Who starry diadems attain;
To dungeon, axe, and stake succeed
Heirs of the old heroic strain.

The zeal of Nature never cools,
Nor is she thwarted of her ends;
When gapped and dulled her cheaper tools,
Then she a saint and prophet spends.

Land of the Magyars! though it be
The tyrant may relink his chain,
Already thine the victory,
As the just Future measures gain.

Thou hast succeeded, thou hast won
The deathly travail's amplest worth;
A nation's duty thou hast done,
Giving a hero to our earth.

And he, let come what will of woe,
Has saved the land he strove to save;
No Cossack hordes, on traitor's blow,
Can quench the voice shall haunt his grave.

" I Kossuth am: O Future, thou
That clear'st the just and blott'st the vile,
O'er this small dust in reverence bow,
Remembering what I was erewhile.

" I was the chosen trump wherethrough
Our God sent forth awakening breath;
Came chains? Came death? The strain He blew
Sounds on, outliving chains and death."

J. R. LOWELL.

ULYSSES

It little profits that an idle king,
By this still hearth, among these barren crags,
Match'd with an aged wife, I mete and dole
Unequal laws unto a savage race,
That hoard, and sleep, and feed, and know not me.
I cannot rest from travel: I will drink
Life to the lees: all times I have enjoy'd
Greatly, have suffer'd greatly, both with those
That loved me, and alone; on shore, and when
Thro' scudding drifts the rainy Hyades
Vext the dim sea: I am become a name;
For always roaming with a hungry heart
Much have I seen and known; cities of men
And manners, climates, councils, governments,
Myself not least, but honour'd of them all;
And drunk delight of battle with my peers,
Far on the ringing plains of windy Troy.
I am a part of all that I have met;
Yet all experience is an arch wherethro'
Gleams that untravell'd world, whose margin fades
For ever and for ever when I move.
How dull it is to pause, to make an end,
To rust unburnish'd, not to shine in use!
As tho' to breathe were life. Life piled on life
Were all too little, and of one to me
Little remains: but every hour is saved
From that eternal silence, something more,
A bringer of new things; and vile it were
For some three suns to store and hoard myself,
And this grey spirit yearning in desire
To follow knowledge like a sinking star,
Beyond the utmost bound of human thought.
　　This is my son, mine own Telemachus,
To whom I leave the sceptre and the isle—
Well-loved of me, discerning to fulfil
This labour, by slow prudence to make mild
A rugged people, and thro' soft degrees
Subdue them to the useful and the good.

Most blameless is he, centred in the sphere
Of common duties, decent not to fail
In offices of tenderness, and pay
Meet adoration to my household gods,
When I am gone.   He works his work, I mine.
   There lies the port: the vessel puffs her sail:
There gloom the dark broad seas.   My mariners,
Souls that have toil'd, and wrought, and thought with me—
That ever with a frolic welcome took
The thunder and the sunshine, and opposed
Free hearts, free foreheads—you and I are old;
Old age hath yet his honour and his toil;
Death closes all; but something ere the end,
Some work of noble note, may yet be done,
Not unbecoming men that strove with Gods.
The lights begin to twinkle from the rocks:
The long day wanes: the slow moon climbs: the deep
Moans round with many voices.   Come, my friends,
'Tis not too late to seek a newer world.
Push off, and sitting well in order smite
The sounding furrows; for my purpose holds
To sail beyond the sunset, and the baths
Of all the western stars, until I die.
It may be that the gulfs will wash us down:
It may be we shall touch the Happy Isles,
And see the great Achilles, whom we knew.
Tho' much is taken, much abides, and tho'
We are not now that strength which in old days
Moved earth and heaven; that which we are, we are;
One equal temper of heroic hearts,
Made weak by time and fate, but strong in will
To strive, to seek, to find, and not to yield.

Lord Tennyson.

YUSSOUF

A stranger came one night to Yussouf's tent,
Saying, " Behold one outcast and in dread,
Against whose life the bow of power is bent,
Who flies, and hath not where to lay his head;
I come to thee for shelter and for food,
To Yussouf, called through all our tribes ' The Good.' "

" This tent is mine," said Yussouf, " but no more
Than it is God's; come in, and be at peace;
Freely shalt thou partake of all my store
As I of His who buildeth over these
Our tents His glorious roof of night and day,
And at Whose door none ever yet heard Nay."

So Yussouf entertained his guest that night,
And, waking him ere day, said: " Here is gold;
My swiftest horse is saddled for thy flight;
Depart before the prying day grow bold."
As one lamp lights another, nor grows less,
So nobleness enkindleth nobleness.

That inward light the stranger's face made grand,
Which shines from all self-conquest; kneeling low,
He bowed his forehead upon Yussouf's hand,
Sobbing: " O Sheik, I cannot leave thee so;
I will repay thee; all this thou hast done
Unto that Ibrahim who slew thy son! "

" Take thrice the gold," said Yussouf, " for with thee
Into the desert, never to return,
My one black thought shall ride away from me;
First-born, for whom by day and night I yearn,
Balanced and just are all of God's decrees;
Thou art avenged, my first-born, sleep in peace! "

J. R. LOWELL.

COLUMBUS

How in God's name did Columbus get over
　　Is a pure wonder to me, I protest,
Cabot, and Raleigh too, that well-read rover,
　　Frobisher, Dampier, Drake, and the rest.
　　　　Bad enough all the same,
　　　　For them that after came,
　　　　But, in great Heaven's name,
　　　　How *he* should ever think
　　　　That on the other brink,
Of this wild waste terra firma should be,
Is a pure wonder, I must say, to me.

How a man ever should hope to get thither,
  E'en if he knew that there was another side;
But to suppose he should come any whither,
  Sailing straight on into chaos untried,
      In spite of the motion
      Across the whole ocean,
      To stick to the notion
      That in some nook or bend
      Of a sea without end
He should find North and South America,
Was a pure madness, indeed I must say, to me.

What if wise men had, as far back as Ptolemy,
  Judged that the earth like an orange was round,
None of them ever said, Come along, follow me,
  Sail to the West, and the East will be found.
      Many a day before
      Ever they'd come ashore,
      From the " San Salvador,"
      Sadder and wiser men
      They'd have turned back again;
And that *he* did not, but did cross the sea,
Is a pure wonder, I must say, to me.
                          ARTHUR HUGH CLOUGH.

JACOB

MY sons, and ye the children of my sons,
Jacob your father goes upon his way,
His pilgrimage is being accomplished.
Come near and hear him ere his words are o'er.
  Not as my father's or his father's days,
As Isaac's days or Abraham's, have been mine;
Not as the days of those that in the field
Walked at the eventide to meditate,
And haply, to the tent returning, found
Angels at nightfall waiting at their door.
They communed, Israel wrestled with the Lord.
No, not as Abraham's or as Isaac's days,
My sons, have been Jacob your father's days,
Evil and few, attaining not to theirs
In number, and in worth inferior much.

Q

As a man with his friend, walked they with God,
In His abiding presence they abode,
And all their acts were open to His face.
But I have had to force mine eyes away,
To lose, almost to shun, the thoughts I loved,
To bend down to the work, to bare the breast,
And struggle, feet and hands, with enemies;
To buffet and to battle with hard men,
With men of selfishness and violence;
To watch by day, and calculate by night,
To plot and think of plots, and through a land
Ambushed with guile, and with strong foes beset,
To win with art safe wisdom's peaceful way.
Alas! I know, and from the onset knew,
The first-born faith, the singleness of soul,
The antique pure simplicity with which
God and good angels communed undispleased,
Is not; it shall not any more be said,
That of a blameless and a holy kind,
The chosen race, the seed of promise, comes.
The royal, high prerogatives, the dower
Of innocence and perfectness of life,
Pass not unto my children from their sire,
As unto me they came of mine; they fit
Neither to Jacob nor to Jacob's race.
Think ye, my sons, in this extreme old age
And in this failing breath, that I forget
How on the day when from my father's door,
In bitterness and ruefulness of heart,
I from my parents set my face, and felt
I never more again should look on theirs,
How on that day I seemed unto myself
Another Adam from his home cast out,
And driven abroad unto a barren land,
Cursed for his sake, and mocking still with thorns
And briers that labour and that sweat of brow
He still must spend to live?   Sick of my days,
I wished not life, but cried out, Let me die;
But at Luz God came to me; in my heart
He put a better mind, and showed me how,
While we discern it not, and least believe,
On stairs invisible betwixt His heaven

And our unholy, sinful, toilsome earth
Celestial messengers of loftiest good
Upward and downward pass continually.
Many, since I upon the field of Luz
Set up the stone I slept on, unto God,
Many have been the troubles of my life;
Sins in the field and sorrows in the tent,
In mine own household anguish and despair,
And gall and wormwood mingled with my love.
The time would fail me should I seek to tell
Of a child wronged and cruelly revenged
(Accursed was that anger, it was fierce,
That wrath, for it was cruel); or of strife
And jealousy and cowardice, with lies
Mocking a father's misery; deeds of blood,
Pollutions, sicknesses, and sudden deaths.
These many things against me many times,
The ploughers have ploughed deep upon my back·
And made deep furrows; blessed be His name
Who hath delivered Jacob out of all,
And left within his spirit hope of good.

Come near to me, my sons: your father goes,
The hour of his departure draweth nigh.
Ah me! this eager rivalry of life,
This cruel conflict for pre-eminence,
This keen supplanting of the dearest kin,
Quick seizure and fast unrelaxing hold
Of vantage-place; the stony hard resolve,
The chase, the competition, and the craft
Which seems to be the poison of our life,
And yet is the condition of our life!
To have done things on which the eye with shame
Looks back, the closed hand clutching still the prize!—
Alas! what of all these things shall I say?
Take me away unto Thy sleep, O God!
I thank Thee it is over, yet I think
It was a work appointed me of Thee.
How is it? I have striven all my days
To do my duty to my house and hearth,
And to the purpose of my father's race,
Yet is my heart therewith not satisfied.

ARTHUR HUGH CLOUGH.

TO AN OAK TREE

EMBLEM of England's ancient faith,
  Full proudly may thy branches wave,
Where loyalty lies low in death,
  And valour fills a timeless grave.

And thou, brave tenant of the tomb!
  Repine not if our clime deny,
Above thine honour'd sod to bloom,
  The flowrets of a milder sky.

These owe their birth to genial May;
  Beneath a fiercer sun they pine,
Before the winter storm decay—
  And can their worth be type of thine?

No! for, 'mid storms of Fate opposing,
  Still higher swell'd thy dauntless heart,
And, while Despair the scene was closing,
  Commenced thy brief but brilliant part.

'Twas then thou sought'st on Albyn's hill,
  (When England's sons the strife resign'd,)
A rugged race resisting still,
  And unsubdued though unrefined.

Thy death's hour heard no kindred wail,
  No holy knell thy requiem rung;
Thy mourners were the plaided Gael,
  Thy dirge the clamorous pibroch sung.

Yet who, in Fortune's summer-shine
  To waste life's longest term away,
Would change that glorious dawn of thine,
  Though darken'd ere its noontide day?

Be thine the Tree whose dauntless boughs
  Brave summer's drought and winter's gloom!
Rome bound with oak her patriots' brows,
  As Albyn shadows Wogan's tomb.

                                SIR WALTER SCOTT.

CLAUD HALCRO'S VERSES

AND you shall deal the funeral dole;
  Ay, deal it, mother mine,
To weary body, and to heavy soul,
  The white bread and the wine.

And you shall deal my horses of pride;
  Ay, deal them, mother mine;
And you shall deal my lands so wide,
  And deal my castles nine.

But deal not vengeance for the deed,
  And deal not for the crime;
The body to its place, and the soul to Heaven's grace,
  And the rest in God's own time.

                              SIR WALTER SCOTT.

PARSON AVERY

WHEN the reaper's task was ended, and the summer wearing
    late,
Parson Avery sailed from Newbury, with his wife and
    children eight,
Dropping down the river-harbour in the shallop " Watch
    and Wait."

Pleasantly lay the clearings in the mellow summer-morn,
With the newly planted orchards dropping their fruits first-
    born,
And the homesteads like green islands amid a sea of corn.

Broad meadows reached out seaward the tided creeks between,
And hills rolled wave-like inland, with oaks and walnuts
    green;—
A fairer home, a goodlier land, his eyes had never seen.

Yet away sailed Parson Avery, away where duty led,
And the voice of God seemed calling, to break the living
    bread
To the souls of fishers starving on the rocks of Marblehead.

All day they sailed: at nightfall the pleasant land-breeze
  died,
The blackening sky, at midnight, its starry lights denied,
And far and low the thunder of tempest prophesied!

Blotted out were all the coast-lines, gone were rock, and
  wood, and sand;
Grimly anxious stood the skipper with the rudder in his hand,
And questioned of the darkness what was sea and what was
  land.

And the preacher heard his dear ones, nestled round him,
  weeping sore;
" Never heed, my little children! Christ is walking on before
To the pleasant land of heaven, where the sea shall be no
  more."

All at once the great cloud parted, like a curtain drawn aside,
To let down the torch of lightning on the terror far and wide;
And the thunder and the whirlwind together smote the tide.

There was wailing in the shallop, woman's wail and man's
  despair,
A crash of breaking timbers on the rocks so sharp and bare,
And, through it all, the murmur of Father Avery's prayer.

From his struggle in the darkness with the wild waves and
  the blast,
On a rock, where every billow broke above him as it passed,
Alone, of all his household, the man of God was cast.

There a comrade heard him praying, in the pause of wave and
  wind:
" All my own have gone before me, and I linger just behind;
Not for life I ask, but only for the rest thy ransomed find!

" In this night of death I challenge the promise of thy
  word!—
Let me see the great salvation of which mine ears have
  heard!—
Let me pass from hence forgiven, through the grace of Christ,
  our Lord!

" In the baptism of these waters wash white my every sin,
And let me follow up to thee my household and my kin!
Open the sea-gate of thy heaven, and let me enter in ! "

When the Christian sings his death-song, all the listening
    heavens draw near,
And the angels, leaning over the walls of crystal, hear
How the notes so faint and broken swell to music in God's ear.

The ear of God was open to his servant's last request;
As the strong wave swept him downward the sweet hymn
    upward pressed,
And the soul of Father Avery went, singing, to its rest.

There was wailing on the mainland, from the rocks of Marble-
    head:
In the stricken church of Newbury the notes of prayer were
    read;
And long, by board and hearthstone, the living mourned the
    dead.

And still the fishers outbound, or scudding from the squall,
With grave and reverend faces, the ancient tale recall,
When they see the white waves breaking on the Rock of
    Avery's Fall !

J. G. Whittier.

JOSEPH STURGE

The very gentlest of all human natures
    He joined to courage strong,
And love outreaching unto all God's creatures
    With sturdy hate of wrong.

Tender as woman; manliness and meekness
    In him were so allied
That they who judged him by his strength or weakness
    Saw but a single side.

Men failed, betrayed him, but his zeal seemed nourished
    By failure and by fall;
Still a large faith in human-kind he cherished,
    And in God's love for all.

And now he rests; his greatness and his sweetness
  No more shall seem at strife;
And death has moulded into calm completeness
  The statue of his life.

Where the dews glisten and the song-birds warble,
  His dust to dust is laid,
In Nature's keeping, with no pomp of marble
  To shame his modest shade.

The forges glow, the hammers all are ringing;
  Beneath its smoky vale,
Hard by, the city of his love is swinging
  Its clamorous iron flail.

But round his grave are quietude and beauty,
  And the sweet heaven above,—
The fitting symbols of a life of duty
  Transfigured into love!

J. G. WHITTIER.

BROWN OF OSSAWATOMIE

JOHN BROWN OF OSSAWATOMIE spake on his dying day:
" I will not have to shrive my soul a priest in Slavery's pay.
But let some poor slave-mother whom I have striven to free,
With her children, from the gallows-stair put up a prayer for
    me! "

John Brown of Ossawatomie, they led him out to die;
And lo! a poor slave-mother with her little child pressed nigh.
Then the bold, blue eye grew tender, and the old harsh face
    grew mild,
As he stooped between the jeering ranks and kissed the
    negro's child!

The shadows of his stormy life that moment fell apart;
And they who blamed the bloody hand forgave the loving
    heart.
That kiss from all its guilty means redeemed the good intent,
And round the grisly fighter's hair the martyr's aureole bent!

Perish with him the folly that seeks through evil good!
Long live the generous purpose unstained with human blood!
Not the raid of midnight terror, but the thought which
    underlies,
Not the borderer's pride of daring, but the Christian's sacrifice.

Nevermore may yon Blue Ridges the Northern rifle hear,
Nor see the light of blazing homes flash on the negro's spear.
But let the free-winged angel Truth their guarded passes scale,
To teach that right is more than might, and justice more
    than mail.

So vainly shall Virginia set her battle in array;
In vain her trampling squadrons knead the winter snow with
    clay.
She may strike the pouncing eagle, but she dares not harm
    the dove;
And every gate she bars to Hate shall open wide to Love!

J. G. WHITTIER.

MY TRIUMPH

LET the thick curtain fall;
I better know than all
How little I have gained,
How vast the unattained.

Not by the page word-painted
Let life be banned or sainted;
Deeper than written scroll
The colours of the soul.

Sweeter than any sung
My songs that found no tongue;
Nobler than any fact
My wish that failed of act.

Others shall sing the song,
Others shall right the wrong,—
Finish what I begin,
And all I fail of win.

What matter, I or they?
Mine or another's day,
So the right word be said
And life the sweeter made?

Hail to the coming singers!
Hail to the brave light-bringers!
Forward I reach and share
All that they sing and dare.

The airs of heaven blow o'er me;
A glory shines before me
Of what mankind shall be—
Pure, generous, brave, and free.

A dream of man and woman
Diviner but still human,
Solving the riddle old,
Shaping the Age of Gold!

The love of God and neighbour;
An equal-handed labour;
The richer life, where beauty
Walks hand in hand with duty.

Ring, bells in unreared steeples,
The joy of unborn peoples!
Sound, trumpets far off blown
Your triumph is my own!

Parcel and part of all,
I keep the festival,
Fore-reach the good to be,
And share the victory.

J. G. Whittier.

THE LIE

Go, soul, the body's guest,
  Upon a thankless arrant;
Fear not to touch the best;
  The truth shall be thy warrant:
Go, since I needs must die,
  And give the world the lie.

Say to the court, it glows,
  And shines like rotten wood;
Say to the church, it shows
  What's good, and doth no good:
If church and court reply,
  Then give them both the lie.

Tell potentates, they live,
  Acting by others' action;
Not loved, unless they give,
  Not strong, but by a faction:
If potentates reply,
  Give potentates the lie.

Tell men of high condition,
  That manage the estate,
Their purpose is ambition,
  Their practise only hate:
And if they once reply,
  Then give them all the lie.

Tell them that brave it most,
  They beg for more by spending,
Who, in their greatest cost,
  Like nothing but commending:
And if they make reply,
  Then give them all the lie.

Tell zeal it wants devotion;
  Tell love it is but lust;

Tell time it meets but motion;
　Tell flesh it is but dust:
And wish them not reply,
　For thou must give the lie.

Tell age it daily wasteth;
　Tell honour how it alters;
Tell beauty how she blasteth;
　Tell favour how it falters:
And as they shall reply,
　Give every one the lie.

Tell wit how much it wrangles
　In tickle points of niceness;
Tell wisdom she entangles
　Herself in over-wiseness:
And when they do reply,
　Straight give them both the lie.

Tell physic of her boldness;
　Tell skill it is prevention;
Tell charity of coldness;
　Tell law it is contention:
And as they do reply,
　So give them still the lie.

Tell fortune of her blindness;
　Tell nature of decay;
Tell friendship of unkindness;
　Tell justice of delay:
And if they will reply,
　Then give them all the lie.

Tell arts they have no soundness,
　But vary by esteeming;
Tell schools they want profoundness,
　And stand so much on seeming:
If arts and schools reply,
　Give arts and schools the lie.

Tell faith it's fled the city;
　Tell how the country erreth;

Tell, manhood shakes off pity;
　　Tell, virtue least preferreth:
And if they do reply,
　　Spare not to give the lie.

So, when thou hast, as I
　　Commanded thee, done blabbing,
Although to give the lie
　　Deserves no less than stabbing,
Stab at thee he that will,
　　No stab thy soul can kill.
Sir Walter Raleigh.

MILTON

Place me once more, my daughter, where the sun
May shine upon my old and time-worn head,
For the last time perchance.　My race is run;
And soon amidst the dead I must repose.
Child, is the sun abroad?　I feel my hair
Borne up and wafted by the gentle wind,
I feel the odours that perfume the air,
And almost can forget that I am blind
And old, and hated by my fellow men.
Yet would I fain once more behold the light
Of day before I die, and gaze again
Upon its living and rejoicing face.
Fain would I see thy countenance, my child,
But I will bend me calmly to my doom,
And wait the hour which is approaching fast.
W. E. Aytoun.

PITT

And thou, blest star of Europe's darkest hour,
Whose words were wisdom, and whose counsels power,
Whom earth applauded through her peopled shores;
Alas! whom earth too early lost deplores:
Young without follies, without rashness bold,

And greatly poor amidst a nation's gold;
In every veering gale of faction true,
Untarnish'd Chatham's genuine child, adieu!
Unlike our common suns, whose gradual ray
Expands from twilight to intenser day;
Thy blaze broke forth at full meridian sway.
O proved in danger! not the fiercest flame
Of discord's rage thy constant soul could tame;
Not when, far striding o'er thy palsied land,
Gigantic treason took his bolder stand;
Not when wild zeal, by murderous faction led,
On Wicklow's hills her grass-green banner spread;
Or those stern conquerors of the restless wave
Defied the native soil they wont to save.—
Undaunted Patriot! in that dreadful hour,
When pride and genius own a stronger power;
When the dimmed eyeball and the struggling breath
And pain and terror mark advancing death;
Still in that breast thy country held her throne,
Thy toil, thy fear, thy prayer were hers alone,
Thy last faint effort hers, and hers thy parting groan.

BISHOP HEBER.

SIMON, SON OF ONIAS

How was he honoured in the midst of the people
In his coming out of the sanctuary!
He was as the morning star in the midst of the cloud,
And as the moon at the full;
As the sun shining upon the temple of the most High,
And as the rainbow giving light in the bright clouds:
And as the flower of roses in the spring of the year,
As lilies by the rivers of waters,
And as the branches of the frankincense tree in summer:
As fire and incense in the censer,
And as a vessel of gold set with precious stones,
As a fair olive-tree, budding forth fruit,
And as a cypress which groweth up to the clouds.
When he put on the robe of honour,
And was clothed with the perfection of glory,

When he went up to the holy altar,
He made the garment of holiness honourable.
He himself stood by the hearth of the altar,
Compassed with his brethren round about,
As a young cedar in Libanus;
And as palm trees compassed they him round about.

APOCRYPHA.

A PSALM OF LIFE

TELL me not, in mournful numbers,
　Life is but an empty dream!
For the soul is dead that slumbers,
　And things are not what they seem.

Life is real!　Life is earnest!
　And the grave is not its goal;
Dust thou art, to dust returnest,
　Was not spoken of the soul.

Not enjoyment, and not sorrow,
　Is our destined end or way;
But to act, that each to-morrow
　Finds us farther than to-day.

Art is long, and Time is fleeting,
　And our hearts, though stout and brave,
Still like muffled drums, are beating
　Funeral marches to the grave.

In the world's broad field of battle,
　In the bivouac of Life,
Be not like dumb, driven cattle!
　Be a hero in the strife!

Trust no Future, howe'er pleasant!
　Let the dead Past bury its dead!
Act—act in the living Present!
　Heart within, and God o'erhead!

Lives of great men all remind us
   We can make our lives sublime,
And, departing, leave behind us
   Footprints on the sands of time;

Footprints, that perhaps another,
   Sailing o'er life's solemn main,
A forlorn and shipwrecked brother,
   Seeing, shall take heart again.

Let us, then, be up and doing,
   With a heart for any fate;
Still achieving, still pursuing,
   Learn to labour and to wait.

H. W. Longfellow.

OH, TIMELY HAPPY, TIMELY WISE

Oh, timely happy, timely wise,
Hearts that with rising morn arise!
Eyes that the beam celestial view,
Which evermore makes all things new!

New every morning is the love
Our wakening and uprising prove;
Through sleep and darkness safely brought,
Restored to life, and power, and thought.

New mercies, each returning day,
Hover around us while we pray;
New perils past, new sins forgiven,
New thoughts of God, new hopes of Heaven.

If on our daily course our mind
Be set to hallow all we find,
New treasures still, of countless price,
God will provide for sacrifice.

Old friends, old scenes, will lovelier be,
As more of Heaven in each we see:

Some softening gleam of love and prayer
Shall dawn on every cross and care.

As for some dear familiar strain
Untired we ask, and ask again,
Ever in its melodious store,
Finding a spell unheard before;

Such is the bliss of souls serene,
When they have sworn, and steadfast mean,
Counting the cost, in all to espy
Their God, in all themselves deny.

O could we learn that sacrifice,
What lights would all around us rise!
How would our hearts with wisdom talk
Along life's dullest dreariest walk!

We need not bid, for cloistered cell,
Our neighbour and our work farewell,
Nor strive to wind ourselves too high
For sinful man beneath the sky:

The trivial round, the common task,
Would furnish all we ought to ask;
Room to deny ourselves; a road
To bring us daily nearer God.

Seek we no more; content with these,
Let present rapture, comfort, ease,
As Heaven shall bid them, come and go:—
The secret this of rest below.

Only, O Lord, in Thy dear love
Fit us for perfect rest above;
And help us, this and every day,
To live more nearly as we pray.

JOHN KEBLE.

LET US NOW PRAISE FAMOUS MEN

LET us now praise famous men, and our fathers that begat us.

The Lord hath wrought great glory by them through his great power from the beginning.

Such as did bear rule in their kingdoms, men renowned for their power, giving counsel by their understanding, and declaring prophecies:

Leaders of the people by their counsels, and by their knowledge of learning meet for the people, wise and eloquent in their instructions:

Such as found out musical tunes, and recited verses in writing:

Rich men furnished with ability, living peaceably in their habitations:

All these were honoured in their generations, and were the glory of their times.

There be of them, that have left a name behind them, that their praises might be reported.

And some there be, which have no memorial; who are perished, as though they had never been; and are become as though they had never been born; and their children after them.

But these were merciful men, whose righteousness hath not been forgotten.

With their seed shall continually remain a good inheritance, and their children are within the covenant.

Their seed standeth fast, and their children for their sakes.

Their seed shall remain for ever, and their glory shall not be blotted out.

Their bodies are buried in peace; but their name liveth for evermore.

APOCRYPHA.

WHAT ENDURES?

NOTHING endures but personal qualities.

What do you think endures?
Do you think a great city endures?
Or a teeming manufacturing state? or a prepared constitution?
    or the best built steamships?
Or hotels of granite and iron? or any chef-d'œuvres of
    engineering, forts, armaments?

Away! these are not to be cherish'd for themselves,
They fill their hour, the dancers dance, the musicians play
    for them,
The show passes, all does well enough of course,
All does very well till one flash of defiance.

A great city is that which has the greatest men and women,
If it be a few ragged huts it is still the greatest city in the
    whole world.

WALT WHITMAN.

WISDOM

But where shall wisdom be found?
And where is the place of understanding?
Man knoweth not the price thereof;
Neither is it found in the land of the living.
The depth saith, It is not in me:
And the sea saith, It is not with me.
It cannot be gotten for gold,
Neither shall silver be weighed for the price thereof.
It cannot be valued with the gold of Ophir,
With the precious onyx, or the sapphire.
The gold and the crystal cannot equal it:
And the exchange of it shall not be for jewels of fine gold,
No mention shall be made of coral, or of pearls:
For the price of wisdom is above rubies.
The topaz of Ethiopia shall not equal it.
Neither shall it be valued with pure gold.

Whence then cometh wisdom?
And where is the place of understanding?
Seeing it is hid from the eyes of all living,
And kept close from the fowls of the air.
Destruction and death say,
We have heard the fame thereof with our ears.

God understandeth the way thereof,
And he knoweth the place thereof.
For he looketh to the ends of the earth,
And seeth under the whole heaven;
To make the weight for the winds;
And he weigheth the waters by measure.
When he made a decree for the rain,
And a way for the lightning of the thunder:
Then did he see it, and declare it;
He prepared it, yea, and searched it out.
And unto man he said, Behold,
The fear of the LORD, that is wisdom;
And to depart from evil is understanding.

JOB XXVIII.

GRISELDA

THIS marquis hath hir spousèd with a ryng
Brought for the same cause, and then hir sette
Upon an hors snow-whyt, and wel amblyng,
And to his palys, with no further let,
(With joyful peple, that hir ladde and mette)
Conveyèd hire, and thus the day they spende
In revel, til the sonne gan descende.
　And shortly forth this tale for to chace,
I say, that to this newe marquisesse
God hath such favour sent hir of his grace,
That it seemed not by any liklynesse
That she was born and fed in rudenesse,
As in a cote, or in an oxe stalle,
But nourisht in an emperoures halle.

　To every wight she waxen is so deere
And worshipful, that folk where she was born,

And from hir birth*e* knew hir yer by yere,
Scarce trowèd thay, but dorst have boldly sworn,
That to Janicle, of which I spak biforn,
No daughter she were, for as by cónjectúre
They thought she was another créatúre.

For though that ever vertuous was she,
She was encresèd in such excellence
Of maners goode, i-set in high bountee,
And so discret, and fair of eloquence,
So benigne, and so digne of reverence,
And coud*e* so the peples hert embrace,
That ech hir loveth that lokith in hir face.

Nought only of Saluc*es* in the toun
Publisshèd was the bountee of hir name,
But eek byside in many a regioún,
If one sayd wel, another sayd the same.
So spredd*e* wide her bounté and her fame,
That men and wommen, as wel yong as olde,
Go to Saluces upon hir to byholde.

Thus Walter lowly, nay but royally,
Weddid with fortunat honestetee,
In Godd*es* pees lyveth ful esily
At home, and outward grace ynough hath he;
And for he saw that under low degree
Was oft*e* vertu y-hid, the peple him helde
A prudent man, and that is seen ful selde.

Nought only this Grisild*es* thurgh hir witte
Knew al the wayes of wifly homlynesse,
But eek when that the tyme requirèd it,
The comun profyt coude she wel redresse;
Ther was no discord, rancour, or hevynesse
In al that lond, that she coude not appese,
And wisly bryng them alle in rest and ese.

Though that hir housbond absent were anon,
If gentilmen, or other of hir contree,
Were wroth, she wold*e* bryng*e* them at one,
So wyse and ryp*e* word*es* hadd*e* she,
And judg*e*ment of so gret equitee,
That she from heven sent was, as men wende,
Peple to save, and every wrong to amende.

GEOFFREY CHAUCER.

WILL

O WELL for him whose will is strong!
He suffers, but he will not suffer long;
He suffers, but he cannot suffer wrong:
For him nor moves the loud world's random mock,
Nor all Calamity's hugest waves confound,
Who seems a promontory of rock,
That, compass'd round with turbulent sound,
In middle ocean meets the surging shock,
Tempest-buffeted, citadel-crown'd.

But ill for him who, bettering not with time,
Corrupts the strength of heaven-descended Will,
And ever weaker grows thro' acted crime,
Or seeming-genial venial fault,
Recurring and suggesting still!
He seems as one whose footsteps halt,
Toiling in immeasurable sand,
And o'er a weary sultry land,
Far beneath a blazing vault,
Sown in a wrinkle of the monstrous hill,
The city sparkles like a grain of salt.

LORD TENNYSON.

NATURE'S GENTLEMAN

HE boasts nor wealth nor high descent, yet he may claim
  to be
A gentleman to match the best of any pedigree:
His blood hath run in peasant veins through many a noteless
  year;
Yet, search in every prince's court, you'll rarely find his peer.
For he's one of Nature's Gentlemen, the best of every time.

He owns no mansion in the Square, inherits no estate;
He hath no stud, no hounds, no duns, no lacqueys at his gate;
He drinks no wine, and wears no gloves, his coat is thread-
  bare worn:

Yet he's a gentleman no less, and he was gentle born.
He is one of Nature's Gentlemen, the best of every time.

His manners are not polish'd, he has never learn'd to bow:
But his heart is gentle,—gentle manner out of it doth grow,
Like a flower whose fragrance blesseth all within its beauteous
    reach,
Or the dainty bloom upon a plum, or the softness of a peach.
For he's one of Nature's gentle ones, the best of every time.

He takes small pains to smoothe his words to fit a courtly
    phrase;
And he would scorn to file his soul for even royal praise;
And he has wrath too when the proud the gentle-soul'd
    distress:
He's not the form—gentility, but very gentleness.
Ay! one of Nature's gentle men, the best of every time.

As true old Chaucer sang to us, so many years ago,
He is the gentlest man who dares the gentlest deeds to do:
However rude his birth or state, however low his place,
He is the gentle man whose life right gentle thought doth
    grace.
He is one of Nature's Gentlemen, the best of every time.

What though his hand is hard and rough with years of honest
    pains,—
Who ever thought the knight disgraced by honour's weather-
    stains?
What though no Heralds' College in their books his line can
    trace,—
We can see that he is gentle by the smile upon his face.
For he's one of Nature's Gentlemen, the best of every time.

W. J. Linton.

DEFIANCE

Monarch of Gods and Dæmons, and all spirits
But One, who throng those bright and rolling worlds
Which Thou and I alone of living things
Behold with sleepless eyes! regard this Eart

Made multitudinous with thy slaves, whom thou
Requitest for knee-worship, prayer, and praise,
And toil, and hecatombs of broken hearts,
With fear and self-contempt and barren hope.
Whilst me, who am thy foe, eyeless in hate,
Hast thou made reign and triumph, to thy scorn,
O'er mine own misery and thy vain revenge.
Three thousand years of sleep-unsheltered hours,
And moments aye divided by keen pangs
Till they seemed years, torture and solitude,
Scorn and despair,—these are mine empire:—
More glorious far than that which thou surveyest
From thine unenvied throne, O Mighty God!
Almighty, had I deigned to share the shame
Of thine ill tyranny, and hung not here
Nailed to this wall of eagle-baffling mountain,
Black, wintry, dead, unmeasured; without herb,
Insect, or beast, or shape or sound of life.
Ah me! alas, pain, pain ever, for ever!

No change, no pause, no hope! Yet I endure.
I ask the Earth, have not the mountains felt?
I ask yon Heaven, the all-beholding Sun,
Has it not seen? The Sea, in storm or calm,
Heaven's ever-changing Shadow, spread below,
Have its deaf waves not heard my agony?
Ah me, alas, pain, pain ever, for ever!

The crawling glaciers pierce me with the spears
Of their moon-freezing crystals, the bright chains
Eat with their burning cold into my bones.
Heaven's wingèd hound, polluting from thy lips
His beak in poison not his own, tears up
My heart; and shapeless sights come wandering by,
The ghastly people of the realm of dream,
Mocking me: and the Earthquake-fiends are charged
To wrench the rivets from my quivering wounds
When the rocks split and close again behind:
While from their loud abysses howling throng
The genii of the storm, urging the rage
Of whirlwind, and afflict me with keen hail.
And yet to me welcome is day and night,
Whether one breaks the hoar frost of the morn,

Or starry, dim, and slow, the other climbs
The leaden-coloured east; for then they lead
The wingless, crawling hours, one among whom
—As some dark Priest hales the reluctant victim—
Shall drag thee, cruel King, to kiss the blood
From these pale feet, which then might trample thee
If they disdained not such a prostrate slave.
Disdain! Ah no! I pity thee. What ruin
Will hunt thee undefended through wide Heaven!

P. B. SHELLEY.

SAUL

SAID Abner, " At last thou art come! Ere I tell, ere thou speak,
Kiss my cheek, wish me well! " Then I wished it, and did kiss his cheek.
And he, " Since the King, O my friend, for thy countenance sent,
Neither drunken nor eaten have we; nor until from his tent
Thou return with the joyful assurance the King liveth yet,
Shall our lip with the honey be bright, with the water be wet.
For out of the black mid-tent's silence, a space of three days,
Not a sound hath escaped to thy servants, of prayer or of praise,
To betoken that Saul and the Spirit have ended their strife,
And that, faint in his triumph, the monarch sinks back upon life."

                Then I, as was meet,
Knelt down to the God of my fathers, and rose on my feet,
And ran o'er the sand burnt to powder. The tent was un-looped;
I pulled up the spear that obstructed, and under I stooped;
Hands and knees on the slippery grass-patch, all withered and gone,
That extends to the second enclosure, I groped my way on
Till I felt where the foldskirts fly open. Then once more I prayed,
And opened the foldskirts and entered, and was not afraid,
But spoke, " Here is David, thy servant! " And no voice replied.

At the first I saw nought but the blackness; but soon I
 descried
A something more black than the blackness—the vast the
 upright
Main prop which sustains the pavilion: and slow into sight
Grew a figure against it, gigantic and blackest of all;—
Then a sunbeam, that burst thro' the tent-roof,—showed Saul.

He stood as erect as that tent-prop; both arms stretched
 out wide
On the great cross-support in the centre, that goes to each side:
He relaxed not a muscle, but hung there,—as, caught in his
 pangs
And waiting his change the king-serpent all heavily hangs,
Far away from his kind, in the pine, till deliverance come
With the spring-time,—so agonised Saul, drear and stark,
 blind and dumb.

Ay, to save and redeem and restore him, maintain at the
 height
This perfection,—succeed with life's dayspring, death's
 minute of night?
Interpose at the difficult minute, snatch Saul, the mistake,
Saul, the failure, the ruin he seems now,—and bid him awake
From the dream, the probation, the prelude, to find himself set
Clear and safe in new light and new life,—a new harmony yet
To be run, and continued, and ended—who knows?—or
 endure!
The man taught enough by life's dream, of the rest to make
 sure.
By the pain-throb, triumphantly winning intensified bliss,
And the next world's reward and repose, by the struggle in
 this.

ROBERT BROWNING.

SOUND, SOUND THE CLARION

SOUND, sound the clarion, fill the fife!
 To all the sensual world proclaim,
One crowded hour of glorious life
 Is worth an age without a name.

SIR WALTER SCOTT.

THERE IS NO GOD

" THERE is no God," the wicked saith,
  " And truly it's a blessing,
For what He might have done with us
  It's better only guessing."

" There is no God," a youngster thinks,
  " Or really, if there may be,
He surely didn't mean a man
  Always to be a baby."

" There is no God, or if there is,"
  The tradesman thinks, " 'twere funny
If He should take it ill in me
  To make a little money."

" Whether there be," the rich man says,
  " It matters very little,
For I and mine, thank somebody,
  Are not in want of victual."

Some others, also, to themselves,
  Who scarce so much as doubt it,
Think there is none, when they are well,
  And do not think about it.

But country folks who live beneath
  The shadow of the steeple;
The parson and the parson's wife,
  And mostly married people;

Youths green and happy in first love,
  So thankful for illusion;
And men caught out in what the world
  Calls guilt, in first confusion;

And almost every one when age,
  Disease, or sorrows strike him,
Inclines to think there is a God,
  Or something very like Him.

                  ARTHUR HUGH CLOUGH.

AT TORCELLO

I HAD a vision; was it in my sleep?
And if it were, what then? But sleep or wake,
I saw a great light open o'er my head;
And sleep or wake, uplifted to that light,
Out of that light proceeding heard a voice
Uttering high words, which, whether sleep or wake,
In me were fixed, and in me must abide.

When the enemy is near thee,
    Call on us!
In our hands we will upbear thee,
He shall neither scathe nor scare thee,
He shall fly thee, and shall fear thee,
    Call on us!
Call when all good friends have left thee,
Of all good sights and sounds bereft thee;
Call when hope and heart are sinking,
And the brain is sick with thinking,
    Help, O help!
Call, and following close behind thee
There shall haste, and there shall find thee,
    Help, sure help.

When the panic comes upon thee,
When necessity seems on thee,
Hope and choice have all foregone thee,
Fate and force are closing o'er thee,
And but one way stands before thee—
    Call on us!
Oh, and if thou dost not call,
Be but faithful, that is all.
Go right on, and close behind thee
There shall follow still and find thee,
    Help, sure help.
                    ARTHUR HUGH CLOUGH.

HOPE EVERMORE

HOPE evermore and believe, O man, for e'en as thy thought
  So are the things that thou see'st; e'en as thy hope and
  belief.
Cowardly art thou and timid? they rise to provoke thee
  against them;
Hast thou courage? enough, see them exulting to yield.
Yea, the rough rock, the dull earth, the wild sea's furying
  waters
    (Violent say'st thou and hard, mighty thou think'st to
    destroy),
All with ineffable longing are waiting their Invader,
  All, with one varying voice, call to him, Come and subdue;
Still for their Conqueror call, and, but for the joy of being
  conquered
    (Rapture they will not forego), dare to resist and rebel;
Still, when resisting and raging, in soft undervoice say unto
  him,
  Fear not, retire not, O man; hope evermore and believe.
Go from the east to the west, as the sun and the stars direct
  thee,
  Go with the girdle of man, go and encompass the earth.
Not for the gain of the gold; for the getting, the hoarding,
  the having,
  But for the joy of the deed; but for the Duty to do.
Go with the spiritual life, the higher volition and action,
  With the great girdle of God, go and encompass the earth.

Go; say not in thy heart, And what then were it accomplished,
  Were the wild impulse allayed, what were the use or the
  good!
Go, when the instinct is stilled, and when the deed is accom-
  plished,
  What thou hast done and shalt do, shall be declared to
  thee then.
Go with the sun and the stars, and yet evermore in thy spirit
  Say to thyself: It is good: yet is there better than it.
This that I see is not all, and this that I do is but little;
  Nevertheless it is good, though there is better than it.

                    ARTHUR HUGH CLOUGH.

LOCHINVAR

O, YOUNG LOCHINVAR is come out of the west,
Through all the wide Border his steed was the best;
And save his good broadsword he weapons had none,
He rode all unarm'd, and he rode all alone.
So faithful in love, and so dauntless in war,
There never was knight like the young Lochinvar.

He staid not for brake, and he stopp'd not for stone,
He swam the Esk river where ford there was none;
But ere he alighted at Netherby gate,
The bride had consented, the gallant came late:
For a laggard in love, and a dastard in war,
Was to wed the fair Ellen of brave Lochinvar.

So boldly he enter'd the Netherby Hall,
Among bride's-men, and kinsmen, and brothers, and all:
Then spoke the bride's father, his hand on his sword
(For the poor craven bridegroom said never a word),
" O come ye in peace here, or come ye in war,
Or to dance at our bridal, young Lord Lochinvar? "—

" I long woo'd your daughter, my suit you denied;—
Love swells like the Solway, but ebbs like its tide—
And now am I come, with this lost love of mine,
To lead but one measure, drink one cup of wine.
There are maidens in Scotland more lovely by far,
That would gladly be bride to the young Lochinvar."

The bride kiss'd the goblet: the knight took it up,
He quaff'd off the wine, and he threw down the cup.
She look'd down to blush, and she look'd up to sigh,
With a smile on her lips, and a tear in her eye.
He took her soft hand, ere her mother could bar,—
" Now tread we a measure! " said young Lochinvar.

So stately his form, and so lovely her face,
That never a hall such a galliard did grace;
While her mother did fret, and her father did fume,

And the bridegroom stood dangling his bonnet and plume;
And the bride-maidens whisper'd, " 'Twere better by far,
To have match'd our fair cousin with young Lochinvar."

One touch to her hand, and one word in her ear,
When they reach'd the hall-door, and the charger stood near;
So light to the croupe the fair lady he swung,
So light to the saddle before her he sprung!
" She is won! we are gone, over bank, bush, and scaur;
They'll have fleet steeds that follow," quoth young Lochinvar.

There was mounting 'mong Græmes of the Netherby clan;
Forsters, Fenwicks, and Musgraves, they rode and they ran:
There was racing and chasing, on Cannobie Lee,
But the lost bride of Netherby ne'er did they see.
So daring in love, and so dauntless in war,
Have ye e'er heard of gallant like young Lochinvar?

SIR WALTER SCOTT.

A BALLAD

THE Druid Urien had daughters seven,
Their skill could call the moon from heaven;
So fair their forms and so high their fame,
That seven proud kings for their suitors came.

King Mador and Rhys came from Powis and Wales,
Unshorn was their hair, and unpruned were their nails;
From Strath-Clwyde was Ewain, and Ewain was lame,
And the red-bearded Donald from Galloway came.

Lot, King of Lodon, was hunchback'd from youth;
Dunmail of Cumbria had never a tooth;
But Adolf of Banbrough, Northumberland's heir,
Was gay and was gallant, was young and was fair.

There was strife 'mongst the sisters, for each one would have
For husband King Adolf, the gallant and brave;
And envy bred hate, and hate urged them to blows,
When the firm earth was cleft, and the Arch-fiend arose!

He swore to the maidens their wish to fulfil—
They swore to the foe they would work by his will.
A spindle and distaff to each hath he given,
" Now hearken my spell," said the Outcast of heaven.

" Ye shall ply these spindles at midnight hour,
And for every spindle shall rise a tower,
Where the right shall be feeble, the wrong shall have power,
And there shall ye dwell with your paramour."

Beneath the pale moonlight they sate on the wold,
And the rhymes which they chanted must never be told;
And as the black wool from the distaff they sped,
With blood from their bosom they moisten'd the thread.

As light danced the spindles beneath the cold gleam,
The castle arose like the birth of a dream—
The seven towers ascended like mist from the ground,
Seven portals defend them, seven ditches surround.

Within that dread castle seven monarchs were wed,
But six of the seven ere the morning lay dead;
With their eyes all on fire, and their daggers all red,
Seven damsels surround the Northumbrian's bed.

" Six kingly bridegrooms to death we have done,
Six gallant kingdoms King Adolf hath won,
Six lovely brides all his pleasure to do,
Or the bed of the seventh shall be husbandless too."

Well chanced it that Adolf the night when he wed,
Had confess'd and had sain'd him ere boune to his bed;
He sprung from the couch and his broadsword he drew,
And there the seven daughters of Urien he slew.

The gate of the castle he bolted and seal'd,
And hung o'er each arch-stone a crown and a shield;
To the cells of Saint Dunstan then wended his way,
And died in his cloister an anchorite grey.

Seven monarchs' wealth in that castle lies stow'd,
The foul fiends brood o'er them like raven and toad.

Whoever shall guesten these chambers within,
From curfew till matins, that treasure shall win.

But manhood grows faint as the world waxes old!
There lives not in Britain a champion so bold,
So dauntless of heart, and so prudent of brain,
As to dare the adventure that treasure to gain.

The waste ridge of Cheviot shall wave with the rye,
Before the rude Scots shall Northumberland fly,
And the flint cliffs of Bambro' shall melt in the sun,
Before that adventure be peril'd and won.
                              SIR WALTER SCOTT.

HELVELLYN

I CLIMB'D the dark brow of the mighty Helvellyn,
  Lakes and mountains beneath me gleam'd misty and wide;
All was still, save by fits, when the eagle was yelling,
  And starting around me the echoes replied.
On the right, Striden-edge round the Red-tarn was bending,
And Catchedicam its left verge was defending,
One huge nameless rock in the front was ascending,
  When I mark'd the sad spot where the wanderer had died.

Dark green was that spot 'mid the brown mountain-heather,
  Where the Pilgrim of Nature lay stretch'd in decay,
Like the corpse of an outcast abandon'd to weather,
  Till the mountain winds wasted the tenantless clay.
Nor yet quite deserted, though lonely extended,
For, faithful in death, his mute favourite attended,
The much-loved remains of her master defended,
  And chased the hill-fox and the raven away.

How long didst thou think that his silence was slumber?
  When the wind waved his garment, how oft didst thou
    start?
How many long days and long weeks didst thou number,
  Ere he faded before thee, the friend of thy heart?
And, oh! was it meet, that—no requiem read o'er him—

No mother to weep, and no friend to deplore him,
And thou, little guardian, alone stretch'd before him—
  Unhonour'd the Pilgrim from life should depart?

When a Prince to the fate of the Peasant has yielded,
  The tapestry waves dark round the dim-lighted hall;
With scutcheons of silver the coffin is shielded,
  And pages stand mute by the canopied pall:
Through the courts, at deep midnight, the torches are
    gleaming;
In the proudly-arch'd chapel the banners are beaming,
Far adown the long aisle sacred music is streaming,
  Lamenting a Chief of the people should fall.

But meeter for thee, gentle lover of nature,
  To lay down thy head like the meek mountain lamb,
When, wilder'd, he drops from some cliff huge in stature,
  And draws his last sob by the side of his dam.
And more stately thy couch by this desert lake lying,
Thy obsequies sung by the grey plover flying,
With one faithful friend but to witness thy dying,
  In the arms of Helvellyn and Catchedicam.

SIR WALTER SCOTT.

THE DYING GIPSY'S DIRGE

WASTED, weary, wherefore stay,
Wrestling thus with earth and clay?
From the body pass away;—
      Hark! the mass is singing.

From thee doff thy mortal weed,
Mary Mother be thy speed,
Saints to help thee at thy need;—
      Hark! the knell is ringing.

Fear not snow-drift driving fast,
Sleet, or hail, or levin blast;
Soon the shroud shall lap thee fast,
And the sleep be on thee cast
      That shall ne'er know waking.

Haste thee, haste thee, to be gone,
Earth flits fast, and time draws on,—
Gasp thy gasp, and groan thy groan,
        Day is near the breaking.
            Sir Walter Scott.

THE LUMBERMEN

Cheerily, on the axe of labour,
  Let the sunbeams dance,
Better than the flash of sabre
  Or the gleam of lance!
Strike!—With every blow is given
  Freer sun and sky,
And the long-hid earth to heaven
  Looks, with wondering eye!

Loud behind us grow the murmurs
  Of the age to come;
Clang of smiths, and tread of farmers,
  Bearing harvest home!
Here her virgin lap with treasures
  Shall the green earth fill;
Waving wheat and golden maize-ears
  Crown each beechen hill.

Keep who will the city's alleys,
  Take the smooth-shorn plain,—
Give to us the cedar valleys,
  Rocks and hills of Maine!
In our North-land, wild and woody,
  Let us still have part;
Rugged nurse and mother sturdy,
  Hold us to thy heart!

O, our free hearts beat the warmer
  For thy breath of snow;
And our tread is all the firmer
  For thy rocks below.

Freedom, hand in hand with labour
    Walketh strong and brave;
On the forehead of his neighbour
    No man writeth Slave!

Lo! the day breaks! old Katahdin's
    Pine-trees show its fires,
While from these dim forest gardens
    Rise their blackened spires.
Up, my comrades! up and doing!
    Manhood's rugged play
Still renewing, bravely hewing
    Through the world our way!

                J. G. WHITTIER.

AVENGE, O LORD

AVENGE, O Lord, thy slaughtered saints, whose bones
    Lie scattered on the Alpine mountains cold;
    Even them who kept thy truth so pure of old,
When all our fathers worshipt stocks and stones,
Forget not: in thy book record their groans
    Who were thy sheep, and in their ancient fold
    Slain by the bloody Piemontese, that rolled
Mother with infant down the rocks; their moans
The vales redoubled to the hills, and they
    To heaven. Their martyred blood and ashes sow
    O'er all the Italian fields, where still doth sway
The triple tyrant; that from these may grow
    A hundredfold, who, having learned thy way,
    Early may fly the Babylonian woe.

                JOHN MILTON.

AMBITION

In full-blown dignity, see Wolsey stand,
Law in his voice, and fortune in his hand:
To him the church, the realm, their powers consign;
Through him the rays of regal bounty shine;
Turned by his nod the stream of honour flows,

His smile alone security bestows:
Still to new heights his restless wishes tower;
Claim leads to claim, and power advances power;
Till conquest unresisted ceased to please,
And rights submitted, left him none to seize.
At length his sovereign frowns—the train of state
Mark the keen glance, and watch the sign to hate:
Where'er he turns he meets a stranger's eye,
His suppliants scorn him, and his followers fly;
Now drops at once the pride of awful state,
The golden canopy, the glittering plate,
The regal palace, the luxurious board,
The liveried army, and the menial lord.
With age, with cares, with maladies oppressed,
He seeks the refuge of monastic rest.
Grief aids disease, remembered folly stings,
And his last sighs reproach the faith of kings.

Speak thou, whose thoughts at humble peace repine,
Shall Wolsey's wealth, with Wolsey's end be thine?
Or liv'st thou now, with safer pride content,
The wisest Justice on the banks of Trent?
For why did Wolsey, near the steeps of fate,
On weak foundations raise the enormous weight?
Why, but to sink beneath misfortune's blow,
With louder ruin to the gulfs below.

What gave great Villiers to the assassin's knife,
And fixed disease on Harley's closing life?
What murdered Wentworth, and what exiled Hyde,
By kings protected, and to kings allied?
What, but their wish indulged in courts to shine,
And power too great to keep, or to resign!

The festal blazes, the triumphal show,
The ravished standard, and the captive foe,
The senate's thanks, the gazette's pompous tale,
With force resistless o'er the brave prevail.
Such bribes the rapid Greek o'er Asia whirled,
For such the steady Romans shook the world;
For such in distant lands the Britons shine,
And stain with blood the Danube or the Rhine;
This power has praise, that virtue scarce can warm,
Till fame supplies the universal charm.
Yet reason frowns on war's unequal game,

Where wasted nations raise a single name,
And mortgaged states their grandsires' wreaths regret,
From age to age in everlasting debt;
Wreaths which at last the dear-bought right convey
To rust on medals, or on stones decay.

On what foundations stands the warrior's pride,
How just his hopes, let Swedish Charles decide;
A frame of adamant, a soul of fire,
No dangers fright him, and no labours tire;
O'er love, o'er fear, extends his wide domain,
Unconquered lord of pleasure and of pain.
No joys to him pacific sceptres yield,
War sounds the trump, he rushes to the field;
Behold surrounding kings their power combine,
And one capitulate, and one resign;
Peace courts his hand, but spreads her charms in vain;
" Think nothing gained," he cries, " till nought remain,
On Moscow's walls till Gothic standards fly,
And all be mine beneath the polar sky."
The march begins in military state,
And nations on his eye suspended wait;
Stern famine guards the solitary coast,
And winter barricades the realms of frost:
He comes, nor want, nor cold, his course delay;
Hide, blushing glory, hide Pultowa's day:
The vanquished hero leaves his broken bands,
And shows his miseries in distant lands;
Condemned a needy supplicant to wait,
While ladies interpose, and slaves debate.
But did not chance at length her error mend?
Did no subverted empire mark his end?
Did rival monarchs give the fatal wound,
Or hostile millions press him to the ground?
His fall was destined to a barren strand,
A petty fortress, and a dubious hand;
He left the name, at which the world grew pale,
To point a moral, or adorn a tale.

SAMUEL JOHNSON.

ROBIN HOOD

O FOR an hour with Robin Hood, deep, deep in the forest
    green,
With fern and budding bramble waving o'er me as a screen,
        In mid noon shade,
        Where the hot-breath'd Trade
Came never the boughs between.

O for an hour of Robin Hood, and the brave health of the
    free,
Out of the noisome smoke to where the earth breathes
    fragrantly,
        Where heaven is seen,
        And the smile serene
Of heavenliest liberty.

O for the life of Robin Hood, to wander an outlaw free
Rather than crawl in the market-place of human slavery:
        Better with men
        In the wildest glen,
Than palaced with Infamy.

My life for a breath of Robin Hood, with the arrow before
    my eye
And a tyrant but within bow-shot reach: how gladly could
    I die
        With the fame of Tell,
        With Robin so well
Embalm'd in history.

O but to rest, like Robin Hood, beneath some forest-green,
Where the wild flowers of the coming spring on my moulder-
    ing heart may lean;
        For England's sward
        Is trampled hard
With the journeyings of the Mean.

W. J. LINTON.

FORTUNE

Turn, Fortune, turn thy wheel and lower the proud;
Turn thy wild wheel thro' sunshine, storm, and cloud;
Thy wheel and thee we neither love nor hate.

Turn, Fortune, turn thy wheel with smile or frown;
With that wild wheel we go not up or down;
Our hoard is little, but our hearts are great.

Smile and we smile, the lords of many lands;
Frown and we smile, the lords of our own hands;
For man is man and master of his fate.

Turn, turn thy wheel above the staring crowd;
Thy wheel and thou are shadows in the cloud;
Thy wheel and thee we neither love nor hate.

Lord Tennyson.

THE QUEST OF THE GRAIL

So to the Gate of the three Queens we came,
Where Arthur's wars are render'd mystically,
And thence departed every one his way.

And I was lifted up in heart, and thought
Of all my late-shown prowess in the lists,
How my strong lance had beaten down the knights,
So many and famous names; and never yet
Had heaven appear'd so blue, nor earth so green,
For all my blood danced in me, and I knew
That I should light upon the Holy Grail.

Thereafter, the dark warning of our King,
That most of us would follow wandering fires,
Came like a driving gloom across my mind.
Then every evil word I had spoken once,
And every evil thought I had thought of old,

And every evil deed I ever did,
Awoke and cried, " This Quest is not for thee."
And lifting up mine eyes, I found myself
Alone, and in a land of sand and thorns,
And I was thirsty even unto death;
And I, too, cried, " This Quest is not for thee."

And on I rode, and when I thought my thirst
Would slay me, saw deep lawns, and then a brook,
With one sharp rapid, where the crisping white
Play'd ever back upon the sloping wave,
And took both ear and eye; and o'er the brook
Were apple-trees, and apples by the brook
Fallen, and on the lawns. " I will rest here,"
I said, " I am not worthy of the Quest; "
But even while I drank the brook, and ate
The goodly apples, all these things at once
Fell into dust, and I was left alone,
And thirsting, in a land of sand and thorns.

And then behold a woman at a door
Spinning; and fair the house whereby she sat,
And kind the woman's eyes and innocent,
And all her bearing gracious; and she rose
Opening her arms to meet me, as who should say,
" Rest here; " but when I touch'd her, lo! she, too,
Fell into dust and nothing, and the house
Became no better than a broken shed,
And in it a dead babe; and also this
Fell into dust, and I was left alone.

And on I rode, and greater was my thirst.
Then flash'd a yellow gleam across the world,
And where it smote the plowshare in the field,
The plowman left his plowing, and fell down
Before it; where it glitter'd on her pail,
The milkmaid left her milking, and fell down
Before it, and I knew not why, but thought
" The sun is rising," tho' the sun had risen.
Then was I ware of one that on me moved
In golden armour with a crown of gold
About a casque all jewels; and his horse

In golden armour jewell'd everywhere:
And on the splendour came, flashing me blind;
And seem'd to me the Lord of all the world,
Being so huge.   But when I thought he meant
To crush me, moving on me, lo! he, too,
Open'd his arms to embrace me as he came,
And up I went and touch'd him, and he, too,
Fell into dust, and I was left alone
And wearying in a land of sand and thorns.

And I rode on and found a mighty hill,
And on the top, a city wall'd: the spires
Prick'd with incredible pinnacles into heaven.
And by the gateway stirr'd a crowd; and these
Cried to me climbing, " Welcome, Percivale!
Thou mightiest and thou purest among men! "
And glad was I and clomb, but found at top
No man, nor any voice.   And thence I past
Far thro' a ruinous city, and I saw
That man had once dwelt there; but there I found
Only one man of an exceeding age.
" Where is that goodly company," said I,
" That so cried out upon me? " and he had
Scarce any voice to answer, and yet gasp'd,
" Whence and what art thou? " and even as he spoke
Fell into dust, and disappear'd, and I
Was left alone once more, and cried in grief,
" Lo, if I find the Holy Grail itself
And touch it, it will crumble into dust."

And thence I dropt into a lowly vale,
Low as the hill was high, and where the vale
Was lowest, found a chapel, and thereby
A holy hermit in a hermitage,
To whom I told my phantoms, and he said:

" O son, thou hast not true humility,
The highest virtue, mother of them all;
For when the Lord of all things made Himself
Naked of glory for His mortal change,
' Take thou my robe,' she said, ' for all is thine,'
And all her form shone forth with sudden light

So that the angels were amazed, and she
Follow'd Him down, and like a flying star
Led on the grey-hair'd wisdom of the east;
But her thou hast not known: for what is this
Thou thoughtest of thy prowess and thy sins?
Thou hast not lost thyself to save thyself
As Galahad." When the hermit made an end,
In silver armour suddenly Galahad shone
Before us, and against the chapel door
Laid lance, and enter'd, and we knelt in prayer.
And there the hermit slaked my burning thirst,
And at the sacring of the mass I saw
The holy elements alone; but he,
" Saw ye no more? I, Galahad, saw the Grail,
The Holy Grail, descend upon the shrine:
I saw the fiery face as of a child
That smote itself into the bread, and went;
And hither am I come; and never yet
Hath what thy sister taught me first to see,
This Holy Thing, fail'd from my side, nor come
Cover'd, but moving with me night and day,
Fainter by day, but always in the night
Blood-red, and sliding down the blacken'd marsh
Blood-red, and on the naked mountain top
Blood-red, and in the sleeping mere below
Blood-red. And in the strength of this I rode,
Shattering all evil customs everywhere,
And past thro' Pagan realms, and made them mine,
And clash'd with Pagan hordes, and bore them down,
And broke thro' all, and in the strength of this
Come victor. But my time is hard at hand,
And hence I go; and one will crown me king
Far in the spiritual city."

LORD TENNYSON.

DREAMS, EMPTY DREAMS

I WAS a stricken deer that left the herd
Long since; with many an arrow deep infix'd
My panting side was charged, when I withdrew
To seek a tranquil death in distant shades.

There was I found by One who had Himself
Been hurt by the archers. In His side He bore,
And in his hands and feet, the cruel scars.
With gentle force soliciting the darts,
He drew them forth, and heal'd and bade me live.
Since then, with few associates, in remote
And silent woods I wander, far from those
My former partners of the peopled scene;
With few associates, and not wishing more.
Here much I ruminate, as much I may,
With other views of men and manners now
Than once, and others of a life to come.
I see that all are wanderers, gone astray
Each in his own delusions; they are lost
In chace of fancied happiness, still woo'd
And never won. Dream after dream ensues,
And still they dream that they shall still succeed,
And still are disappointed. Rings the world
With the vain stir. I sum up half mankind,
And add two-thirds of the remaining half,
And find the total of their hopes and fears
Dreams, empty dreams.

WILLIAM COWPER.

THE MILLENNIUM

THRONES, altars, judgment-seats, and prisons; wherein,
And beside which, by wretched men were borne
Sceptres, tiaras, swords, and chains, and tomes
Of reasoned wrong, glozed on by ignorance,
Were like those monstrous and barbaric shapes,
The ghosts of a no-more-remembered fame,
Which, from their unworn obelisks, look forth
In triumph o'er the palaces and tombs
Of those who were their conquerors, mouldering round.
These imaged to the pride of kings and priests
A dark yet mighty faith, a power as wide
As is the world it wasted, and are now
But an astonishment; even so the tools
And emblems of its last captivity,

Amid the dwellings of the peopled earth,
Stand, not o'erthrown, but unregarded now.
And those foul shapes, abhorred by god and man,—
Which, under many a name and many a form
Strange, savage, ghastly, dark and execrable,
Were Jupiter, the tyrant of the world;
And which the nations, panic-stricken, served
With blood, and hearts broken by long hope, and love
Dragged to his altars soiled and garlandless,
And slain amid men's unreclaiming tears,
Flattering the thing they feared, which fear was hate,—
Frown, mouldering fast, o'er their abandoned shrines:
The painted veil, by those who were, called life,
Which mimicked, as with colours idly spread,
All men believed or hoped, is torn aside;
The loathsome mask has fallen, the man remains
Sceptreless, free, uncircumscribed, but man
Equal, unclassed, tribeless, and nationless,
Exempt from awe, worship, degree, the king
Over himself; just, gentle, wise: but man
Passionless?——no, yet free from guilt or pain,
Which were, for his will made or suffered them,
Nor yet exempt, though ruling them like slaves,
From chance, and death, and mutability,
The clogs of that which else might oversoar
The loftiest star of unascended heaven,
Pinnacled dim in the intense inane.

P. B. SHELLEY.

JOY, SHIPMATE, JOY!

Joy, shipmate, joy!
(Pleas'd to my soul at death I cry)
Our life is closed, our life begins,
The long, long anchorage we leave,
The ship is clear at last, she leaps!
She swiftly courses from the shore,
Joy, shipmate, joy.

WALT WHITMAN.

CHRONOLOGICAL INDEX

287

1792-1866.—*Keble:* Oh, Timely Happy, Timely Wise

1792-1822.—*Shelley:* The Ideal; Prometheus; Defiance; The Millennium

1793-1835.—*Hemans:* A Dirge

1800-1859.—*Macaulay:* The Prophecy of Capys; Ivry; Naseby; Horatius; War-Horse; The Battle; The Armada

1802-1839.—*Praed:* Marston Moor

1807-1882.—*Longfellow:* Sir Humphrey Gilbert ; A Psalm of Life

1807-1892.—*Whittier:* The Pipes at Lucknow; Disarmament; Parson Avery; Joseph Sturge; Brown of Ossawatomie; My Triumph; The Lumbermen

1809-1892.—*Tennyson:* Of Old Sat Freedom; Christmas; The Charge of the Light Brigade; England; Sir Galahad; The War Song; Thy Voice is Heard; Home they brought ; Our Enemies have Fallen ; The Sailor Boy; Ode on the Death of the Duke of Wellington; Jephthah's Daughter; Iphigenia; The King; To the Queen; Dost Thou Look Back? ; Ulysses;

Will; Fortune; The Quest of the Grail

1812-1889.—*Browning:* The Patriot; Childe Roland; Saul

1812-1897.—*Linton:* The Brave Women of Tann; Nature's Gentleman; Robin Hood

1813-1865.—*Aytoun:* Milton

1814-1889.—*Mackay:* Cheer, Boys, Cheer

1819-1861.—*Clough:* Hope; The Academy at Venice; Columbus; Jacob; There Is No God; At Torcello; Hope Evermore

1819-1891.—*Lowell:* The Fatherland; Freedom; O Mother State; Columbus; Kossuth; Yussouf

1819 - 1892. — *Whitman:* Dying Heroes; What Endures? Joy, Shipmate, Joy

1819 - 1875. — *Kingsley:* The Knight's Leap

Lee: The Soldier's Tear

Sir A. Conan Doyle: The Song of the Bow

H. Cadett: War

H. Newbolt: Drake's Drum; Admiral Death

Percy's Reliques: Chevy Chace

Anon: The Island; John Dory; Lament over Sir Philip Sidney

INDEX TO FIRST LINES